"YOU ARE FIRST"

This compass, common to navigators from the time of Columbus until about 40 years ago, was used by the Stephens brothers on the *Dorade* (design No. 7) in the transatlantic race of 1931 and in subsequent *Dorade* cruises. The courses in the yacht's log were given in 32 points according to that compass, not in degrees of the circle as are today's.

"YOU ARE FIRST"

The Story of
Olin and Rod Stephens
of Sparkman & Stephens, Inc.

FRANCIS S. KINNEY

DODD, MEAD & COMPANY
New York

1 2 3 4 5 6 7 8 9 10

Library of Congress Cataloging in Publication Data
Kinney, Francis S
  "You are first".

  Includes index.
  1. Stephens, Olin. 2. Stephens, Rod. 3. Sparkman &
Stephens. 4. Yacht-building. 5. Yacht racing.
I. Title.
VM139.K56   338.7′61′62382   78-8148
ISBN 0-396-07567-3

Contents

"YOU ARE FIRST"

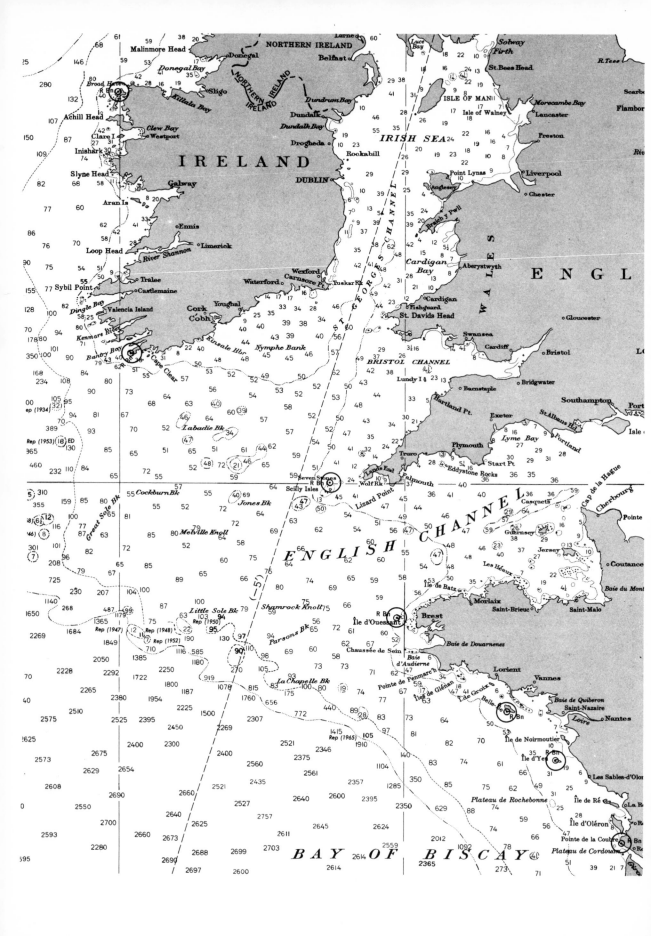

1 Dorade, Design No. 7

The Scilly Islands are the first land a vessel approaching England from the Atlantic can pick up. They are off Land's End, the rocky southwestern tip of Cornwall. Entering the English Channel, a vessel on a course bound for Plymouth must round Lizard Point, about 55 nautical miles after passing the Scillies. There on a high green headland stands a lighthouse tower with a signal station next to it, affectionately called by seamen "The Lizard."

At 5:45 A.M. on Tuesday, July 21, 1931, the signalman on duty there sighted a small white yawl, close-in beneath his station and almost becalmed. At 11 P.M. the night before she had picked up the Lizard light and ghosted along in light air to come as close as possible to exchange signals clearly. The signalman took a look at her through his spyglass, then hoisted two international code flags. They were the letters "E" and "C", one above the other, barely fluttering in the light breeze from the north-northwest. Their meaning:

"WHAT SHIP IS THIS?"

Quickly on the little white yawl up went code flag "H." Its meaning?

"DORADE."

After a brief interval that flag was lowered and the station keeper watching the yawl saw the letters "CTV" hoisted. He checked his book of international code flags and saw the meaning:

"WHICH AM I?"

Then without the slightest hesitation he went to his flag locker and pulled out the flags "NAX" to hoist in answer. They meant:

"YOU ARE FIRST."

The beginning of some history for the world of boating was made at that moment.

The signalman continued to observe this lovely sailboat through his "glass," because he was curious to see if her crew acknowledged his final hoist of code flags.

He saw pandemonium break out immediately aboard that vessel! Men were leaping up and down on her deck, dancing, shouting, slapping each other on the back, and yelling. That was the crew. There was one young man wearing spectacles holding the tiller, who the signalman thought must be the skipper, just standing there quietly and grinning.

What about this white yawl? And what about this young man wearing spectacles who merely stood there quietly at that happy moment and grinned like a Cheshire cat? That's what this story is all about, that boat and her designer. Let's start first with the boat, because she radically changed sailboat design for the next 33 years.

Dorade (named after a fast dolphin that swims in the Caribbean Sea, correctly spelled *Dorado*) was the product of a united family enterprise: the father and the boat's owner, Roderick Stephens, Sr., a wonderful father who shrewdly backed his sons, and these two sons, Olin her designer, skipper, and navigator, and Rod, the practical sailor, who had supervised her construction and the design of her sail plan, rigging, and deck layout. The fourth member of this unbeatable team was the topflight yacht broker Drake H. Sparkman.

She was yawl rigged. She measured 52'-0'' length overall, 37'-3'' length datum waterline, 10'-3'' beam, and 7'-7½'' draft, with a total sail area of 1,209 square feet as designed (later reduced to 1,150 square feet.). She had no power as built. Her builder was the Minneford Yacht Yard, Inc., in City Island, New York, in the year 1929. Originally she had a bowsprit and set a flying jib above it. Later this was removed and her main boom and mainmast were shortened, making her stiffer and easier to handle. Her shrouds and stays were spliced around the hollow spruce masts (mast tangs were adopted later). There was no wheel, but a tiller 5'-6'' long was used. Her displacement was 37,800 pounds as designed. When launched, she floated 3'' deep, which, when calculated, meant that she was almost 4,000 pounds heavier than her weight estimate. The spacing of her steam-bent white oak frames was quite close, much closer than Nevins' Rules specified for this size boat: They were spaced 9'' from center to center, but later Nevins called out a spacing of 11¾'' for a boat of her displacement. This was perhaps one of the reasons she was heavier than others her size. Another was that she was so carefully and strongly built under Rod's supervision.

"When you go aboard *Dorade*," wrote a contemporary yachting journalist, "the one thing that strikes you is the usefulness of everything on board, and the

DORADE
(Rosenfeld)

4

DORADE

Sail Area 1,150 sq. ft.
Displacement 37,800 lbs.
L.O.A. 52'-0''
D.W.L. 37'-3''
Beam 10'-3''
Draft 7'-8''

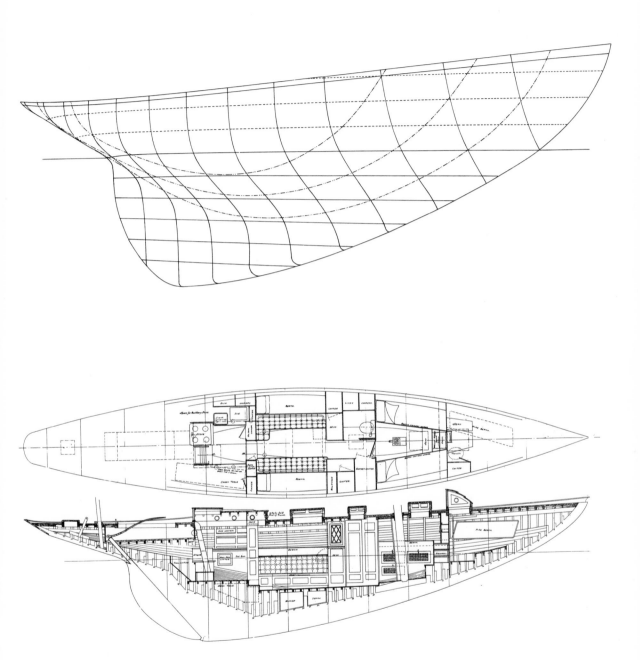

total elimination of everything else. Wherever experience has shown a cleat, a snatchblock, a fair lead, or a handhold would be useful, right there is one to be found, and not half an inch from where it should be. Every cleat is turned at the proper angle, every block and lead runs exactly true. Her rigging is so well proportioned, light and strong. There is strength where it is needed, but no weight where weight would only add to the wear and chafe. She is a sailor's delight."

Belowdecks, critics have commented on the narrowness of *Dorade*'s berths, and there is no doubt they are narrow and deep. In fact, they are just exactly the kind of berth in which you can sleep comfortably at sea, without rolling around like a ball on a billiard table.

How could two young brothers create such a superb design, which was to give them instant success at the very start of their careers? Let's go back to the very beginning.

The firm of Drake H. Sparkman, yacht broker and marine insurance, was created in 1928. The company needed a naval architect who could fulfill a client's desire to build a new boat, particularly the kind of boat that would win races.

"A winning boat is priceless" is the basic philosophy of successful yacht design thought. It is creating such boats that leads to success.

Drake Sparkman had a weather eye out for a man who could fulfill this need. And so he was impressed when he read in the January, 1928, issue of *Yachting* magazine this description of a proposed new six meter: "The ideas of young designers should see the light of day in the hopes that they might succeed, where more experienced naval architects have progressed but little in the past year or so. It is with this idea in view that we publish the accompanying plans from the board of Olin J. Stephens II of New York, which show a six-meter boat with possibilities."

The magazine went on: "In explanation of the design, Mr. Stephens has the following to say.

"'The design is intended primarily for light weather. In any design the most important factors of speed seem to be long sailing lines and large sail area, with moderate displacement and small wetted surface. Then comes beauty, by which is meant clean, fair, pleasing lines. Though per se beauty is not a factor of speed, the easiest boats to look at seem the easiest to drive.

"'To produce long sailing lines there are two methods available. First, by using a long waterline with fine ends; second, a shorter waterline and full ends. The former method has been used in this design. The waterline is about the longest of any exisiting American Six. Though this long waterline would ordinarily result in small sail area, this has been avoided by reducing the girth and girth difference measurements to the very minimum, which also lessens the wetted surface. The measured sail area is good while with overlapping jibs of various size, it may be said to be ample for the lightest weather.'"

Having headlined the piece showing the drawings "A six-meter boat design with interesting possibilities," *Yachting* concluded: "To predict what a boat will or will not do, from a study of her designs, is a dangerous undertaking, as experienced designers and critics well know. Nevertheless this design shows a great deal of promise, and it would be decidedly interesting to see her built and tried out."

This helped Olin obtain a job first with Henry J. Gielow, then with Philip L. Rhodes. He worked at his drawing board for them to learn the practical tricks of the trade. Later Phil Rhodes and he would be competitors for over 40 years. (Few people realize that the second boat in this transatlantic race of 1931 was the little gaff-rigged cutter, *Skäl*, designed by Phil Rhodes.)

Drake Sparkman soon took Olin into his firm on a trial basis. He found Olin his first client. His first client's design won races, and the firm name was changed to Sparkman & Stephens, Inc. Rod, younger and still at college, was to join them later.

When *Dorade* sailed into Plymouth, England, that day in 1931, she was not only first to finish this transatlantic race from Newport, Rhode Island, but she was first by two days boat for boat, and on corrected time by almost a four-day margin.

The race had started on July 4 at Newport. There were ten oceangoing sailboats entered. *Dorade* was the third smallest. Two of the entries were English boats.

For their crew aboard *Dorade*, Olin and Rod invited the same friends who had sailed with them on the previous year's Bermuda Race and had in fact grown up sailing with them. These young men, whose average age was 22 years, were:

Owen P. Merrill (Jim), who worked as a designer for Olin and whose father had designed, built, and sold the yawl *Trad* to the Stephens.

John D. Fox (Johnny the Wolf), their Scarsdale school friend.

Hartwell Moore (Buck), the son of Bob Moore who had shared Mr. Stephens, Sr.'s, dream of a transatlantic crossing.

Edward S. Koster (Ed or Nick), from Scarsdale, who volunteered to cook, as he had on the Bermuda Race.

The seventh member of the boat's company was the man who paid all the bills, Mr. Stephens, Sr. (who passed away in his ninetieth year in 1975), then 46, nicknamed by his shipmates "The Commodore," in pleasant deference to his election that year as Vice Commodore of the Larchmont Yacht Club.

After careful thought the Stephenses had decided to take the great circle course, the shortest distance from one point to another on the earth's spherical surface. Geometrically speaking *Dorade*'s great circle course was at the edge of the plane where the three points—Newport, Rhode Island, Plymouth, England, and the center of the earth—intersect the earth's surface to form a circular line. This is best illustrated by stretching a string on a globe between two fingers; when you pull the string tight it is at its shortest: a great circle course. Today it is approximately the route the airlines take when flying from New York to London.

Crew of DORADE '31

By choosing this course leading inside Sable Island, they would miss the benefit of the fair current in the Gulf Stream and would be near icebergs. But the advantage of the shorter distance outweighed that consideration. Nothing ventured nothing gained, so they took the chance.

It is most interesting to read *Dorade*'s log picturing the instances, the experiences, the weather, the condition of the sea, all from the very cryptic remarks. The 16 days of the voyage recorded in the log show an entry for every hour of every day. All courses are magnetic and are laid in points of the compass and in half or quarter points, not degrees. This is the way navigators did it at that time and as far back as the time of Columbus. The writing is in pencil by whomever was just off watch (ink sprayed with water smudges, but pencil does not). The book itself is quite small—a stenographer's pad about 4″ wide by 9″ high. Picture the scenes to yourself while reading the following entries (author's notes in parentheses):

Saturday, July 4, 1931, 12 noon
    Wind: S.E., light (4 to 8 mph.)
    Remarks: *Cynara* cast off tow line off Brenton's Reef.
    (Because *Dorade* did not have an engine, she was towed out to the starting line.)

1 p.m.
Course: S.E. ½ E.
Wind: S.S.W., light (a broad reach)
Crossed line at start in this order: *Mistress, Highland Light, Dorade, Water Gypsy, Landfall, Lismore, Skäl, Maitenes II, Ilex, Amberjack.*

6:30 p.m., W.S.W., light (air)
Doused spinnaker, set and doused it again. Set mizzen.
(Once past Gay Head and Nomans Island darkness hid the fleet standing out to sea. It was then that Olin and Rod committed *Dorade* to a different course from the rest, which took her along the Vineyard's South Beach out past Nantucket and east between Nova Scotia and Sable Island. It would have been a shorter distance to go through Vineyard and Nantucket sounds, but the current was against them at that time.)

Sunday, July 5, 9 a.m.
(Steering) E. × S. ½ S.
N.E., moderate (breeze)
Ballooner set in place of jib topsail and genoa.

12 midnight, course N.E. × N.
Wind: E., light. (It veered from N.E. to E., so *Dorade* tacked inshore.)
Wonderful phosphorescence. (A beautiful sight to behold, lighting up our wake in the dark.)

Monday, July 6, 2 a.m., (steering) E.N.E.
S.E., moderate (13 to 19 mph breeze)
Wind backing. Headed for England at last!

Tuesday, July 7, 5 a.m., course E. × N.
S.E., moderate (breeze blowing)
Average speed: 8.2 knots
School of porpoises from 4 to 4:30 a.m. Pumped bilge.

10 p.m., 8.5 knots
Sea smooth. Steering beautifully. (A consistently good trait of this great yawl in all sea conditions.)

Wednesday, July 8, 6 a.m.
9.2 knots
Practically sailing herself. Fog!

7 a.m., 9.4 knots
Sighted three whales, one big, two small passed close aboard. Fog setting in thick. (A great anxiety to her skipper and navigator, requiring constant vigilance.)

11 a.m., (steering) E. × S. ½ S.
S., moderate. (A reaching breeze, the fastest point of sailing.)
9.5 knots
Passed close aboard the fishing schooner *Isabel J. Corkum*. Weather has cleared up. Sun is shining! Warm on deck.

8 p.m., 9.9 knots
Coming in thick. (Pea soup fog again.)

Thursday, July 9, 6 a.m.
Excellent coffee made by the Commodore (Mr. Stephens, Sr.).

7.a.m., Commodore reading detective stories to the watch.

10 a.m., course E. × S.
Wind: S.W., light
Too thick for sights. (That meant dead reckoning, instead of celestial navigation, had to suffice.)

11:30 a.m. Steamer sounded fog horn—abeam to starboard. (The fear of being run down by a steamer in the fog is always present, but she is probably passing abeam on a parallel course.)

8 p.m., Foggy. Rod sounding Lothrop (horn). Very pistol (with flare) at hand. (Nevertheless, they took no chances.)

10 p.m. Thick, and sounding horn.

11:30 p.m. Jibed, set mizzen staysail. (A great sail to set on a yawl, because it is easy to handle, being set flying, and adds almost a knot to the speed.)

Friday, July 10, 1 a.m., (steering) E. × N.
N.W., moderate (breeze)
Quite thick out. Have man forward for lookout.

2 a.m. Still foggy.

5 a.m. Visibility improving. Pumped bilge. Sponged foot lockers and emptied icebox drain.

8 a.m. Cape Race (should be) abeam (now, we believe).

12 noon
Course: E. ½ N.
N.W., light (air)
Got noon sight. (and thus fixed our position.)

1 p.m. Shipmate (coal stove) in service. (A great comfort, this old-fashioned cast-iron stove that burns wood, coal, or charcoal briquettes.)

7 p.m. Practically flat calm.

Saturday, July 11, 2 a.m.

Set spinnaker. Wind picking up.

3 a.m., (steering) E.S.E.
W.S.W., very light (air)
Took off mizzen. Sea calm.

4:15 p.m., 6.3 knots
Passed directly over what appeared to be a pinnacle rising from the bottom. The surrounding water was quite green. It was not more than 50 ft. square.

4:50 p.m. About 100 yards to port sighted a small patch of green water, about 50 ft. × 100 ft. Most likely another shoal spot. Olin and Jim had taken sights about 3 p.m., and as the day was calm and conditions perfect, Olin took another sight, which checked our previous ones.

Sunday, July 12, 8 a.m.

The Commodore, after first trick, performs wonders with egg and bacon in form of sandwiches with coffee. Mate adds a bit more chafing gear, and then goes into action against the shipmate (won't draw). Going to put a blower on next time. The beards improve daily, as does the mileage, the meals, and the hair on the top of the doctor's head.

3:30 p.m. Spinnaker dropped into water. All hands hauled it back aboard. No damage. Found belaying pin to which spinnacker halyard was fast had let go. All back okay in little time.

4 p.m., course E. × S. ½ S.
Wind: W., moderate
9.0 knots
Rolling quite a lot. (Because she is running before the wind.)

8 p.m., 9.3 knots
Have seen two sharks in last half hour.

Monday, July 13, 6 a.m.

W., moderate (breeze)
Hit 10.8 knots on the gauge. Spinnaker dropped. Called all hands. Hauled in safely. Halyard chafed through at head block. Rod to masthead, reeved double halyard.

8 a.m., W., fresh (breeze, 19–25 mph)
Set heavy spinnaker.

4 p.m.
(Steering) E. × S.
W.N.W., (still) fresh
9.8 knots
Hit 10.85 twice. Grand sailing!

10:30 p.m. A school of racing dolphins, or porpoises, suddenly came up from astern, marked by streaks of lively phosphorescence, traveling in all directions and at speeds of as much as 16 to 20 knots. They played around *Dorade* for about 20 minutes. A very remarkable sight!

Tuesday, July 14, 2 p.m.
Wind: S.W., fresh
Best speed so far 11.4 knots for the Commodore! 11.35 knots for Rod. 11.3 for John.

3 p.m. Overcast. Lumpy (seas running).

8 p.m. (Saw a) school of porpoises diving in and out of the water so gracefully, and so close to us. It was lovely to watch their motions.

Wednesday, July 15, 4 a.m., S.W., fresh. (A reaching breeze again.)
9.7 knots
Clear. Sun rose above horizon as deck watch came on duty.
Very fine.

5 a.m., S.W., fresh (breeze) all morning
Oatmeal, coffee and triscuit served by the Commodore.

12 noon. 201 miles noon to noon. 1,030 miles to Scilly Islands. 1,150 miles to Plymouth. (Over halfway there.)

11 p.m., W.S.W., moderate
9.2 knots
Phosphorescence returns, also one porpoise. Fine sailing. (Quite a sight—trailing a sparkling wake that shone in the dark.)

Thursday, July 16, 12 noon
S.W., fresh. (*Dorade* attaining her highest speed.)
Set new record of 11.7 knots!

2 p.m., course S.E. × E. ¾ E.
S.W., fresh (breeze)
11.2 knots. (Boiling along!)
Seas pretty large.

6 p.m., wind S.W., strong. Blowing hard, 40 to 45 (mph)
Doused mizzen and mizzen staysail. (To ease her.)

10 p.m., S.W., strong (25 to 32 mph)
Jib slatting a lot. Hope it will stand strain.
Raining a little. (Driving *Dorade* hard.)

Friday, July 17, 3 a.m.
W.S.W., moderate. Breeze leaving us.
Set mizzen staysail. Shook out mizzen reef.

5 a.m. Rod went to masthead to reeve through a new spinnaker halyard.

Saturday, July 18, 3 a.m.
S.W. × W., fresh (breeze)
11.1 knots
Doused light spinnaker and balloon jib. Set heavy spinnaker, storm jib, forestaysail.

6 a.m. Lumpy (seas). Blowing hard and rolling a lot.

7 a.m., S.W. × W. fresh +. Breezing up.
11.2 knots.

10 a.m., wind N.W. × N., fresh
Streamed log reading 2,267.0 nautical miles (from Newport).

11 a.m. Steamer *George Washington* close aboard. 470 miles from Scilly Islands. (Expected landfall.)

1 p.m., course E. × S. ½ S.
N.W. × W., fresh (breeze)
Clear. Bright. Lumpy (seas).

11 p.m., wind N. × W., fresh. Very puffy.

12 p.m. Sighted steamer.

Sunday, July 19, 12 noon
2,483.6 nautical miles (log reading from Newport).

1 p.m. Cunarder, four stack, *Majestic*, we think. Passed abeam westward bound. Squall.

9 p.m. Moon and stars showing through clouds. Sea sloppy. Beautiful sailing.

10 p.m. Squalls occasionally passing. Two steamers to leeward.

12 p.m. Passed 100 fathom curve about 10:40 p.m., we think. (Approaching land.)

Monday, July 20, 2 a.m.
Course: E. × S. ¼ S.
Wind: N.N.W., fresh
Sighted steamer to weather. Damm wet and cold! (On such a northern course, never underestimate the cold.)

7 a.m., wind N., fresh
Sun shining. Grand sailing.

10 a.m. Sighted two steam trawlers.

4 p.m. 38 miles to Scillies by (sextant) observation (of the sun).

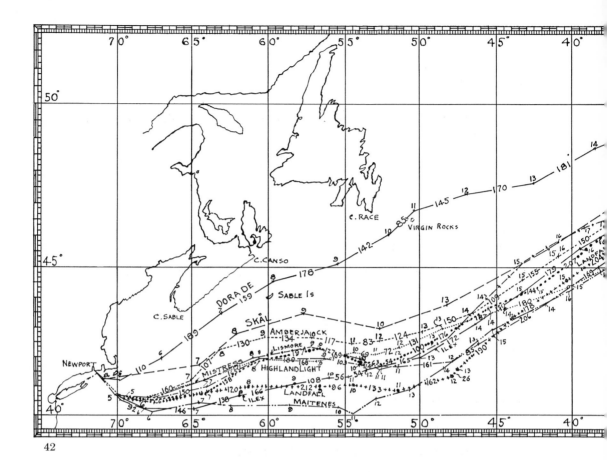

6.35 p.m. Land about 2 points on starboard bow. Scillys!
(LAND HO!)

9.25 p.m. Seven Stones abeam (the lighthouse marking the Scilly Isles.)

11 p.m. Lizard (Point) above horizon on port bow.

Tuesday, July 21, 1931, 2 a.m.
Wind very light and abeam.

3 a.m., course S.E. × S.
Close under the Lizard and becalmed. (Very frustrating to lose steerage way and not move.)

5 a.m. Almost flat. Current helping us along.

5:20 a.m. Fisherman comes along side to greet us. Reports we are first boat! Gives us some crabs.

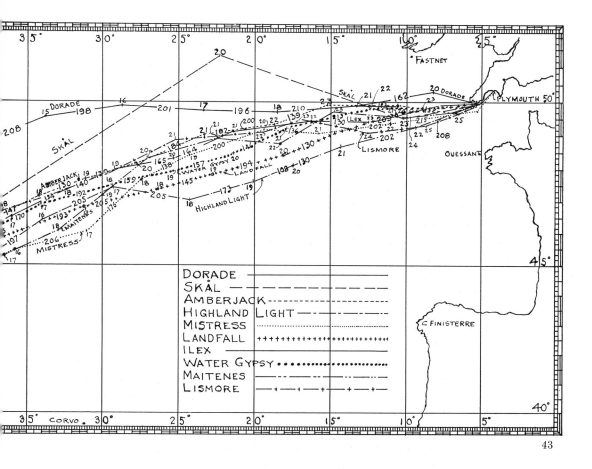

5:45 a.m. Signals (spelling out victory. Still one of the happiest moments of all in Rod's long sailing experience.)

8:00 a.m. Manacle Rock bell abeam. Wind up and down the mast (a flat calm).

2 p.m. About 15 miles to go. Southwester. Can see big boats racing off Plymouth.

3:50 p.m., wind S.W., light
7.2 knots
Off Ram Head, Plymouth Sound. Sixteen days 55 minutes from Newport, Rhode Island, U.S.A. Crossing finish line!

In summary, *Dorade*'s course was east, at times a little to the north or a little to the south. Except for a moderate northeaster the second day, the wind was fair just about all the way, being between west and southwest. It varied in strength between moderate and fresh, driving her at 11 knots for five hours one night. *Dorade*'s mainsail was hand stitched which made it much stronger, because when sewing the seams the sailmaker would give the thread a yank on every stitch, tightening it so it would not come out. The stitches were flush with the cloth and thus less vulnerable to chafe. It held beautifully through these strong breezes.

There was lots of fog, and this made celestial navigation difficult. A small but important thing that Rod saw to during her construction was to place the sextant box handy to the cockpit. For a worrisome period, when shoal spots were observed, they badly needed a sight to check their dead reckoning position. The sun just then burst through a hole in the clouds, and at the same time the horizon was visible. The sextant was grabbed and a sight taken just in the nick of time, before the fog returned. It proved they were where they thought they were, on a shortcut inside the Virgin Rocks, well off Cape Race, Newfoundland.

Why such a course? Because it saved 100 miles.

But for that quick sight of the sun, possible because the sextant lived near the cockpit, prudence would have dictated constant vigilance, slower speed, and a change of course to the safe but longer route. Little things like that are what help win ocean races.

However, in no way a little thing was the outstandingly excellent and accurate navigation practiced aboard *Dorade*. Her crew always knew where they were within a mile or two, and so could sail the shortest distance across the ocean.

Twice chafe of the spinnaker halyard caused that sail to drop overboard. Each time it was quickly retrieved by all hands. Each time Rod went aloft to reeve a new line. No easy task it seemed, because the motion of the boat is magnified many times up there, swinging the masthead in giant arcs. Yes, wooden ships and iron men are still with us. That iron man's name is Roderick Stephens, Jr.

Two days later two of the largest boats sighted each other as they entered the English Channel. They had a bow-to-bow race to the finish in Plymouth. The second one to finish was *Landfall*; only fourteen minutes later, *Highland Light*. Imagine sailing all the way across the Atlantic and having two boats finish only 14 minutes apart. Needless to say, their skippers thought they would be the first boats to finish the race.

As *Landfall* approached Plymouth, someone aboard spotted a small white yawl sailing out in their direction. "Looks like *Dorade*," he said. Whereupon her owner, Paul Hammond, replied, "Don't even joke about such a thing." When she drew closer and they knew she really was *Dorade*, they realized much to their chagrin that she had won.

As *Dorade* sailed into Plymouth two days before the largest boats, a launch went by in the opposite direction. This little boat had been sent out to greet *Dorade* but did not recognize her. When the launch man looked at the little white yawl and noted how well maintained she was, he said to himself, "That boat couldn't possibly have sailed across the Atlantic." So he kept on going in search of some battered craft.

On corrected time the next boat after *Dorade* came in almost four days later. She was the second smallest boat in the race: the *Skäl*. Designed by Phil Rhodes, she too had decided on the northern route. As you can see from the chart of the Atlantic, her course was not nearly as far north as *Dorade*'s. On corrected time the order of the boats was as follows:

First: *Dorade*. 52′ yawl. Roderick Stephens, Sr., owner.
Second: *Skäl*. 48′ gall-rigged cutter. Richard E. Lawrence, owner.
Third: *Amberjack II*. 46′ schooner, smallest in the race. Paul Rust, owner.
Fourth: *Highland Light*. 61′ powerful tall-masted cutter.
Fifth: *Mistress*. 60′ schooner.
Sixth: *Landfall*. 71′ ketch, biggest in the fleet.
Seventh: *Ilex*. 59′ English cutter, 32 years old. Sailed by the Royal Engineers.
Eighth: *Water Gypsy*. 50′ Alden schooner.
Ninth: *Maitenes II*. 49′ English sloop.
Tenth: *Lismore*. 70′ gaff-rigged ketch. Lost tops of both masts.

That summer in England *Dorade* went on to win the Fastnet Race. Then at the end of the summer she was shipped home by steamer. When the crew arrived in New York they were given a ticker tape parade from the Battery to City Hall up Broadway. Such an honor has never before or since been given to any yachtsman. To welcome this sailing family with origins in the Bronx, and to cheer their victories at sea, was a lift for New Yorkers during the Great Depression.

Next *Dorade* won first in Class B in the 1932 Bermuda Race. Then in the summer of 1933 she sailed across the Atlantic again from City Island to Norway, primarily to go back to the Fastnet Race in England, but in between to have some lovely cruising on the coast of Norway. She sailed to Bergen, south around to Oslo, then over to the Fastnet, which started and finished at Cowes. This she again won. Next she sailed back to Larchmont, New York. Her skipper was Rod, with five aboard. Her mate going over was Sherman Hoyt, who did not return with her. Sam Lane (later lost at sea going to Bermuda) was her mate coming back.

There is a medal awarded by the Cruising Club of America, which is described in their club book as follows: "Feeling that there were many noteworthy voyages made in small boats, and frequent examples of meritorious seamanship displayed by amateur sailors of all nationalities that went unrecognized, it seemed to the members of the Cruising Club of America that this organization was the fitting one properly to record and reward such adventure upon the sea.

"Therefore at the annual meeting on February 27, 1923, the following resolution was passed, founding a medal that it was hoped might prove an incentive for carrying on the spirit of adventure in upholding the best traditions of seafaring that are our heritage from the past.

"'Moved and seconded that the Club found, out of funds to be sought for the purpose, a medal to be known as the Blue Water Medal of the Cruising Club of America to be awarded annually at the discretion of the Board of Governors for the year's most meritorious example of seamanship, the recipient to be selected from among the amateurs of all nations.'"

In 1933 this medal was awarded to *Dorade*, Roderick Stephens, Jr., United States, for his three-month, 8,000-mile transatlantic crossing from New York to Norway and return, including victory in the Fastnet Race. This was one of a total of five Atlantic crossings he had made under sail. In addition to a very few Cruising Club members like Rod (who in 1949 and 1950 was its commodore), other recipients of this medal were nonmembers from several different countries, including France, Denmark, England, Argentina, Belgium, Sweden, and Canada.

The events aboard *Dorade* during her passage to Norway in 1933 are related below, some seen through the eyes of her 22-year-old amateur cook, the late David Leason, and some recollected by her skipper, Rod, elaborating on the terse entries in her log.

4 days out, May 24, 1933

As I sit me down to write this, I have just washed and dried the dishes after preparing a delicious meal.

So far I have had swell luck with my cooking and everyone seems to enjoy it a lot, and functioning regularly which is the main thing on a small boat. Whatever is left over from one meal I dump into the soup pot for the next, and no questions asked. So much for cooking.

We are now 150 miles southeast of Halifax and it is cold as hell. The sea is a little rough, but the wind is steady and I wire the pots to the stove and all is well. Seeing that this is really only 3½ days out, we have gone, according to our position, 540 miles from City Island, which is damn fine going, believe me. We are up off the fishing banks, and there is nothing but fog, fog, fog.

7 days out

Impossible to write yesterday because of sea. The good weather we were blessed with finally gave out and we are in for it now with a northwest gale beating us down into the steamer track. According to Rod's wind gauge, the force is about 52 miles per hour, which, with high waves, is some wind! We hove to all last night with mizzen and staysail both sheeted down hard and the tiller lashed. It improved conditions last night, a bit, but not much. It is wet, cold, rough, and nasty, but I love it. It's a cinch dollars and cents make no difference out here—it is muscles and a strong stomach. Of course when I get wet clear through and stay that way for the next few days, I may not enjoy it so much, but so far it's fine.

My right hand is swollen and blistered from scalding hot coffee, but aside from that I am in first-rate condition. I have cut two new holes in my belt in the last four days and feel much better for it. Just now there was the cry of "Steamer!" from on deck, and I grabbed the movie camera (me being official cameraman) and came on deck in time to get some beautiful shots of the *City of Durban*, who came off her course, hove to alongside us, and hailed us. We gave our destination and asked for our position. He gave it to us and said he would report us to the "Herald Trib".

8 days out

Here we are, at it again! What a sea! I never knew anything could be as high as these waves. But this damn little boat rides them like a duck. It is now 9 P.M. and I am scribbling this before I turn in.

We passed a French square-rigger, about 70 years old, today—she was fishing, anchored in 40 fathoms—240 feet of water. Imagine that! The men all gazed at us unbelievingly as we sailed round her, and here and there one would cross himself.

The barometer is dropping like a chunk of lead and I think we are in for a dirty two or three days. Despite the pitch and roll I have finished shaving—in cold salt water—and the thermometer reads 38°! Wow!

I am pretty sleepy now and will quit for tonight. We saw a school of whales. The sun rises at 3:15 A.M. and sets at 9:30 up here—isn't that something! I have two suits of woolen underwear on, and two sweatshirts and a flannel shirt. The helmsman wears approximately the same, plus a fur flying suit (one that went to the pole with Byrd and was given to us), and oilskins and rubber boots.

9 days out, 8:30 P.M.

The sailing is beautiful, it is as calm as a mill pond—the boat is going about six knots, just enough to keep the rigging from slapping and banging around on deck. For the past two hours we have been listening to England and Spain on the radio. You can hear it 100 yards away, it comes in so beautifully. I, sitting at the tiller, watched the most beautiful sunset I have ever seen. It was every delicate shade ever compounded, and a lot that never could be duplicated. The whole pattern was one of ribs and bars of clouds that were crossed, making squares and crosses in the sky, getting smaller until the sun sank—a huge reddish purple ball. Then everything slowly turned color, different colors as they got farther away, and then all settled down into a purplish gray. We all set on deck and couldn't say a word—not a single word did we say for over an hour and a half—that explains how beautiful it was more than I ever could—when you can keep five boys who don't care for much of anything spellbound for that long it must have been good.

We have gone 1,200 miles, or a little less than one third of the way, and it seems as if we had just started.

10 days out

You couldn't ask for a more beautiful day at sea. The waves are huge, but they are swells, and the boat rides them like a chute-the-chute. We have been making 9 knots for the past 14 or 15 hours, and things look good for a sustaining wind tonight.

A minor mishap in the cooking this evening. I prepared a beautiful pièce de résistance of creamed chicken and peas and was just about to serve it when along came an unexpected roll, and down it went, all over the galley floor. I hastily and skillfully scooped it up and served it on schedule.

Rod says this about that, "There were five of us on board, two in each watch, with watch off below where the cook always stayed. The spilled food was served to the watch on deck! This was welcomed by them, because it was food for five. Unbeknownst to those on deck, the three men below cooked themselves some eggs!"

Porpoises played all around the boat today all day long, and believe it or not nicked small chunks out of the log line. I had one pet which came back repeatedly to have me scratch his back with a deck broom, which I did for about a half hour before growing tired of the sport (me, not him!).

Today is the first day we have passed without sighting a steamer. We saw one large fishing schooner to leeward of us, but she was quite a bit away, and we didn't attempt to signal her.

I was on deck at about 10:30 last night, after I wrote you yesterday, and saw northern lights that were northern lights—they looked like a dawn battery of powerful searchlights flaring straight up in the air, stretching out for what must have been hundreds of miles.

11 days out

Dorade made 36 miles in four hours—an average of 9 knots, so you can see how we are driving along. Today's run of 194 miles from noon to noon puts us about 1,600 miles from City Island, so you see we have been stepping right along, seeing that we are cruising and not racing.

It makes me smile to think of the difference between your life back home, and mine, about 900 miles from the nearest possible land. There is a sense of security and safety on this boat that there could never be anywhere else. There are no cars or street cars or fire engines or Mack trucks—nothing day after day but cold dark blue waves, and damn big ones.

We figure that we should, with luck, hit Norway about the 14th of June. It will be interesting to find out just how wrong we are.

13 days out

Today we carried away the port upper spreader.

Rod says, "We were running with two spinnakers set, which was not a good arrangement. The port one collapsed momentarily and wrapped itself around the upper spreader, then suddenly filled and broke off the spreader. I went aloft and brought the two broken pieces down with me. We had some bronze plates which I fashioned to fit, and put one on top and one below the break, then riveted the two together, thus repairing the broken spreader. Then I went aloft again and installed it."

At night a fully loaded rocket pistol that is visible for miles is handy to the helmsman, so it is very safe, but each moment has its own particular thrill, believe me.

Another two weeks should well see us there.

15 days out

Practically impossible to do anything yesterday, let alone write. The same strong breeze is driving us farther and farther along toward Norway—we have gone over 2,000 miles, today, and checked our position as the sun came out long enough to take a sight.

18 days out

We have had two of the finest days for sailing that anyone could possibly wish for—good fair wind, bright sun, friendly looking furry clouds, cheerful bright sea that turns greener and greener as we near land—or possibly it's because we are off the coast of Ireland! We are exactly opposite Dublin on the chart and about 400 miles offshore. We intend cutting north between the Shetland Isles and the mainland of Scotland over through the North Sea to Bergen. We figure about 950 miles further to go—a mere drop in the bucket compared to what we've gone—today's distance at noon (it is now 5 o'clock) was 2,369 miles from City Island.

We are all busy at present, Rod overhauling his charts and navigation equipment, Ducky sleeping (just now getting up to the accompaniment of many grunts, groans, curses, and mumblings about the evils of four-hour watch in general and this one in particular), Sherman doing dead reckoning and figuring the percentage of error in our log and speedometer—one devil of a job—Porter at the tiller, and myself writing.

19 days out

Passed the two most wonderful days I have passed at sea. It seems we are deep in the Gulf Stream, and the water is warm and the sun beats down on us. It greatly improves our morale. Now the boat is completely dry—on deck and below. It is infinitely more comfortable all around now, and we have regained our spirits along with a sort of mental "second wind" toward the completion of our trip. We had 48 biscuits for supper and are stuffed and content.

20 days out

LAND HO!

This afternoon at 4:30 we sighted our landfall—and what a welcome sight. Our navigation was perfect—we sighted it dead ahead of us within ten minutes of when Rod figured we would—right on the nose! The island we sighted was St. Kilda, off the northwestern tip of Scotland, an uninhabited extinct volcano 1,373 feet high, and we saw it from the top of the mast from a distance of about 42 miles, and I prepared a huge meal of six slices of bacon, four eggs apiece, 48 muffins, two individual fig puddings with hard sauce, and brandy and coffee.

According to Rod's statistics, we went 80 miles farther than they did in the ocean race, and it took us two days longer. Without pushing the boat, being as comfortable as possible, having hove to part of one night, we did it in 20 days! We are all rested, all cuts, bruises, scratches, bumps, and scalds healed, well, happy, and contented, and here we are—I never dreamed that a passage over the North Atlantic this time of year in a 50-foot boat could be as comfortable, as easy, and as satisfactory.

We saw waves that looked like mountains, waves that looked like ripples, felt winds of 50 miles an hour and more, and felt no wind at all, had days of vision for over 30 miles, and had foggy days where you had to feel your way forward with one hand on the lifeline and one hand grasping in front of you—black as pitch.

We are now going through Pentland Firth, which is between the mainland of Scotland and the Orkney Islands. I just wish you could see the sight. It is sunset, and the sharp sheer cliffs right down to the water's edge (we are a mile offshore) half in purple light, half in deeper purple shadow, with huge fields of heather stretching back as far as the eye can see, and beyond that a perfectly huge range of mountains that almost covers the sky. Here and there is a hut, probably a fisherman's, and in one inlet that is abeam of us now is a castle that is in ruins. Through the glasses we can see the wall still standing in places, quite distinctly.

We are traveling about 15 knots past the land, because we have a 9-knot current running with us, and are passing along the coast quite rapidly. It is beautiful sailing.

The sun is just on the water's edge, and it is 10:15 P.M. It stays light until 1:30, when the sun is well up in the sky again.

23 days out

It is amusing to see what the crew does to bring a breeze. I shaved off my mustache, Rod threw away some winter underwear, Porter made the sea an offering of seven cents in Norwegian money, Ducky played the harmonica with his mouth and the accordion with his hands, and Sherman wore a curly black Russian winter hat all day long in the hot sun! Isn't that ridiculous?

We are all a pasty white in color—none of us having a vestige of burn left from City Island, and seeing that we have seen the sun for about 15 minutes at a time since then and considering the extreme weakness of that sun in these latitudes, the reason is easily seen.

24 days out, June 13, 1933, 9:10

LAND HO! The skipper just sang it out not less than three minutes ago—Porter saw it being at the tiller and told Rod. I ran on deck and sure enough over the evening mist on the calm water I could make out the dim outline of a mountain which doesn't rock, sway, or move, but stands still!

Then followed for *Dorade*'s crew a never-to-be-forgotten cruise behind rocky islands, through narrow straits, and in and out of Norwegian fjords surrounded by mountains. In places small fields at the water's edge had an unusual look, where hay was cured in the sun by hanging it vertically on wire fencing to dry at the best angle for the sun, never very high above the horizon. Behind the farms, where the land is too steep for cultivation, were forests of evergreens mounting to the timberline, and above that bare rock. What a magnificent sight, this coast of Norway.

Dorade sailed south from Bergen in a big "U" to Oslo. Then to Cowes, England, to compete in the Fastnet Race. Won it. Then sailed westward back home across the Atlantic again, mostly close hauled.

The names of the crews aboard *Dorade* for the transatlantic passages and the Fastnet Race in that summer of 1933 are listed in Rod's old photo album.

City Island to Norway to England—1933
Rod Stephens, Jr., skipper and navigator
Sherman Hoyt, mate
Porter Buck
Ducky Endt
Dave Leason, cook

Fastnet Race—1933
Rod Stephens, Jr., skipper and navigator
Sherman Hoyt, mate
Porter Buck
Ducky Endt
Dave Leason, cook
Bob Going
Phil Gick

Cowes back to Larchmont—1933
Rod Stephens, Jr., skipper and navigator
Porter Buck, first mate
Joe Appleton (from *Brilliant*)
Albie Pratt (from *Grenadier*)
Sam Lane (from *Grenadier*)
Dave Leason, cook

There is something very good that all of us sailors have inherited from *Dorade*. Namely, the Dorade vent, a ventilator that takes in spray or rain with air, separates the water from the air, and delivers the air below nice and dry. It is well known to all who have boats. It is a high cowl ventilator mounted on the top of a rectangular box. The cowl ventilator extends down into the box several inches, but ends several inches above the bottom. The downtake spout for air is a piece of pipe extending up from the bottom of the deck. Important features, overlooked by many, are the size and location of scuppers for this box—holes that should be in the after side of the box at deck level near the corners. They let out the water that has come through the cowl ventilator with the air. Since water cannot run uphill, it cannot go down the downtake spout into the cabin,

DORADE *Vent*

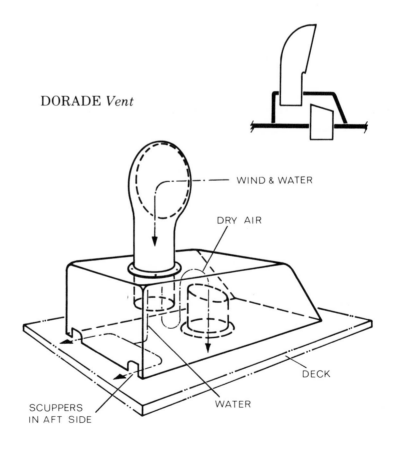

WIND & WATER

DRY AIR

DECK

SCUPPERS
IN AFT SIDE

WATER

but runs out the scuppers harmlessly on deck. The downtake spout should extend at least halfway up from the deck to the top of the box before its open top is ensured of taking in air without water. Of course, it is very important to have this downtake pipe made watertight where it comes through the deck.

In studying the early pictures of *Dorade*, I noticed that the ventilators were high cowls only, not Dorade vents. I asked Rod how this Dorade vent evolved. He explained the process step by step.

"At first before we started across the Atlantic in April, 1933, she had cowl vents on high necks. The cowls were arranged to turn at the tops of these necks. Next I put in a low baffle just inside the mouth of the cowl with a scupper hole at the base of this plate. It didn't work very well as far as keeping the water out. Then I got the idea of putting a box over the tube, which I cut off above the deck. Then the idea of having the cowl tube come into this box forward of the deck tube came to me. At that stage the box had screw-in cover plates for two holes, one above the downtake and one above the cowl tube's forward position. Later we simplified this scheme by eliminating the hole above the downtake."

Thus Rod invented the Dorade vent and in his usual modest way called it after his boat, not himself.

What's become of *Dorade*? After she was sold by the Stephens family—Olin and Rod became too busy to use her so they sold her—she went to the West Coast. There in 1936 she won the Honolulu Race from San Francisco across the Pacific to Hawaii. Now she is owned by Mr. J. Franklin Eddy, who keeps her in very shipshape condition in her present home port, Seattle, Washington. In fact, he is so proud of her he has the license plate on his car not in numbers but in the letters D O R A D E.

Mr. Stephens, Sr., Olin, and Rod

2 *Oh Youth*

The Stephens family—father and grandfather—had been in the anthracite business. The firm the grandfather put together was known as the Stephens Fuel Company and was very prosperous, operating from the Bronx in the City of New York. The firm was sold in 1929, luckily before the stock market crashed in the fall.

Prior to that the family had decided that it was too hot in the summertime living in the Bronx, so they took to going to Lake George in the Adirondack Mountains. This was to be the first experience on a fair size body of water for young Olin and Rod.

The boys were always pushing off from the family's sandy beach in one kind of boat or another, be it a small canoe to be paddled or a rowboat to be propelled by oars. On this beautiful lake they learned that when water was taken into a boat, she would swamp and sink. That when capsized, she was difficult to right and bail out. How to row. Feathering your oars for the least resistance. And all such things a boatman learns in his boyhood. Mr. Stephens, Sr., soon realized that a lake with boundaries all around was limiting for the boys. So in 1920 the family decided to go to Cape Cod during the summer months. There they encountered salt water for the first time, with its unlimited horizons, beyond which they were later to sail across the Atlantic Ocean.

The cottage they rented was on Sandy Neck, a quiet, isolated peninsula that shelters Barnstable Harbor from the open waters to the north. The Stephens had to somehow get to the town of Yarmouth, which was 2 miles away in a direct line across the harbor but 10 miles by road. The trouble was, there was not a road, so a boat was very much of a necessity. The result was that Mr. Stephens bought a 16′ sloop named *Corker*, with no power, neither inboard nor outboard, to propel her when she got becalmed.

One morning, while Mrs. Stephens and their five-year-old daughter Marite stayed ashore, Mr. Stephens and the boys boarded *Corker* and set sail with a dinghy in tow. Olin was then 12 years old, Rod not quite 11. *Corker* headed for Yarmouth from Sandy Neck, but never made it. The tide was falling, unbeknownst to *Corker*'s crew, and stranded them on the sand flats. (This was not the last time that Rod was to run aground. It happens to the best of sailors, and it happened to him a number of years ago when *Mustang* ran aground on a falling tide, which left her high and dry entering the sandpit at Lloyd Neck in Long Island Sound.) Well, the father and his two sons left the boat on the sand flat and walked the rest of the way, pushing and pulling the dinghy over the flats. He said cheerfully, "We'll come back for her this evening."

Mr. Stephens, Sr., who was then 35, resisted the urge to run things himself and let his sons do practically all the sailing. He helped out by hoisting the mainsail, heaving in the anchor, and handling other jobs a good crew does. His idea was simply that he did not want either of his sons to grow up not knowing how to do things for themselves. As it turned out, few fathers have hit upon a happier way of training their offspring. Not only did this method enable Rod and Olin to succeed as sailors, but it determined the careers that both of them have successfully pursued all their lives.

The next summer the family returned, but this time Mr. Stephens bought a boat that was 10′ longer: a 26′ day sailer called *Token*. The Stephens sailors decided they would go to Provincetown in her. This was the first mistake they made, because the town was 40 miles away, and because they planned to return in the same day. No 26′ sailboat should endeavor to do that; it's just too far. The second mistake they made was that when everybody was aboard, there were six people. Olin later confessed, "All in all, it was just what I've since come to call a drowning party." There was Mrs. Stephens, their sister Marite (now Mrs. Robert R. Sheridan of Dorset, Vermont), Rod, Olin, and two friends.

The boat had a fair breeze on the way to Provincetown and made pretty good time. They anchored, went ashore for lunch, then returned and started sailing home. It was a beat to windward, and it blew harder and harder, and they seemed to be getting nowhere. With too many bodies and too little boat, it became apparent that the craft was not performing well. It had a weak motor that was of little or no help. Soon the gathering storm was too much for the boat. The men reefed the mainsail. That appeared to be more sail than they could carry. So they lowered it altogether, and bounced around under the jib alone. Finally buffeted by wind and waves and getting nowhere, they dropped the jib. Luckily a fishing boat was nearby, and they waved wildly to her in distress. She towed them back to Provincetown. It was a day rich in lessons, and neither of the Stephens brothers has ever had to be towed into port again.

In 1922 Mr. Stephens, Sr., joined the Larchmont Yacht Club, not far from Scarsdale, where the family had moved. He replaced *Token* with a centerboard yawl about the same size, which was the first boat the family had owned that had a cabin with berths and a self-bailing cockpit. One Friday evening in the early summer the three Stephens men took possession of this boat, which had been named *Trad* by her designer, builder, and owner, Mr. Edward Merrill of Riverton, New Jersey. They went aboard her there and brought her through the old Delaware and Raritan Canal, which runs from the Delaware River through New Jersey, alongside Lake Carnegie at Princeton, then to New York Harbor. From there they sailed her to the American Yacht Club on Long Island Sound, arriving Sunday evening.

Rod always remembers this cruise in idyllic terms. While moored at the entrance to the canal, they spent their first night afloat. The next night they anchored at the back of Staten Island. It was their first exposure to the kind of existence that lures the sailing yachtsman: whole days and nights afloat, free from the ties and cares of the land, isolated in his own world.

In Scarsdale it was fascinating to pour over charts covering the east coast from Larchmont to Martha's Vineyard and Nantucket. The boys were fascinated with the harbors along the coast. Three weeks later they set sail for Edgartown, this time accompanied by an experienced yachtsman, a friend of Mr. Stephens, Sr., named Charlie Dayton, who had also been in the anthracite business. Mr. Dayton impressed the boys with his quiet levelheadedness, and he taught them a lot about boats and sailing. There is one remark he made that neither Olin nor Rod has ever forgotten: "Eternal vigilance is the price of safety."

At Edgartown that summer (where the family rented a house on the bluff south of the Yacht Club) *Trad* was fun to sail because she was a good all around boat. And Edgartown is a great place to learn how to sail because there is almost always a steady breeze each day. The average wind speed there is 14 miles an hour, which does not seem like much. But when you take into account days of flat calms, it is quite high; in fact, it is the second windiest place on the Atlantic coast after Cape Hatteras. The big event as far as yachting goes on the island of Martha's Vineyard, where Edgartown is located, is when the New York Yacht Club cruise comes into Edgartown or Vineyard Haven. The boys, now 15 and 14 years old, were very impressed to see this fleet of large schooners, yawls, ketches, and sloops come in and anchor.

Again Mr. Stephens, Sr., changed his boat the next year, buying a larger, huskier, and stiff boat named *Souwester*. She was designed by the then technical editor of *Motorboat* magazine, Bill Atkin. Bill Nutting, the editor of *Motorboat*, had sailed to England in her predecessor *Typhoon*, which had naturally enjoyed much publicity in the yachting press. Both boys had avidly absorbed the book that Nutting wrote about his voyage. In *Souwester* Bill Atkin had modified the design of *Typhoon* by filling out the bow and fining down the stern. She was one of two boats built to take part in a projected single-handed transatlantic race. Her prospective Irish owner backed out of the deal at the last minute, so Mr. Stephens, Sr., bought her. This made the boys feel they had a very important boat.

She turned out to be a dud to sail. For hour after hour they would take her back and forth across Long Island Sound, making almost no progress to windward at all. On one cruise along the Sound they made good only 17 miles against the wind in twelve hours of sailing! She was sold with almost greater enthusiasm than when she had been bought.

During the fall, winter, and spring Rod and Olin attended Scarsdale High School. There Rod became captain of the football team. Later Mr. Stephens was fond of telling his friends, "while Rod was captain of the team they never lost a game."

The next boat the family owned was a little schooner, a Royal Nova Scotia one design about 25′ long with a small cabin. This was another not-so-good vessel, following the choices of *Corker, Token, Trad,* and *Souwester.* Her name was *Scrapper.* Mr. Stephens bought her as he bought the others, largely on the basis of his sons' unfailingly enthusiastic recommendations. In May, 1925, Rod and Olin and a Scarsdale school friend named Johnny Fox sailed her across Long Island Sound from Larchmont and spent the night anchored in Cold Spring Harbor. The weather was wet and bitter cold, and the boat's cabin top leaked. The next day three miserable, bedraggled teenagers sailed back to Larchmont. They tumbled into the changing room at the Larchmont Club and took long, hot showers. They were just drying themselves and Rod was saying, "I wouldn't go on a boat now if you paid me," when an adult club member, Sherman Hoyt, then considered the best small boat helmsman in the country, peered around the door and called, "We need a couple of guys to make up the crews of the new six meters. Any offers?" In immediate unison Rod and Olin shouted, "Yes Sir!"

This was to be the inspirational beginning for Olin, because six meters were, and still are, one of the very finest sailboats to race. Their performance is supreme. Compared to the almost misbehavior of the other boats that the boys had sailed, six meters were just about perfect. Olin was told to join a six called *Redhead* sailed by Clinton Crane, an amateur designer of great repute. Rod went aboard *Lanai,* sailed by Sherman Hoyt. Both boats, designed by Mr. Crane, had been launched only a few days earlier; this was their first trial. Each was around 34′ long and had an open cockpit and no cabin. Their speed and responsiveness, the way they thrust to windward! These were sensations utterly foreign to Rod and Olin, who had known only the poor performance of their other boats.

The two had a close match at first. But gradually the skill of Sherman Hoyt began to tell, and *Lanai* opened such a widening lead that her skipper invited Rod to steer her over the last mile. Rod no longer felt the driving rain that had made him so miserable three hours earlier. As *Lanai* raced acrosss the Sound, he felt the free yet precise control of her tiller as she neared her maximum speed. Then when they swept across the finish line, the excitement of winning, even a friendly trial, unforgettably pervaded his whole being.

In his way Olin shared his brother's feelings. He later said, "It provided a new lesson. From that time on I was thoroughly bitten by the six-meter bug." But the afternoon sailing provided for Olin something that would prove to be an even greater reward: the friendship of Clinton Crane. At that time he was in his early fifties, a quiet, dignified man, soon to be commodore of the Seawanhaka Corinthina Yacht Club in Oyster Bay. At the turn of the century Mr. Crane had earned a degree in naval architecture at the University of Glasgow. For a time he had worked in the United States as a yacht designer, then had joined a leading company, The St. Joseph Lead Company, as its president and later chairman. He designed yachts only as an amateur, although with considerable success.

In the summer of 1926 the Stephens family acquired their next boat, *Alicia*. She was one of eight schooners known as the Sound Schooner Class, swifter than any of the family's earlier boats. On weekends when Rod and Olin could not inveigle their way into a six-meter crew, they raced her at Larchmont, New Bedford, and Edgartown. By this time Charlie Dayton had taught them to use a chart, a compass, and a set of parallel rules. They became proficient at piloting. *Alicia* won some races that summer.

On their own the boys decided to take a cruise from Edgartown to Gloucester. They rounded Cape Cod and ran into fog and no wind. Next morning, after they had been anchored, the sun burned away the fog, and a light breeze came in from the east. They set sail and spotted a fleet of boats: the New York Yacht Club's summer cruise rounding the Cape. Olin laid the course from the Cape to Gloucester, their destination, and they headed for Gloucester on a reach. Soon they noticed a New York 40 sloop coming up fast behind them. Since she crossed their stern, this did not seem right to Rod. "Say, Olin," he called, "if they're heading for Marblehead shouldn't we be on a course 3° or 4° the other side of them?"

His brother told him to say on the course he had laid and to ignore the other boat. Soon after they had run most of the day, they made their landfall: Gloucester came up dead ahead. As they sailed into harbor, they saw on the horizon astern the New York 40 suddenly making a big change in course and heading down the coast toward them, presumably to Marblehead. She had sailed 25 miles too far west. Another maxim was engraved in Rod's memory: "If you have checked your own equipment, trust it."

Another episode that had to do with the compass was when they were on a passage to Nova Scotia in a 28′ schooner owned by Bob Moore. At the start of the voyage her compass proved to be wildly inaccurate. The reason: Mr. Moore had installed new galvanized steel fuel tanks without considering their effect on the magnetic field of the compass. So they put into New Bedford to seek out a compass adjuster. A good one by the name of George Systere came aboard, swung ship, used his astrolobe, and with compensating magnets corrected the compass. Then he invited the crew to his own boat for a drink and a singsong. Mr. Systere played an accordion, which so fascinated Rod that a few months later he bought one and taught himself to play it.

Olin was now 17, Rod 16. The problem of their education and their future had engaged their father for quite some time. It was obvious to him now that neither of his sons had any interest in the anthracite business. His two sons went to Scarsdale High School, where both acquitted themselves well in academic subjects. Olin spent much of his time in history classes, preferring to concentrate on subjects such as American history and mathematics. He did well in these, especially the latter. But in chemistry he did not fare so well. All his spare time at home was devoted to drawing boats. By now with the help of books and the intense application of his mind to his subject, he had taught himself the essentials of theoretical yacht design. His mind was constantly filled with ideas to make boats sail faster and to improve them generally. Now more than ever he is still a very single-minded man regarding his profession.

Rod excelled in all sports, much to his father's pleasure. Not only was he captain of the football team as the quarterback, but he made the basketball and the baseball teams as well.

Olin was persuaded to go to the Massachusetts Institute of Technology by his father, to take a degree in naval architecture. However, Olin had no interest in the big ship architecture that dominated the MIT course. He wanted to make a start in yacht designing as soon as possible and not waste time on the other compulsory subjects there. Founded on and largely supported by money from the du Pont family, which made its fortune from chemicals, MIT insisted that all freshmen students should take chemistry—not Olin's favorite subject. In deference to his parents, and before graduating from Scarsdale High School, he traveled to Boston for a preliminary interview with the head of MIT's department of naval architecture. Hearing of Olin's interest in sailboats, the professor showed him plans he had drawn for an oceangoing yacht. The hypercritical young Olin examined her lines, made some slight pleasantry, and went home even more convinced that MIT would waste his time.

Nevertheless, in the fall of 1926 he presented himself at the college to take a four-year course in naval architecture. From the outset he did not enjoy it. Soon after returning to college from the Christmas vacation in 1926, Olin suffered a slight attack of jaundice. It was necessary for him to return home to recuperate, and there he spent the days designing a six meter. He never returned to MIT. It turned out that this was the very best thing he could have done, for he has since far outstripped his MIT freshmen classmates in receiving honors. They include an honorary degree of Master of Science from Stevens Institute of Technology in 1945 and a Master of Arts degree from Brown University in 1959. He was awarded the Society of Naval Architects and Marine

Engineers David W. Taylor Gold Medal in 1959, and their Certificate of Commendation in 1974. He has been quite active in the Society, being presently chairman of Panel H13 on sailing yachts and a member of the committee on fellows and hydrodynamics. He is also chairman of the International Technical Committee of the Offshore Rating Council and is author of "Measurement Parameters of the International Offshore Rating Rule" and many articles on yachting subjects. And he is a trustee of Mystic Seaport, Inc.

STORMY WEATHER   (Rosenfeld)

3 Early Designs

In the spring of 1927 Olin and Rod persuaded their father to buy a six meter. He did so, obtaining *Natka* at a reasonable price because she had not been too successful. She had placed sixth out of eight in the Scandinavian-American Cup in 1925, so the qualities of speed, steering, and handling that make a boat a winner were evidently poor. Not expecting too much from her, Olin and Rod found great satisfaction when, with hard work and some luck, they managed now and then to win or to place against the newer, faster boats. Learning to get the most out of a boat that was not as fast as her sisters was valuable experience. Even more valuable in the long run were the contacts and the friendships that racing a six meter brought the Stephens brothers. At that time the sixes were the most active open racing class, providing hot competition on Long Island Sound and attracting many of the country's prominent yachtsmen. International contests in the sixes took place between the United States, Britain, Scandinavia, and other European countries.

They were not a one-design class. Meter boats such as twelves, tens, eights, and sixes put design and construction to the test, as well as the crew's sailing ability. They usually have different lengths, different dimensions for beam, for displacement and for sail area. These differences are compensated for by the use of a formula* so that, for instance,

---

* $\dfrac{\text{Length} + 2\,\text{Girth Diff.} + \sqrt{\text{Sail Area}} - \text{Freeboard}}{2.37} = 6 \text{ meters}$

great length is offset by less sail area or larger displacement. The designer's only concern is that the collective measurements of his boat when passed through the formula shall produce the result of, in this case, six meters (when used to produce 5.5, or 8, or 10, or 12 meters, it governs those classes also). The rule was devised in 1906 by the International Yacht Racing Union, at that time a European-based group. American interest in meter boats developed only after a rule modification in 1919.

Although in the late 1920's meter boats were considered only suitable for more or less sheltered waters such as Long Island Sound, the Clyde, or the Baltic, a busy one-way traffic in them developed down the exposed Atlantic coast from Nova Scotia to Long Island Sound. It began in 1927 when a syndicate of Long Island yachtsmen ordered 14 identical ten meters from Starling Burgess's design to be built in Germany at a bargain price by Aberking and Rasmussen of Bremen. Unlike the smaller sixes, the ten meters ran 60′ long, had cabins with full accommodations, five or more berths, a galley, a head, etc. Nonetheless, they were bought for inshore racing and cruising. In 1928 no less than 8 identical eight meters and 4 identical twelve meters, all from the same designer and builder, joined the fleet in Long Island Sound.

At that time U.S. law required no duty on yachts imported on their bottoms. Therefore all new boats were shipped to Halifax and sailed to Long Island Sound.

In May, 1927, when the first group of ten-meter boats arrived, two brothers in the Roosevelt family, Philip and John, invited Olin and Rod to help them bring their new "ten" down from Halifax. On the northbound steamer Phil Roosevelt showed the Stephens brothers how to take sextant sights of the sun and stars, teaching them the rudiments of celestial navigation.

The new ten meters left Halifax towed by a big diesel-powered schooner, but the convoy soon ran into high seas and heavy weather. Cast off from their tow and separated, the meter boats continued the voyage under their own reduced sail. Subsequent letters to the yachting press from pleased owners soon expressed surprise at the sea-keeping ability of the narrow, deep-keeled ten meters. True they sailed on their ears when heeled by a strong breeze, but they made fast progress to windward, a very important feature in winning sailboat races. The following season Olin sailed aboard a new eight meter the entire distance from Halifax to New York. Its performance did not surprise Olin but merely confirmed his ideas. It must have been the inspiration for *Dorade*'s narrow, deep shape.

Through the years after *Dorade*'s outstanding victory, there were many ocean-racing yachtsmen who were very critical in their opinions of her. Especially caustic were the proper Bostonians, who had been brought up on and were quite sure that Alden schooners were the very best type to sail on the ocean.

No doubt about it, they were good seagoing boats because their designs were based on the well-known Gloucester fishing schooners. These vessels had

Six-Meter Goose

to sail out with cracked ice in their holds and stay out over the Grand Banks or George's Bank until their dorymen had caught enough cod to fill the schooner's hold. Then there was always a race to see which boat could arrive home at the wharf first. They had to be fast as well as seaworthy, because the first load of codfish to arrive brought the highest price.

These critics of *Dorade* called her "just a six meter" or "too narrow so therefore too tender" or "little or no room below, making her uncomfortable." There is a grain of truth in what they said, but she was so fast, and finished first so often, that she revolutionized the design of sailing yachts thereafter.

Sailing his own designs, John Alden had twice won the Bermuda Race: first in his schooner *Malabar IV* in 1923, then in another of his schooners, *Malabar VII,* in 1926. These vessels were beamy and stood up to the wind. They were even fast with the wind on the beam or astern. But making good progress to windward is most important in a sailing boat, and at this they were not particularly good. Their heavy construction did not help. The builders of these schooners were mostly in Maine, where they preferred to use sawn- instead of steam-bent frames. Of course a sawn frame means that you go across the grain, when the curve is cut in certain places, so they cannot be very long. Consequently they lay one piece alongside another (as you would to make a wall of bricks) and bolt them together longitudinally. Hence they are twice as thick as a steam-bent frame, which has the grain going in the curve because it is straight grained to begin with, and then bent after being saturated with steam in a steam box, which saves a great deal of weight. On the meter boats, built with steam-

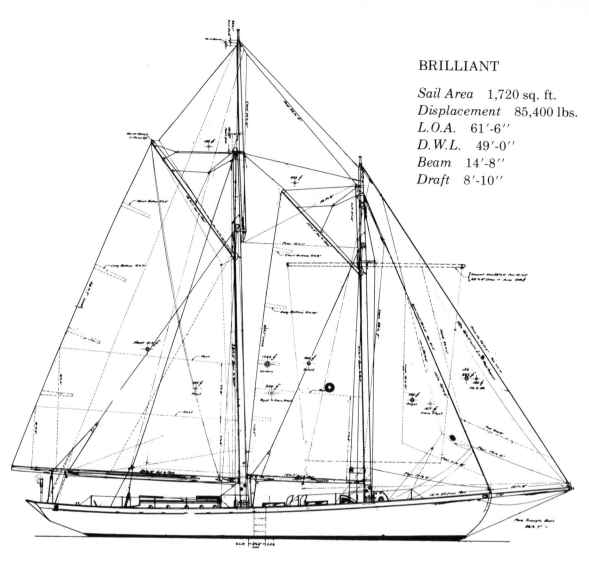

BRILLIANT

Sail Area 1,720 sq. ft.
Displacement 85,400 lbs.
L.O.A. 61'-6''
D.W.L. 49'-0''
Beam 14'-8''
Draft 8'-10''

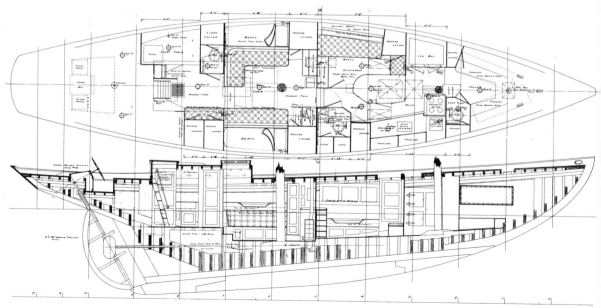

bent frames, this weight saving was put into their lead keels. This heavy ballast keel, together with their narrow beam, enabled them to have great power to windward.

Before *Dorade*'s victory in the transatlantic race of 1931, and although Olin had published a design of a six meter in yachting magazines, the first design he sold was of a very small boat. He was commissioned to do it entirely through the salesmanship of his prospective patron, who later added the name Stephens to his own when the new firm was incorporated.

As a yacht broker Drake Sparkman believed that "no deal is too small." In later years he recalled a client who first bought a dinghy from him for $700. A year later the same client bought a sailboat costing $7,000. Two years after that this client traded for one costing $15,000. Ultimately the same client ordered a yacht designed by Sparkman & Stephens that cost $90,000.

The committee of the Larchmont Yacht Club in the fall of 1928 decided to sponsor a new small class boat for its junior members. As in any popular sailing area, yacht clubs along both sides of Long Island Sound from time to time vie with one another in launching new classes of racing boats. It is a matter of practical club politics: The club that first sponsors a successful design will have a larger fleet and a greater influence in running the class racing. In general, the boat's success will rub off on the club. So Larchmont, sensing that the time was right for a new junior boat on Long Island Sound, quietly cast around for designs.

As it happened, member Drake Sparkman had one immediately available drawn by fellow member Olin Stephens, a junior himself. Mr. Sparkman at first whisper of the club's proposal had gotten Olin to produce a design and persuaded a boat builder named Buckhout in Poughkeepsie, up the Hudson River from New York City, that if he moved quickly and built the first boat, he could possibly have the monopoly over the construction of what might become a highly popular class. Buckhout built the boat. The Larchmont Yacht Club accepted the design. Then further lobbying resulted in its being sponsored by the Junior Yacht Racing Association of Long Island Sound.

As *Yachting* magazine described her, "The design shows a well modeled little craft with nice sheer and moderate overhangs. The iron keel and buoyant flaring sections indicates stiffness and dryness. The modern efficient rig should make for good speed and ease of handling in all weathers. The cockpit is quite roomy and comfortable for a boat this size, and double plank bulkheads making watertight compartments fore and aft make the boat unsinkable. The need for such a class as this for juniors has long been felt in many localities. As there is no reason why this design should not be acceptable anywhere along the Atlantic coast, it is hoped that other junior associations will build duplicates in the future."

Such good publicity augered well for the success of the design, but it would not make the new design partnership of Sparkman & Stephens suddenly rich. Measuring 21'-6" overall, 15'-0" datum waterline, 5'-10" beam, and 3'-6"

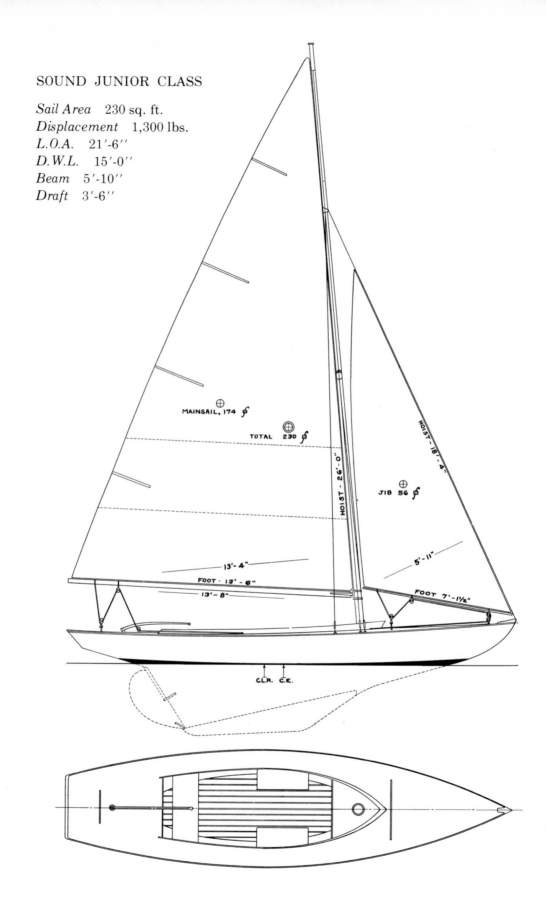

SOUND JUNIOR CLASS

Sail Area 230 sq. ft.
Displacement 1,300 lbs.
L.O.A. 21'-6"
D.W.L. 15'-0"
Beam 5'-10"
Draft 3'-6"

MAINSAIL, 174 □

TOTAL 230 □

JIB 56 □

HOIST - 26'-0"

HOIST - 18'-4"

13'-4"

FOOT - 13'-6"

13'-8"

5'-11"

FOOT 7'-1½"

C.L.R. C.E.

draft, with 230 square feet total sail area, the Manhasset Bay One Design as it is now called (originally Sound Junior One Design), took Buckhout's yard a month to build. From each boat priced at $1,000, the designer received a royalty of $25. It was a start, and nothing could diminish Olin's quiet exultation seeing his first creation launched. It gave him the greatest pleasure to know that when she was first launched she floated exactly on her designed waterline. Best of all, on her trial trip she sailed well and "without vices." It is the plans of this little sloop that are lettered "Design No. 1, Sparkman and Stephens, Naval Architects," and dated "July 1929."

The last two summers Rod and Olin had sailed a good deal together, and Rod had ultimately expressed hope that he could find work with Olin that would involve boats. Olin thought it would be a great idea. They made a good team on a boat, they never argued, and for a long time they used to take it in turns to steer. But after the purchase of *Natka,* and after sailing her a few times, Rod suggested that Olin should always steer and navigate and handle tactics, while he controlled the foredeck and the sails.

At Larchmont they surprised themselves by racing their six-meter *Natka* and winning second place in the class in the club's Regatta Week. Larchmont has always had the largest regatta every summer anywhere in the United States. The second largest is at Marblehead, and the third largest is the Edgartown Regatta. There are a lot of sailboats on the southern California coast, so it may be that nowadays the regatta there is larger than these on the East Coast.

Olin and Rod next took a boat called *Kalmia* in the 500-mile Gibson Island Race, starting at New London, Connecticut, and ending up at Chesapeake Bay just beyond Annapolis. *Kalmia* was the smallest boat competing. They drove her through some rough weather past some of her bigger rivals, and she won her class. Later Drake Sparkman found a client who wanted Olin to design a larger version of *Kalmia.* Race success did produce clients.

Interest was soon stirring in the coming year's British-American Cup Races for six meters. Since Britain had won the last match on the Clyde in 1928, rivalry for places on the American team would be strong. Drake Sparkman again found a client for Olin. This time Olin persuaded the owner not to wait until the winter to have the boat built, but to have work started on it immediately in the fall to give himself ample time for crew training. The design was a slightly modified version of the six meter that had first appeared in *Yachting* the year before. One day soon thereafter Drake returned jubilantly from lunch at the New York Yacht Club and called Olin to tell him he had secured yet another commission, this time for an even bigger sloop, 30′ on the waterline.

Olin's new six-meter design was named *Thalia.* Unfortunately, as the punsters were quick to say, "*Thalia* was a failure." She was beamy and fine ended and incapable of high speed in strong winds, because she created her maximum wavelength too soon. But her trials in the fall were promising enough for Clinton Crane, over the next four months, to steer five would-be clients in Olin's direction. Four of them ordered six meters. The fifth ordered an eight meter, as a candidate to represent the United States in trying to wrest the Canada's Cup from the Canadians on Lake Ontario the following summer. Now at last the work was rolling in!

Meantime Rod had not returned to his studies of mechanical engineering at Cornell. He worked with Olin at his office at Nevins Yard, where he made himself useful. He and Olin had known the yard owner, Henry Nevins, for several years. They had first spoken to him while nosing around the yard as boys on winter Sundays, when it was too cold to sail. And they had come to know him better when their father laid up the six-meter *Natka,* which they had owned, at the yard. Rod and Mr. Nevins got along so well that the yard owner called Rod's father and made a remarkable request. "Would you object" he said, "if I proposed to Rod that he should quit college and come to work for me? I'll teach him more in three or four years about building boats than he'll learn in 10 years at college. He has a tremendous aptitude, and he could have a great future here, because I have no one to take over when I'm gone."

Mr. Stephens, Sr., said he would leave it to his son to decide. Rod was nonplussed. Thanking Mr. Nevins, he pointed out that he was due back at college in three weeks.

"Just think it over," said Mr. Nevins.

The more Rod thought about the proposition, the more attractive it seemed. He told his dean at Cornell that the Nevins job appealed to him because most of all he wanted to work with small boats. Being a dean this man naturally said, "To make a success in life one should not take a job simply because one likes the work."

"That," Rod argued, "seemed like bad advice. If you find work that's more enjoyable each day, that way you'll surely stay more ahead of the game."

The college dean gave Rod a leave of absence, confident that this promising athlete would be back on campus before the end of the next term.

Just like Olin, Rod never returned to college. And just like Olin, as it turned out, it was the right thing to do.

The great success of Sparkman & Stephens derives from the Stephens brothers knowing exactly what they wanted to do and not wasting the last three years in college, but starting their careers early in life. Rod's experience working at Nevins Yard was far more valuable to the team effort of Sparkman & Stephens than would have been three more years of mechanical engineering.

As design work began rolling in, suddenly in a matter of a few months Olin found himself outgrowing his space at Nevins Yard. So Drake Sparkman rented a larger office for him opposite the boat yard at 205 City Island Avenue, City Island, New York City, and hired a retired draftsman, named McCormack, to do his final drawings. It was time, too, to consider the future of the partnership. On October 28, 1929, five men met at Sparkman & Stephens' East 44th Street offices to turn the partnership into a corporation. They were Drake Sparkman, his younger brother James, and James Murray, the three of them salesmen. Then Olin and his father. The incorporation was confirmed on November 11, 1929.

With the collapse of the stock market on Wall Street reverberating on other markets around the world, it seemed to be the least propitious time to start a new company, particularly one dealing exclusively with high-priced luxury items. But in fact, people with money to buy boats still seemed to have enough to buy more and larger ones. Certainly the yacht brokerage business showed no sign of diminishing.

The failure of the stock market did threaten one vital side of Olin's work. He heard a rumor that the British-American Cup series of races for six meters might be canceled. In addition to *Thalia,* not long launched, Olin now had three six meters on his design board or under construction at Nevins Yard: *Comet* and *Meteor,* sisterships for two yachtsmen sailing on Lake Michigan, and *Mist,* designed for John Roosevelt. Yet another contract was almost ready to be signed incorporating the client's ideas and some of Olin's. Fortunately, a few days later Olin was relieved to hear the British-American Cup match would take place after all. And shortly afterward in 1930 he clinched the contract for his fifth six-meter design.

In quick succession in the early months of 1930 his new creations came down the ways at the Minneford and Nevins yards. First *Kalmia*'s big sister, one named *Balkis,* and Bob Moore's *Cynara.* Then the bigger *Alsumar.* Then three of the six-meter designs, *Mist, Comet,* and *Meteor.* With Olin and Rod sailing *Comet* before she was shipped to Lake Michigan, the twin six meters won three first places, two seconds, and three thirds in their first seven races.

Minneford launched *Dorade* that May. She joined a record fleet of 41 yachts for the 600-mile race from New London, Connecticut, to Bermuda. When she started, the first four days gave the fleet a reach in a moderate breeze all the way to the island. But a faulty sextant ruined any chance of winning for *Dorade* and her crew. The resulting nagivational error took them too far east, and as they approached the island they found they had a longer beat to windward before they reached the finish line than Olin had estimated. Still, with the handicaps worked out, *Dorade* came third overall, second in her class, and won the prize awarded to the leading boat with an all-amateur crew. She crossed the finish line nearly 12 minutes ahead of a new 60′ schooner designed by Sherman Hoyt, and only 46 seconds behind another new schooner called *Teragram.* The magazine *Boats* predicted that *Dorade*'s performance would soon "alter the whole concept of the ocean racer and make a profound change in defiance of the sailing world of her time."

The second-place boat in that Bermuda Race was John Alden's latest schooner design, *Malabar X.* It was gratifying to the crew aboard *Dorade* that they had beaten most of the other bigger schooners, boat for boat.

The next boat was a six meter named *Cherokee.* She had problems. Meter boats must float precisely to their marks, and it was noticed that *Cherokee*'s waterline was dipping under water at the stern. At her launching and rigging she had floated exactly right, but since then her wooden hull must have absorbed more water than normal. Extra fittings added in and around her cockpit had weighed her down enough to increase her waterline length and to disqualify her as a six-meter.

When *Dorade* was first launched she floated 3″ deep. All that was done was to simply paint her boot top 3″ higher. Because she floated deep, her handicap or rating turned out slightly different from what Olin had calculated. Any increase in a six meter's measurements will result in her not complying with the formula. One solution was to reduce *Cherokee*'s sail area. Another was to cut 30 or 40 pounds off the aft end of the lead keel. But Olin believed that to interfere with her ballast or sail area might mar her performance. On the other hand, to cut off the stern of the boat might make her look marginally less beautiful but would not influence her sailing ability. So at Nevins Yard Rod supervised the amputation of some 18″ off *Cherokee*'s stern. He carefully weighed it to ensure that enough had been removed to make her float correctly again, then had her hull closed off with a new transom stern. The American team beat the British, with Corny Shields skippering *Cherokee*. She scored a first place, two thirds, and a fourth. Olin regarded *Cherokee* with much affection as having secured his position as a successful designer of meter boats.

Despite the stock market collapse, the first year of Sparkman & Stephens, Inc., proved to be successful, both at sea and on the books. The design office had kept busy with two more six meters, a 38′ sloop, and a 43′ motor cruiser. This last order came through a new salesman, W. Porter Buck.

In the last three months of the year Olin's already brimming cup was overflowing. He and his old girl since childhood, Susie Reynolds, had always agreed that they would marry as soon as he had made a fair start. The first year of Sparkman & Stephens, Inc., fulfilled that requirement. They were married in Scarsdale at the Presbyterian church, where Mr. Stephens, Sr., was an elder, and where both bride and groom had attended the Sunday school. Susie did not want Olin to wear his spectacles for the ceremony. But Olin, naturally shortsighted and unable to see clearly across a room, much less a church, said that maybe he might not recognize her at the altar and might take the wrong girl's hand. She relented.

That December the current issue of *Yachting* magazine had a portrait of Olin on the opening Hall of Fame page with a caption that began: "To have achieved a reputation as a clever helmsman, successful racing skipper, and at the same time to have earned a name as a naval architect with many fast yachts to one's credit is something that does not often fall to the lot of anyone at the age of 20. Hence it is with satisfaction that we present this month the portrait of Olin J. Stephens II of whom all the above can be said."

The minute any two yachtsmen board their boats for a quiet sail around the bay, they are almost certain to be overcome by a desire to race. The Stephens brothers have long endeared themselves to their clients not only by

CHEROKEE
(Rosenfeld)

providing them with boats that win races, but by demonstrating that they themselves share the universal passion for competitive sailing. The Stephenses have always delighted in getting their seats soaking wet on the spray-swept decks of racing yachts, whether engaged in a midafternoon sprint around a nearby buoy or two in the Sound, or in a grueling transatlantic ocean race. Their seamanship is so superb that several prominent yacht owners have put off entering major races until they were assured of having at least one of the brothers in their crew.

On deck and in the thick of the race, the Stephenses run true to form. No matter how acute the crisis of the moment can be, Olin sits at the tiller or wheel quietly calculating the strategic advantages of a starboard tack perhaps, or pointing out in the steady voice he preserves even during times of intense inner excitement, the effect of the boat's low resistance characteristics on its ability to go to windward. Rod meanwhile is in ceaseless motion, dashing fore and aft as he shifts the sails in response to every change in the wind, scrambling up into the rigging to scout the surface of the water for signs of a better breeze elsewhere, barking orders and in general showing up in the binoculars of rival skippers as the most animated subject on the horizon. The brothers have been in the thick of things during almost every Bermuda Race for the last 50 years, for it is the Kentucky Derby of the yachting world.

Olin, whose interest in sailboats is so objective that he prefers not to take on the responsibilities of owning one, went along as second mate aboard *Bolero,* a lovely 73′ yawl of S & S (Sparkman & Stephens) design built shortly after the war for John Nicholas Brown, at that time Assistant Secretary of the Navy. In 1956 she was first to finish out of 89 starters, and she established a new course record in the 635-mile Bermuda Race.

Right after the war, in the 1946 race to Bermuda, Rod skippered his own N.Y. 32 Class sloop, *Mustang,* winning second place in Class B. Again in 1950 she won second in Class B, and two years later in the same race won first in that class. In 1962 they once more won second in Class B.

That 1956 race to "the onion patch," as Bermuda is known, had 27 S & S boats in it. Out of the 21 trophies that were awarded, 13 went to them.

The days when J. P. Morgan is supposed to have said that "any man who asks how much it costs to own a yacht can't afford one" are mostly a thing of the past. A much more drastic change has come over the whole sport of sailing since the war. The fact is that the increase in the number of large sailing yachts has been overshadowed by a far greater increase in the number of smaller sailing craft. These boats, that were so big it required a crew of a dozen paid hands to sail them, are now almost extinct. And the sport is being taken over more and more by enthusiasts of moderate means who go in for production-built fiberglass stock boats. They are not usually built in a shipyard at the water's edge, but in a factory-like building anywhere inland.

The *Blue Jay,* a little 13′ centerboard sloop that S & S designed in 1947,

LIGHTNING CLASS

Sail Area   177 sq. ft.
Weight   700 lbs.
L.O.A.   19'-0''
Beam   6'-6''
Draft   4'-11''

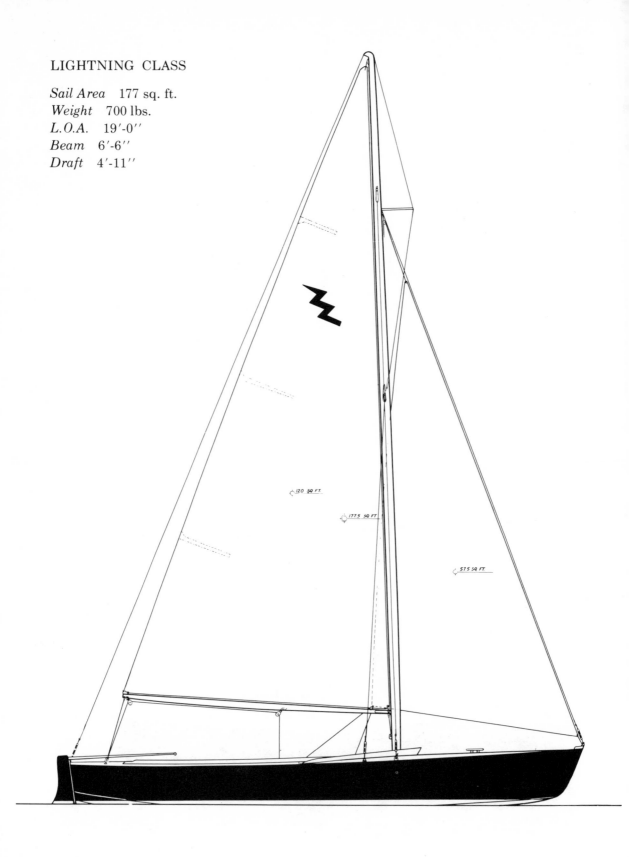

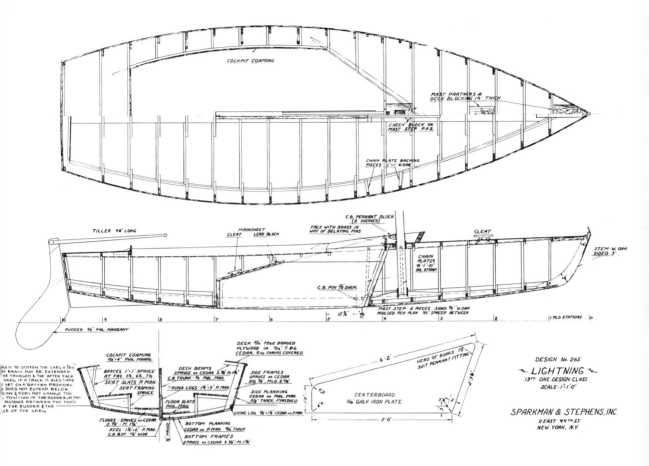

and the *Lightning*,* a spry 19′ centerboard sloop designed in 1939, have become very popular one-design classes.

Sparkman & Stephens prefers to rely for the major part of its sailboat business on well-to-do customers who want yachts rather than day sailers, and want them designed to suit their individual tastes. Sailing yachts as a rule run from 30′ up in length. Most have at least four bunks, a complete galley, toilet facilities, electric lights, and an auxiliary motor. In 1957 S & S had about 100 personnel in the design office. They designed many extremely prosaic vessels such as tugs, minesweepers, coastal tankers, and freighters. In fact, at that time most of the staff was regularly assigned to such jobs. It is a matter of record

* The Lightning class was a good design, but to the Stephens brothers not a good business arrangement. Sparkman & Stephens, failing to appreciate the potential size of the market, let the plans go for a few hundred dollars to the Lightning Class Association, a nonprofit outfit made up of Lightning owners from all over the world—Italy, Peru, Hawaii, and elsewhere. To date there are well over 7,000 Lightnings. It does not cheer Sparkman & Stephens to reflect that if the company had held on to the plans and charged its established royalty for each Lightning to reach the market, it would by now have realized a little more than one hundred thousand dollars on this design alone.

INTERCLUB DINGHY

L.O.A. 11'-6''
D.W.L. 11'-6''
Beam 4'-7''
Draft 1'-8''

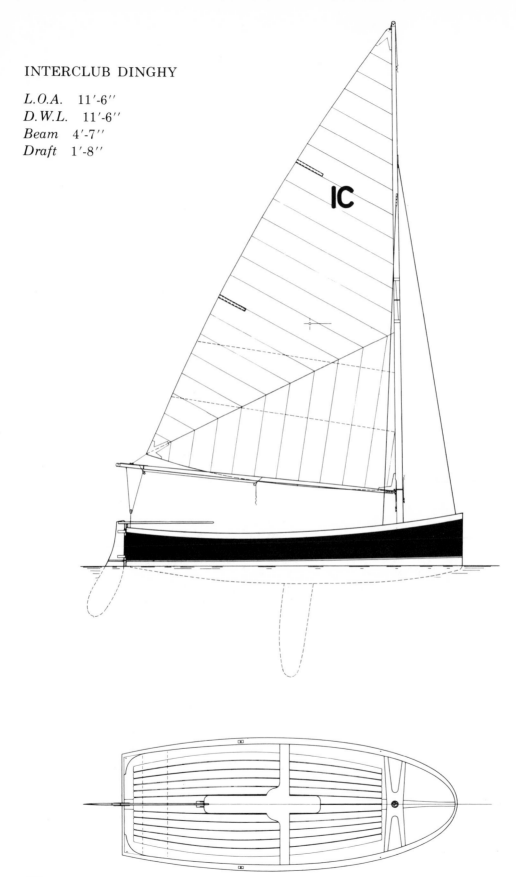

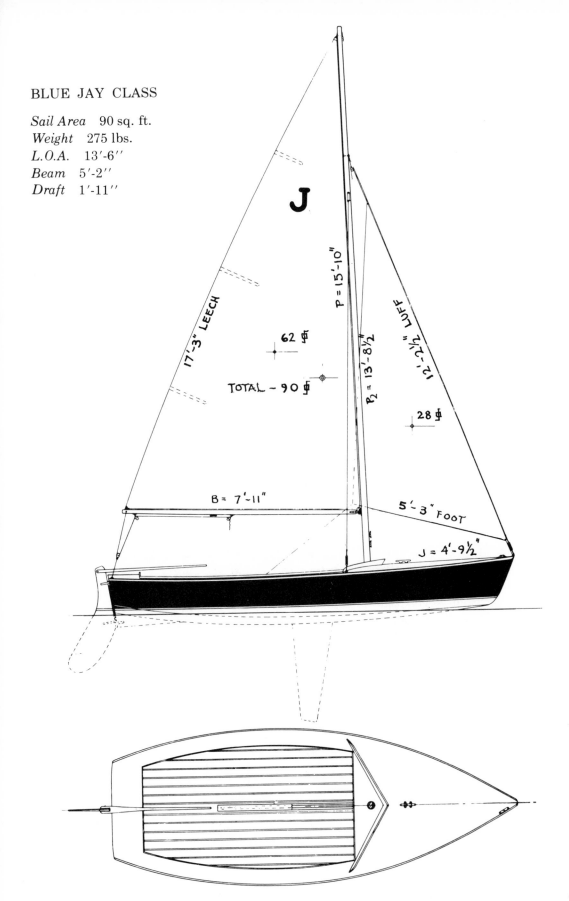

BLUE JAY CLASS

Sail Area 90 sq. ft.
Weight 275 lbs.
L.O.A. 13'-6''
Beam 5'-2''
Draft 1'-11''

J

17'-3" LEECH

P = 15'-10"

12'-2½" LUFF

P_2 = 13'-8½

62 ₁ɟ

TOTAL – 90 ₁ɟ

28 ₁ɟ

B = 7'-11"

5'-3" FOOT

J = 4'-9½"

that in 1957 S & S, having a payroll of about 120 people and with almost no requirements in the way of raw materials, realized from its combined brokerage, insurance, and designing activities a gross income of around a million dollars.

Nowadays designing for companies that produce boats on a mass production basis has been taking part of the place of designing individual boats for clients.*

Mr. Stephens, Sr., did not have to wait long for assurance that his investment in his sons' careers was a sound one. Even in 1932, when there was barely a ripple in the yacht market, Olin was kept moderately busy. His biggest job that year was to design a $90,000 schooner, called *Brilliant*, for Walter Barnum. She was a fast one and has won many races, especially schooner races, which are held now in New York Harbor. Today she is still in commission at the Mystic Seaport to take young people for sails and instruction from time to time.

Olin was called on to design an 11' Class sailing dinghy for the junior members of the Larchmont Yacht Club. Next a yawl named *Stormy Weather*, along the lines of *Dorade* but with greater beam, for Philip Le Boutillier, at that time the president of Best & Co. department stores. The seven other sailboats in 1934, including a 70' yawl, made Rod's assignment of inspecting and supervising their construction quite a busy occupation. No fewer than 20 boats designed by the firm were under construction during that year in half a dozen yards up and down the Atlantic seaboard.

In 1935 Rod skippered *Stormy Weather* in another transatlantic race, winning on corrected time. Then, like *Dorade* did before, she went in the Fastnet Race and won that easily. She also sailed home across the Atlantic.

Naturally Rod wanted to make *Stormy*'s owner, Mr. Philip Le Boutillier, Sr., happy with this new boat. The acid test came when she and *Dorade* sailed in company for the first time, in a 25 mph easterly in Long Island Sound off Larchmont. Under these conditions the Sound gets fairly rough, because the wind and seas have about a 100-mile fetch in which to build up. At first *Dorade* had a slight edge. Rod noticed that *Stormy* had furled her mizzen because it luffed, so he put the helm up, eased *Dorade* off, and went back and told them to set it again. They did. Then to Rod's delight the beamier *Stormy Weather* slowly got going beautifully, beating to windward even with her prototype, the swift *Dorade*. Fait accompli!

Stormy Weather did soon turn out to be a better boat than *Dorade* in many ways, because of her proportionately greater beam. She could perform better

---

* Nautor in Pietarsaari, Finland, has sold as of May, 1977, a total of 588 boats of S & S design, the most popular being the Swan 38 (88 built) and the Swan 36 (86 built). Here in the United States the Tartan Marine Company in Grand River, Ohio, has sold as of this same date 1,653 boats that S & S designed. Their most popular class is the Tartan 27 (623 built), next the Tartan 30 (462 built), and the Tartan 34 (435 built). These two companies together have produced and sold 2,241 fiberglass stock boats from the drawing boards at S & S. Soon to come on the market will be two stock fiberglass boats built in Japan by Fuji Yacht Builders, the Fuji 40 and the Fuji 32, both of S & S design.

under sail on every point of sailing, in almost every sea condition and strength of wind. But there was one exception. That was going to windward in a light breeze with a big ground swell running. The narrow *Dorade* could outsail her only in those particular conditions.

About that time the yachting magazine *Rudder* wrote of the 26-year-old Olin, "The day does not appear far distant when he will be called in to create a defender or maybe a challenger for the America's Cup, the dream of every naval architect."

It so happened that one day in August, 1936, Harold S. Vanderbilt, the outstanding American big boat sailor of his time, got Olin on the telephone and, after telling him the New York Yacht Club had received a challenge for the America's Cup from the Royal Yacht Squadron of Cowes, asked if he would be willing to collaborate with the well-known naval architect W. Starling Burgess in designing a yacht to defend the Cup.

A staggering sum of money has been spent by British, Australian, French, and Swedish yachtsmen, as well as Americans, in the course of their century-long rivalry for possession of this ugly baroque silver pitcher bolted through a table into the floor of a special room in the New York Yacht Club. It is only worth about $500. Known as the America's Cup, it is not named after our country but after the schooner *America*. The whole thing started in 1851 when, before the eyes of Queen Victoria, the schooner *America,* belonging to a New York Yacht Club syndicate headed by John C. Stevens, won a 60-mile race open to all classes of yachts from all nations. This first race took place around the Isle of Wight, and the Cup was put up by the Royal Yacht Squadron of England. At certain intervals during the ensuing 126 years British, Australian, and French challengers have tried many times with no success to return it to their country. In 1977 a Swedish boat suffered the same fate.

America's Cup races in recent decades have been nothing like the come-one, come-all affair at which Queen Victoria was a mortified spectator. For one thing, they are held on this side of the Atlantic. For another, only two yachts compete, one representing the United States and the other the challenging club. And they are built according to certain agreed-on specifications.

The reason Queen Victoria was so mortified at that first race around the Isle of Wight was that when she saw *America* finishing she waited, and waited, and waited, and finally asked one of the officers nearby, "And who is second?" The officer promptly replied, "Your Majesty there is no second."

That swift schooner *America* was designed by a man named Steers. She was revolutionary for her time, having a fine bow and superb sails. Up to that time most vessels were of the shape called a cod's head and mackerel tail type. The schooner *America* literally reversed this. This shape, plus the fact that her sails were far superior, allowed her to finish so far ahead of her competitors and to bring the cup home to the New York Yacht Club, where it still remains.

Nowadays, instead of the large J Class boats that were used when Harold Vanderbilt called Olin, the races are held in 12-meter sloops about half the size

STORMY WEATHER

Sail Area 1,332 sq. ft.
Displacement 44,800 lbs.
L.O.A. 53'-11''
D.W.L. 39'-9''
Beam 12'-6''
Draft 7'-11''

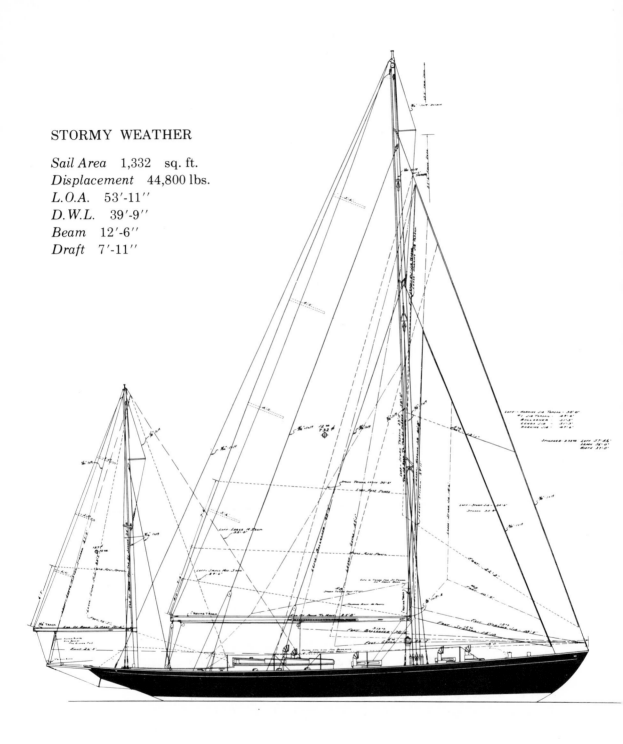

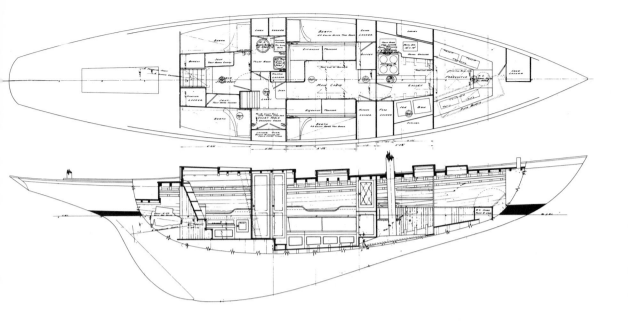

of the old J's. They still cost just as much—around a million dollars is what the J's cost in their time. A person who walks around the model room of the New York Yacht Club can plainly see what has happened to money: a million dollars could pay for a J boat in 1937, but in 1958 the same amount of money could only buy a 12 meter, a little craft compared to the J's.

Sir Thomas Lipton, the English tea merchant, is commonly supposed to have spent an average of a million dollars apiece on his five fruitless attempts to recapture the America's Cup.

Well, at the time Mr. Vanderbilt called up Olin he had already defended the America's Cup twice, once in 1930 and again in 1934 with yachts designed by Starling Burgess. Faced now with the challenge of a new boat, *Endeavour II,* owned and sailed by T. O. M. Sopwith, the British airplane manufacturer, he wanted the best and most original brains he could get to design a defender, as well as the most adept sailors he could get to handle her. Having seen the Stephens brothers in action, he strongly implied to Olin that, as part of the deal, he and Rod must consent to serve on the crew. Olin hardly had to consult his brother before accepting.

Olin and Starling Burgess agreed to design two hulls each, then test 5′ models of all four of them in a tank to determine which of the four to concentrate on. The tests were conducted over a period of six weeks in the fall of 1936. At length the collaborators made their choice (they had a gentlemen's agreement not to disclose which of them had designed the hull they favored). They both then settled down to an arduous period of working out refinements

GESTURE

Sail Area   1,454 sq. ft.
Displacement   48,580 lbs.
L.O.A.   57'-4''
D.W.L.   40'-0''
Beam   12'-7''
Draft   8'-2''

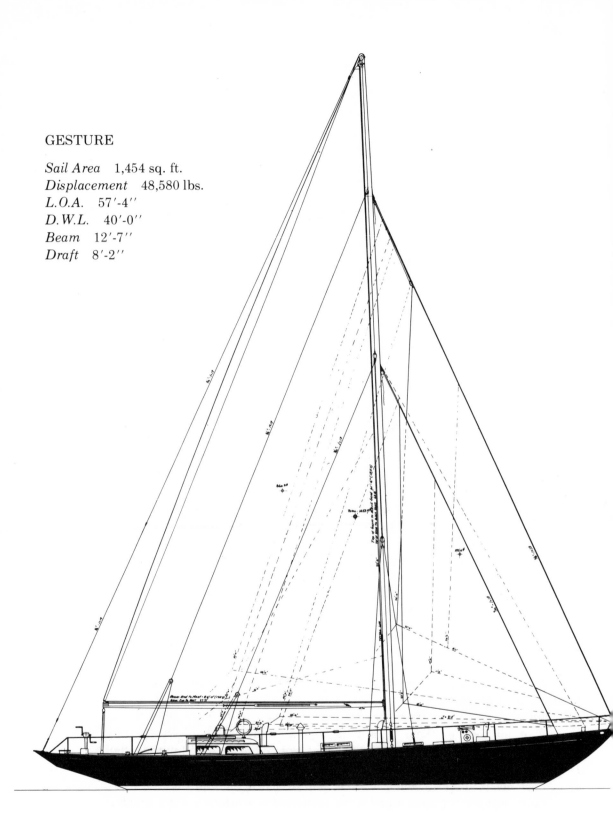

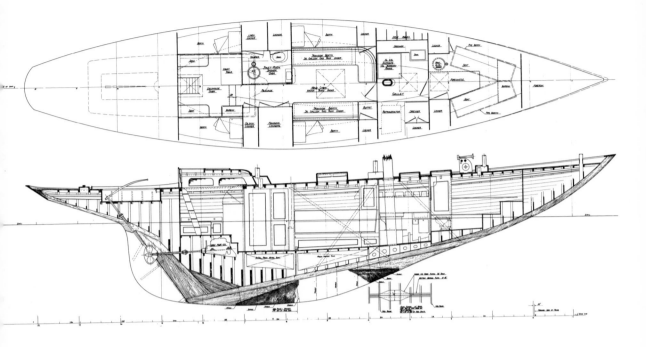

and pondering the multitude of detailed structural problems they would have to solve if the finished yacht were ever to sail as they wanted her to.

Simultaneously Rod set about working up a deck plan, plotting the location of winches, cleats, blocks and leads, and other parts of the rigging. The sail handling gear, which had been either invented outright or drastically adapted from existing types, was so extraordinary that veteran yachtsmen studying a model of the finished boat at the New York Yacht Club are still astonished by it.

Ranger's particulars are boggling to today's mind not used to such large sloops. She was 135'-2'' length overall, 87'-0'' length on the waterline, 21'-0'' beam, had a draft of 15'-0'', carried a total sail area of 7,950 square feet, and displaced 372,990 pounds. Comparing her with a twelve meter, let's say *Intrepid,* she was about double the size: *Intrepid*'s length overall was 68'-0'', her waterline length 45'-0'', her beam 12'-0'', her draft 8'-1'', her total sail area 1,750 square feet (about one fourth of *Ranger*'s), and her displacement in pounds 66,357 (less than one fifth of *Ranger*'s).

Tuning up *Ranger* in practice runs was a matter of racing her in preliminary trials alongside two other J boats, *Rainbow* and *Yankee.* This is the only way to test a sailboat's speed, for you cannot find out whether it is faster than a certain boat without sailing alongside that boat. After she had easily beaten both *Rainbow* and *Yankee,* she raced in the big event itself. The Stephens brothers were among the six amateur members of the crew. Rod was in charge of the yacht's complement of 26 paid hands, almost the entire population of a Norwegian fishing village, who had been imported especially for that summer of racing *Ranger.*

ZWERVER

Sail Area 1,347 sq. ft.
Displacement 42,255 lbs.
L.O.A. 56'-9''
D.W.L. 39'0''
Beam 11'-9''
Draft 8'-0''

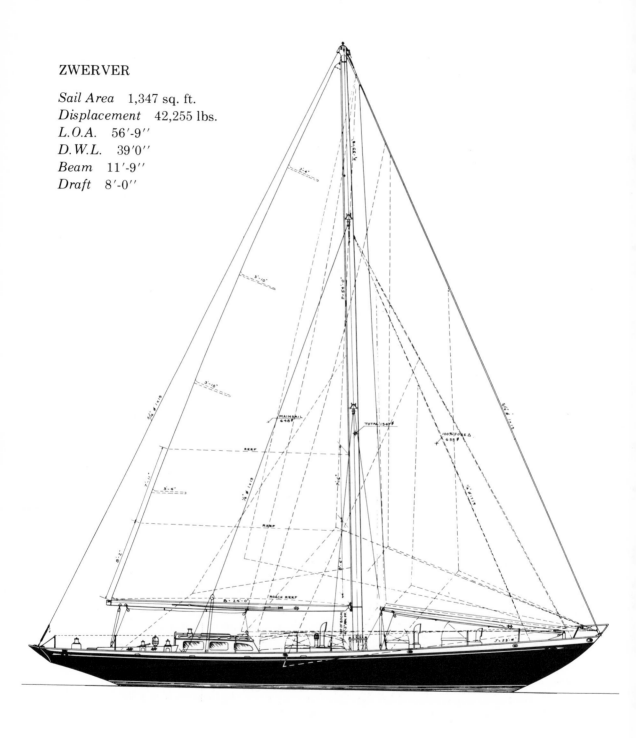

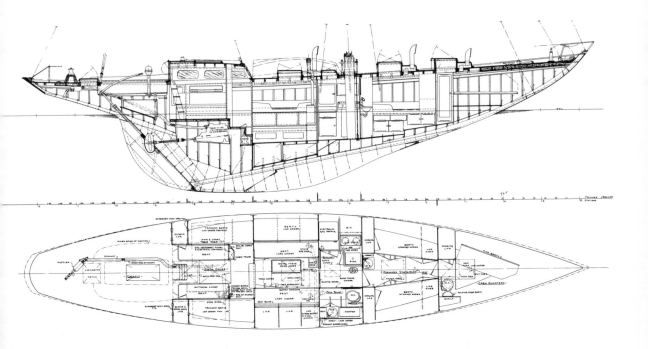

Olin was reverse helmsman, spelling Mr. Vanderbilt at the wheel and alternating with him as tactician in *Ranger*'s afterguard. Earnest and unobtrusive, Olin hardly moved from the afterdeck all summer long, staring intently this way and that through spray-fogged eyeglasses as he prepared for every conceivable contingency. For example, he might spend a whole afternoon plotting how in a given set of circumstances he could blanket or backwind a competitor, racing maneuvers that call for an almost reptilian combination of patience and cunning. Whenever there was an obvious move to make that summer, at least four people would immediately point it out to Mr. Vanderbilt. Rod said not long ago, "If nobody was sure what to do next, Olin would tell Mr. Vanderbilt what he thought was the best bet, and he almost always turned out to be right."

As for Rod himself, as supervisor of the paid hands he was responsible for seeing to it that the headsails and spinnakers adding up to more than 12,000 square feet of canvas were broken and set with split-second precision. He also had to keep a constant check on the myriad mechanical contrivances, from belowdecks to the masthead. Wearing red trousers with an assortment of tools flapping from a belt around his waist, he seemed to be everywhere at once.

The Cup match was to be decided on the basis of four out of seven 30-mile races held off Newport between July 31 and August 5, 1937. During each race hundreds of pleasure craft carrying spectators, journalists, and newsreel cameramen followed the two big boats around the course. The first four races ended with Mr. Vanderbilt's yacht crossing the finish line well in the lead. The America's Cup remained in this country.

Thus ended the career of perhaps the most magnificent sailing yacht of all time, *Ranger*.

The late Mr. Roderick Stephens, Olin J. Stephens II, and Roderick Stephens, Jr., on the occasion of the presentation in 1968 of the Marine Aluminum Ocean Racing Trophy to Olin Stephens for his oustanding contributions to ocean racing with aluminum.

4 Olin and Rod

Olin is a man who has mastered the art of getting other people to do what he wants in producing boat designs. He is a good administrator with a trained eye for the proper shape of a boat. Competitive, genuinely modest and unassuming, he likes to keep track of how each calculation and each drawing is coming along. Because it seems as if he wears rubber sole shoes when he moves about the office, it is often quite startling to find him at your side having a look at your work. Then, if the lines he sees are pleasing, he says, "That's good, Frank, just as you've drawn it." If not, perhaps he will say, "I would like that sheer line better if the low point were just a hair further aft." Or else, "Mario, the loftsman at Minneford's says he has never worked with a better set of offsets than you've given him."

Not only is the talent of being artistic needed for good design, but also the inquisitive, scientific mind of a mathematician. These two characteristics are combined in Olin's makeup. Now his current thinking is of how a computer can be used to predict performance of a new boat.

I remember almost having an auto accident when giving him a ride from Greenwich to our design office, after we had met to review preliminary plans of the new *Palawan* at the home of her prospective owner, Tom Watson. Olin began to expound on the relationship between a tiller and a wheel, working out lever arms and resulting moments. I was driving toward a Y intersection at about 55 mph and wasn't sure which fork to take. Finally I interrupted a little late to ask, "Left or right, Olin?" He pointed right just in the nick of time for me to swerve in that direction, saying, "Sorry, Frank, I hadn't realized you didn't know the way."

Rod is a man who knows how to build things. Without very much help he built his own house in Scarsdale with the skills he learned helping to build wooden boats at Nevins and other yards.

For a number of years he owned a 45' sloop of the New York Yacht Club 32 Class named *Mustang*. It was always a familiar sight when in port to see him aloft in a bosun's chair tuning the rigging. You always knew from a distance that the boat must be *Mustang* and that the rigger up there must be Rod.

The name *Mustang* on Rod's boat was not after a horse, nor did it have anything to do with a navy man who comes up through the ranks. Rod wanted a single name that had a good sound to it when hailed across the water. He was sitting in his as yet unnamed boat, one of the New York 32 Class (sail number N.Y. 17) of S & S design when a plane buzzed the yard in which the boat lay. There was a roar close overhead. "What kind of a plane is that?" he asked. Someone answered, "It's a P51, a Mustang."

"That's it. *Mustang,* that's the name for my boat," he immediately replied.

He is a very positive person. In dealing with the many boat builders on his inspection trips around the world, at which he spends 50% of his time now, he always explains the reason he would like something done a particular way. Because of the intelligence of the various builders he deals with, they get to understand the need to do things his way and to cooperate, because he gives them the reason and it is a good one 95% of the time, it seems.

Except for being skipper and owner of *Mustang* during the 1950's, and except for being skipper of *Stormy Weather* in the 1935 Transatlantic Race, and before that of *Dorade* in the 1933 Transatlantic, Rod has favored taking charge of the foredeck of sailboats when racing. Way back in his youth he decided to let Olin be skipper, when the two were sailing together. This combination of talents produced marvelous teamwork in winning both races and designing commissions.

Rod has always been a topflight athlete. While captain of his high school football team in Scarsdale, the team never lost a game. Later he became a figure skater. Then later in life he became an excellent skier. To maintain his leg muscles for skiing, he runs upstairs to the office after lunch every day, two steps at a time—the full twelve floors. In his early days of sailing he could go up a mast hand-over-hand without being hoisted in a bosun's chair. If ever there was a human dynamo, he's it.

It can be said of both brothers that they are perfectionists. Olin and Rod are rarely satisfied, if ever, and insist that the designers under them do their best at all times. The optimum must be achieved in all phases of their work. This goes for sailing as well.

On one of the Block Island races many years ago I was fortunate in finding myself aboard *Mustang* as one of her crew. There were some prominent people, including Ken Davidson and Carleton Mitchell, in each watch.

The race itself was pretty easy stuff, being a close reach from Larchmont down the Sound out and around Block Island, then a broad reach back to Stamford. The wind was just the right strength for fine sailing at the time until we were about 7 miles from the finish. Then it dropped to almost a flat calm. It was the middle of the night.

Until then Rod had been quite easygoing about everything. But when the wind dropped, he leapt into action. He moved all over the deck, rattling out orders in machine-gun style as he assisted in changing to lighter and lighter sails, with lighter and lighter sheets, afterguys, and forward guys, and also with lighter and lighter snapshackles. It paid off. With the lightest of zephyrs, *Mustang* began to move almost imperceptibly past becalmed boats with dropping sails and cursing crews. She finished third, I believe, hours ahead of the next boat.

When recounting the story to one of my friends, who had also raced with Rod, this friend told me of another.

It seems that there was a great but friendly racing rivalry between Rod on *Mustang* and Harvey Conover on *Revonoc*. One day in a thick fog when it was calm and neither crew could see the other boat, but were close enough to hear across the water everything that went on, they each considered anchoring because of a supposed head current.

Rod knew the current was not foul at that time in that place, but he thought he would have some fun. He quietly whispered to his crew what he wanted to do and then went into action. When all was ready, a strong voice was heard from *Mustang*:

"All right on the foredeck. Let go the anchor."

Then another sound, "splash," as the anchor was thrown over.

Then, "Let out plenty of scope."

Hearing these happenings through the fog, Harvey Conover thought *Revonoc* should do the same. He did. But he never heard *Mustang* again.

Unbeknownst to him, Rod had not lowered *Mustang*'s anchor more than a couple of feet below the surface, and had very quietly heaved it aboard again. *Mustang* kept moving away toward the finish line on a fair current, while *Revonoc* discovered the mistake too late to catch up. Outfoxed!

Both brothers leave the doors to their offices open, thereby becoming more accessible to their employees. They never seem to mind being interrupted by questions from someone on the team of designers who has a problem to be solved. Together the employer and the employee learn from these open-door encounters.

By dictating their letters into IBM tape recorders from assembled notes on the subject at hand, they have become independent of their stenographers. It is easy to stop the dictation and the tape to answer someone's question, which makes them that much more accessible. Of course the employees would never think of butting in when they are on the telephone, or when someone else is with them. To warn when the telephones are in use, there are white lights, one above each door, which light up when that respective phone is in use. This saves time for all hands.

A person's first impression on entering the S & S design office (on the twelfth floor of 79 Madison Avenue, at 28th Street, in New York City) is that of a vast open space with lots of light and air. This is needed for the designers at their boards. Right in the center sits Gil Wyland (now semiretired) surrounded by a glass enclosure. He is the chief engineer. At one end are three offices: one for Olin, one for Rod, and one in between for Walter Schaub, the accountant. Near the switchboard at the entrance is a conference room, as well as Gil Wyland's glass enclosure. Bill Mav, short for Mavrogiannis, and Stige, short for Bill Stiger, work at the western end of the room. The former is directly responsible for the day-to-day work of designing, while the latter is the company's electrical engineer, writes specs, and inspects S & S boats abuilding in the United States. This leaves Rod free to do the inspecting of boats being built abroad. Rod is the one who travels the most and the farthest, away from the office on inspection and trial trips almost half of the time. My other colleagues on the team of designers here are Hank Uhle, Howard Pierce, Mario Tarabocchia, and Alan Gilbert. No design would be complete without the work of these men.

There are many half models and full tank test models all around, representing about all the different shapes a boat can take. Sailboat models abound, but this does not mean that the firm has not done plenty of power-boats. It has. Many a fast one and many a large luxurious one have been designed by the people at S & S. The firm is composed of 25 persons, including the yacht brokers, who recently moved into their present quarters in this same large room.

For an office not quite like that of the headquarters of a large corporation or a bank, some rather important and prominent people come to it. There was one particular day, October 20, 1970, when 79 Madison Avenue was surrounded by police, who banned all parking on the block and kept pedestrians on the move. Shortly before 11 A.M. ten men from three cars entered the building. That group was a bodyguard, a mixture of FBI and Scotland Yard men for the Right Honorable Edward Heath, member of Parliament, later to become prime minister of Great Britain. He had come, interrupting diplomatic business at the United Nations building, to discuss with Olin the design of his new ocean-racing sloop, the second *Morning Cloud.* She was the boat in which in 1971 as prime minister he captained a team of three British yachts to victory against 17 other international teams in the Admiral's Cup Races.

Within half an hour in Room 1207 on the twelfth floor, which has on its door SPARKMAN & STEPHENS, INC., another two men arrived, His Highness the Aga

Khan accompanied by his private secretary. They were there to talk over a new 90', 45-knot motor yacht S & S was designing for him.

Olin is partial to foreign cars. He likes to drive his six-cylinder BMW, which he owns now. He has owned several Porsches since the late 1960's, and prior to that a Mercedes in 1952 and another in 1966. These he feels are better cars than the BMW, especially the Mercedes acquired in 1952, which ran very smoothly but did not have as much power as the later one.

After one of his European trips, partly for business and partly for vacation, we were all lunching at our round table at the Prince George Hotel. Olin remarked with a sheepish grin, "I was trying out my new Porsche on the Autobahn and got it up to 110 mph."

We almost fell off our chairs in surprise. It was so unlike him, we thought.

Later I asked him which of these different cars he likes best.

"Each one was better engineered but worse built than the one before," he answered.

In Sheffield, Massachusetts, a town in the southwest corner of the state in the foothills of the Berkshire Mountains, Olin owns a home to which he escapes. It is surrounded by about 130 acres of fields and woodland. A farmer mows the fields on his place, which keeps them green and neat.

Rod, on the other hand, has had several compact-design Oldsmobiles. He prefers the old-fashioned stick shift rather than the automatic drive because there are some steep hills in Scarsdale where he lives, and he finds he has better control with that type. In the winter if you see an Olds in that area with snow tires on all four wheels, chances are it belongs to Rod. He correctly equips his car for the best control on snow-covered roads going downhill as well as uphill. Olin does the same on his BMW.

When Rod bought one new car, he specified that the side rear vision mirror be located by the buyer, him. Just as a yacht designer would locate the compass on his own boat, there must not be a large angle between the view ahead and the sight line to the mirror (or the compass), and it must not block vision ahead or to the side.

One day when I was new on the job, Olin came out and said quietly to me, "From now on we will put down the client's name on the drawing as Mr. So-and-So. I don't want to use So-and-So Esquire anymore. Just because someone has a lot of money is no reason why he should be called Esquire." I had always wanted to flatter the owner by using *Esq.,* but ever since then the title block on each drawing has read Design No. such and such, name of plan, dimensions, description, and then for Mr. So-and-So.

Both brothers have opinions about the relationship of jibs to mainsails on sloops. Olin says that sloops designed with a foretriangle and mainsail each of equal size do not seem to perform as well as sloops with these two sails of unequal size. That is, a sloop with a large jib and a small main, or a sloop with a small jib and a large main, will sail better than one on which the total sail area is divided 50-50 between jib and main.

Rod has some very practical opinions about how to prevent a dismasting in a squall regarding these two sails on a sloop rig. Whether inexperienced or just plain lazy, the average skipper of a sloop when confronted by a squall will decide to drop the mainsail and keep on sailing with his large, genoa jib set. This is a mistake, Rod feels. By doing it that way he greatly increases his chance of losing the mast. Why? Because the tension on the jibstay may become so inordinately great in a very strong puff of wind that it increases the compressive strain on the mast to its ultimate, then this overstressed mast buckles and gives way.

If, on the other hand, such a skipper confronted with that situation had dropped his big jib when he could have and continued sailing by the main alone, luffing a little, no harm should come to his mast. Why? Because the principal force then is not compression but one of bending on the mast, and the shrouds can easily do their job of handling this strain.

It would seem then that the old-fashioned sloops that could sail well with the main alone were a pretty good design at that. The Herreshoff design "S" boat was a good example of Olin's theory and Rod's practicality regarding these thoughts.

Rod thinks that good design creates one item to do several jobs. This is especially true the smaller the boat is. For instance, an icebox top can double as a chart table. A galley sink can double as a washbasin. A locker door can also serve to close off a passageway. A forestaysail boom pedestal can be a ventilator. A cockpit coaming can keep out spray and incorporate stowage pockets, as well as being a base for winches and cleats. In the head on some stock boats the flexible telephone-type shower fixture can be afixed above to take a shower or held at the wash basin to wash one's hands, so it does two jobs. If there are two doors with their hinges near a corner, they should swing on a common hinge to behave properly, otherwise they may jam at their handles. Thus a single common hinge does a better job than two sets. Now for some more prosaic items:

When it comes to plumbing, Rod insists that sinks and washbasins must be located so that they are high enough to drain directly overboard. On a sailboat this means more than having them just high enough to drain when the boat is upright, but high enough to drain when the boat heels under sail. Rod says you must not have one way outboard off the centerline, because that will move it down underwater when the boat is heeled. Then a fountain of seawater will shoot up, flooding the interior of the boat and sooner or later sinking her. Rod has learned all this from firsthand experience, and makes his colleagues in the office and the builders in the yards adhere strictly to the correct way.

Toilets deserve expert location for easily understood reasons. Rod points out it is unfortunate that the ones with foot pedal valves on the intake lines always seem to be faulty. Or, that is, this particular type of valve is faulty. When the bowl is not far enough above the waterline, the boat may be swamped and sink unless the seacock at the through hull intake is shut each time. It has happened to many an otherwise good boat, even at her home mooring! And the discharge line needs to be looped well above the water even when the boat's heeled to prevent a siphoning back effect.

Olin is always thinking about shapes that will move through the water with the least resistance. Different parts of a sailboat have different shapes. Thus at the surface a boat needs to pass over large waves and through small waves. Water is noncompressible, so it presents a hardness not found in air, which is compressible. At the surface, then, the question for the designer is: Will there be less resistance if the bow is shaped to cut through the wave? Or shaped to push it ahead? Certain Dutch boats are shaped to push the waves ahead, and how they can beat to windward in a sea is quite a mystery.

On the other hand, the fine, sharp, hollow, waterlined bow shape of certain old designs like the schooner *America* seemed to slice through so nicely you would think they would develop the least resistance. The answer is that somewhere between these two extremes lies the optimum configuration.

The shape in terms of an entire sailboat hull has a lot to do with its speed. For example, the longer the displacement type boat is, the faster she goes. This does not mean for overall length but for waterline length. So if the waterline is lengthened to make her a short-ended boat, not minding the fact that she may not appear as beautiful without long overhanging ends, she will be swifter.

The reverse transom and near horizontal horn timber on so many boats today has to do only in part with a handicap rule. Many think it is entirely a result of measurements for the IOR rule, but this is not so. It is there to flatten the stern wave and cause it to form farther aft, when it does form. The farther apart a displacement boat's bow and stern wave are, the faster these waves allow the boat to move.

It is the speed of waves that interested Admiral Taylor (a medal struck in his name was awarded to Olin as an honor awhile back), who discovered that if you took the distance between crests, found the square root of that distance, and multiplied it by 1.34, you could accurately predict the speed of those particular waves. So the bow and stern waves lock a displacement type boat to that maximum speed, unless she manages to surf in a gale of wind. This a boat does if she is light enough and long enough—that is, has a light displacement-length ratio.

On the line drawings of our most successful sailboats the bow sections are much closer to a "U" shape than a "V". *Stormy Weather* certainly is that way. Her name brings to mind a remark that is noteworthy. John Alden, the famous Boston designer of the many well-known Alden schooners said of *Stormy Weather* when he saw her hauled out in a shipyard for the first time, "There isn't one line I would change on that boat." High praise indeed for the young Stephens brothers, who were revolutionizing yacht design. Their many well-known yawls were soon to make the Alden schooner designs obsolete.

Talking about the "U" sections at the bow, if you put that kind of a bow at the forward end with the flat stern mentioned before, on a light yet strong hull you will most likely have a flyer, which can surf. How to do it? That's the art of yacht designing. To get his team of designers to do it is one of the secrets of Olin's success.

There are trends in the ownership of sailing yachts, which the Stephens brothers have taken part in and to which they have contributed. After a decline in popularity of the schooner rig, the yawl became *the* rig to have for good reasons. It was easier to handle, faster to windward, and more versatile in respect to control of the boat. This change was brought about principally by the success of *Dorade.*

After the centerboard yawl *Finisterre* won the Bermuda Race three times—which had never been done by any other boat before and has not been done since—centerboard yawls became *the* type to have. This trend abruptly came to an end when *Revonoc* was lost at sea. That was a sad time for Rod, who directed the Coast Guard's search for his old friend throughout the Bahamas and off the Florida coast to no avail.

Next came sloops and cutters, because they were the best performers going to windward, and with masthead rigs could set the largest possible spinnakers, which made them the fastest downwind rigs as well as upwind.

At the present time there is a group of very wealthy yachtsmen who want to break speed records and be the owners of the boats that are first to finish, regardless of their corrected time resulting from whatever handicap rule is used. They have the longest, lightest for their size, leanest for their length, least wetted surface size-wise ketches. Ketches such as *Windward Passage,* designed by Alan Gurney, really started this trend in the United States. S & S designs

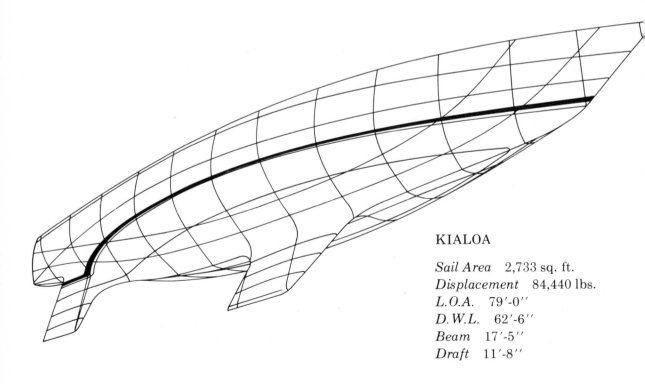

KIALOA

Sail Area   2,733 sq. ft.
Displacement   84,440 lbs.
L.O.A.   79'-0''
D.W.L.   62'-6''
Beam   17'-5''
Draft   11'-8''

such as *Kialoa* and *Tempest* sail at fantastic speeds, even surpassing famous clipper ship records on long passages. Mr. Kilroy, owner of *Kialoa,* said she had gone 20 knots for a time. Unbelievable.

But is it really unbelievable? I think I can prove that it could happen, but first Rod's remarks on the subject.

He sailed a good deal on the 135′ J boat *Ranger,* a much larger vessel than *Kialoa.* When asked about her top speed under sail, he simply shook his head slowly, saying, "We never could quite reach 14 knots. 13.8 or 13.9 was tops." *Ranger* was a heavy boat and never was sailed in a gale of wind for fear of losing her rig. And the seas in summertime off Newport, where she was moored, never would reach the size of those in southern latitudes called the Roaring Forties.

I think *Kialoa* did sail 20 knots, and here is my table based on Admiral Taylor's formula for the speed of waves ($\sqrt{\text{wave length}} \times 1.34$) to back up this claim.

Wavelength Crest to Crest	For a Wave Speed of
20.0′	6 knots
35.6′	8 knots
55.6′	10 knots
80.1′	12 knots
109.0′	14 knots
142.5′	16 knots
180.4′	18 knots
222.6′	20 knots

So I believe she was surfing down a wave that was 223 feet long from crest to crest. *Quod est demonstratum.*

My colleague Bill Stiger crewed aboard *Tempest* in a recent Bermuda Race. During a rough period when the boat was jumping almost from wave to wave, a man was sent forward to help lower and change one of the big jibs. When the bow of *Tempest* shot off the crest of a wave and dropped into the trough ahead, this man felt the bow drop out from under him. He stayed in midair! When the bow met the backside of the next wave, it came up quickly underneath him, and he landed on the strong pulpit rail. Fortunately he was not hurt, but the tubing was bent a lot. Stige thinks, after having raced on the old 70-footers such as *Baruna,* that they were much more comfortable in a sea way because of their weight and slower speed. But that's the price the owners of these new lightweight ketches must pay for their fantastic speeds.

The remarkable disparity of tastes and temperaments of the two Stephens brothers have long mystified people in the yachting world. Rod, they feel, is the more understandable of the two. He is miserable away from boats and salt water. When he is deeply involved in what is his avocation as well as his vocation, he takes his sailing both seriously and lightly. On the one hand he used to sail his own 45′ sloop *Mustang* with driving determination in as many racing classics as he could find time to enter. On the other, he was an enthusiastic member of a group of convivial Long Island Sound yachtsmen who called themselves the Cruising, Boozing and Snoozing Club, and has won three of the eleven one-man-to-a-boat races, which are known as the Single-handed Creepstakes.

Olin, a man many people consider the best sailboat designer in the country but who by preference spends his weekends on his 130-acre farm in New England, owns no boat. He numbers few yachtsmen among his close friends. He has been tutored in modern painting by several artists at the New School for Social Research. John Heliker, a Greenwich Village artist, was Olin's first painting instructor and has known him well for a long time. He also studied under Yasuo Kuniyoshi, learning modern painting techniques.

When Olin is not relaxing on his farm where he and his family spend their weekends in summer, he lives most of the year in a pleasant colonial-style house in Scarsdale, where he and his wife entertain infrequently, asking only a few friends in at a time. Among those who are likely to be invited are an architect, the director of an art gallery, and several painters. But no yachtsmen! At times, according to his niece Betsy, he likes to produce some delicious French dishes; he is an excellent gourmet cook.

Olin had diligently, if intermittently, tried to teach himself to paint, striving to produce pictures of the old barn and fishing wharf type. But he never succeeded in coming up with results that any school would care to claim. Without saying much about it to Rod, he began attending a one-night-a-week painting class that Heliker, an Abstract Impressionist, was conducting in a fourth-floor, cold-water flat in Greenwich Village. It was at Heliker's suggestion that he took some lessons from Kuniyoshi at the New School. And then he studied under Easton Pribble, a painter who lived on the second floor of Heliker's building. Under the influence of these preceptors, Olin has abandoned barns and fishing wharfs to work comfortably in the impressionist, Abstract Impressionist, and Neo-Cubist styles. He does not mention this side of his life to sailing men.

I asked Olin the other day how he was getting along with his modern painting. "I'm not active now, but I did enjoy it," he said. "And Susie and I do go to the galleries on Saturdays, when we can."

Olin is also a collector of paintings. He has been buying modern art on and off since 1939 and how had a goodly number of pictures including a Maurice Prendergast, a Marston Hartley, and Jean Marin. His other aesthetic preferences reflect the same general outlook, and so does his intellectual interests: Bach and Bartok, Maritain and Kafka. And lectures on philosophy and cultural history by Heinrich Blucher, also at the New School. Not surprisingly in a man of such taste, he favors automobiles of foreign make.

At the very beginning of their careers the Stephens brothers decided not to drink. Nor do they smoke. But of course if you are a yachtsmen and you raft your boat up with other boats, the drinking always starts. Because the brothers knew they would attend so many gatherings of yachtsmen, they decided once and for all to abstain.

KIALOA   (Barlow)

The Cruising Club of America, which except for a beach on Block Island has no home it can call its own, is considered the top group of offshore sailors in the United States. It advises its members to ask themselves several questions about candidates for admission, among them: "Would you enjoy the company of the candidate glass-in-hand in the cabin of a small yacht?" The members have been enjoying Rod's company in such surroundings since 1936 despite the fact that the glass in his hand is never filled with booze. He is by nature the sort who requires no alcohol to fit into a crowd of drinking sailors. Indeed, in the cabin of a small yacht his company is likely to be considered more enjoyable than that of anyone else's present, as with his accordion slung over his neck and a pleasant smile on his face he asks, "What'll it be next?"

"How about 'When I Wore a Tulip'?" someone may shout.

"I don't know all the chords for it, but let's give it a try," Rod will probably reply, tossing off his glass of milk. "Here we go!"

Rod is recognized as an authority by the editors of periodicals specializing in his field. The magazine *Yachting* has published a number of long articles by him bearing such informative titles as "Pointers on Handling Light Sails," "Suggestions on Spinnakers," "Further Notes on Nylon Sails," "A Primer on Construction Details," and "Rod Rigging." His advice is constantly being sought by enthusiastic but less gifted sailors.

One Saturday morning a few summers ago a telephone rang in his home. He found himself talking to a client aboard a yacht hundreds of miles off Cape Hatteras, who was calling ship-to-shore to say that he was having trouble in a race and what should he do next? Rod can no longer recall exactly what he told the man, but it may have been something like, "Before you douse the spinnaker, overhaul the halyard, flaking it down starting with the bitter end." That's the way he talks.

Rod remained a highly eligible bachelor until 1947, when at the age of 38 he married Marjorie McClure from Scarsdale, a girl he had known since his teens. She has become almost as fond of sailing as he is. Their honeymoon gave her a good notion of what married life would be, for it was a 700-mile cruise from Florida to North Carolina aboard a boat Rod was bringing north for a friend. They have a daughter, Betsy, who first boarded *Mustang* in a basket at age three weeks. After she became mobile, she did her sailing encased in a balsa wood life preserver roped to *Mustang*'s lifelines. Rod, when he was not racing, spent practically every weekend during the season cruising on *Mustang* with his wife and daughter.

When Rod built his house himself, by long habit in supervising the construction of boats, he was so finicky about the quality of the materials he used that the local lumberyard owner finally exclaimed, "Look, Mr. Stephens, this building doesn't have to float!"

The decor of Rod's house emphasizes its owner's almost total absorption in sea and sailing vessels. Plates have sailboat motifs. A brass clock in the study tolls the time in ship's bells rather than in hours. And most of the pictures on the walls are of sailing ships underway.

Olin made a great contribution in 1932 to yacht designing. At that time Professor Kenneth Davidson, a naval architect on the faculty of Stevens Institute of Technology in Hoboken, New Jersey, decided to try to work out a close relationship between towing tank promise and ultimate performance. His idea was simplicity itself: to compare in minute detail behavior of a certain vessel under actual sailing conditions with that of a model of the same boat under exactly simulated conditions in the Stevens' swimming pool. To help with his field work, Davidson needed an expert sailor who knew enough about sailboat design to make relevant observations and record them with hair-splitting accuracy. Having read of Olin's success with *Dorade,* he called him to ask if he would be interested.

Olin was delighted to help. During the fall of 1933 he spent many weekends with stopwatch in hand and pad and pencil by his side, often accompanied by Ken Davidson, sailing about in *Gimcrack,* a 34' sloop of Olin's design, to collect the required information. When all the results were in, Davidson worked out a set of factors that must be applied to the readings of towing tank instruments in order to arrive at an accurate interpretation of the test. Thanks to this study, tank testing is now regarded as a fairly reliable means of predicting the performance of a finished boat. It is a further testimonial to the soundness of Professor Davidson's corrections that they are taken seriously.

For the 1977 America's Cup Race, Olin decided that since thousands of models 4- to 5-foot long had been tested in the tank at Stevens (named the Davidson Tank in honor of the late Professor Davidson), different models' resistances were getting too close to compare. They are measured at about three fourths of a pound on the towing carriage scale there. Olin felt it was high time to use a much larger model in the same procedure, registering the more accurately measured higher resistance. Particularly when an expensive boat such as an America's Cup defender needed a model built of her and tested.

So the model of the our latest S & S 12 meter, named *Enterprise,* is 23' long—a fair size boat itself. The tank at Stevens is not big enough to tow that size model, so it has been tested with very reassuring results in a much larger tank in Maryland.

During all this tank testing, some yachtsmen took the position that the secret of boat design lay in the tanks themselves, not in the abilities of the men who designed the boats that were tested there. Olin's reply to those thoughts in 1957 was, "The tank can't design a boat." He continued, "It can't draw a single line on a piece of paper. It only answers questions, and the designer must know the right questions to ask. And there are a lot of questions it can't answer, too, such as what specifically is at fault in an unsatisfactory model. All it can tell in such cases is what the total result will be under given conditions."

He went on to say, "I always wish there were some more scientific way of doing it, but the tank can't prove that. Sailboat designing started out as 90% art and 10% science. And someday let's hope it will be the other way around. We're only about halfway there now." That was in 1957. I'm sure he would add now that we are more oriented scientifically than we were then. Witness the fact that the model for the new twelve is 23′ long.

When Olin collaborated with Starling Burgess in the design of the J boat *Ranger* for Mr. Vanderbilt, they agreed not to reveal which of them was responsible for the hull they ultimately chose. Starling Burgess died in 1947. The mystery remained until about 1956, shortly after it was reported in an article in *Sports Illustrated*. The reporter wrote that Vanderbilt, who had been in a better position to know the answer than anyone other than the designers themselves, believed *Ranger*'s hull to have been based on one of Olin's two models. Olin then composed a letter to Mr. Vanderbilt that set the unofficial record straight.

"Briefly, the model, No. 77C, from which *Ranger* was built, was a Burgess model." He wrote, "To Starling's credit he scrupulously carried out the agreement we made not to name the individual responsible for the lines of this model. Til now I have felt justified in taking the same position. Possibly I should not have kept quiet for so long, as I have apparently mislead you, and possibly others, although not intentionally."

Olin always wears a bow tie, and he almost never takes off his coat in the office. His employees only saw it off once in the summer of 1977, when the air-conditioning broke down. Wearing it is probably in anticipation of meeting a client. "I can't seem to get along without those extra pockets," he claims.

Olin has two sons. The oldest, now in his early forties, is Olin J. Stephens III. He is in the real estate business in Newfane, Vermont, where he lives. The other son is Sam R. Stephens, now in his mid-thirties. He is a builder living in Ackworth, New Hampshire, specializing in restoring old houses. He has worked on places his brother Olin bought and sold.

Fortunately for designers in the firm, the sons are not interested in their father's business, or it probably would be held entirely by the Stephens family. As it is now, there are 18 shareholders—mostly the men who work at Sparkman & Stephens, as well as Olin and Rod. So in that way it is a profit-sharing business.

While Olin concerns himself primarily with hull shapes, which is a very complicated matter, Rod is involved with the sail plan, the deck plan, and construction details. The sail plan of a boat gives only a two-dimensional view; that is, the sails are outlined flatly as a profile on the paper. This can also be said of the deck plan. It shows a plan view, which is a view looking down. To coordinate the seemingly simple drawings takes all the knowledge and experience at a designer's command. Rod is a master at this.

To choose the proper size of a sail, one must consider the stability for which the boat must be designed. Generally speaking, a boat for a windy place such as

San Francisco Bay may be stiff, and would have a smaller total sail area than a boat for a place such as Long Island Sound, which has mostly light breezes. Then, too, there is the shape of the sails. What is the best overlap for jibs? What is the best size for a storm jib? Or a storm trysail? Then, most important of all, the sheet leads. What is the proper angle from the clew of a jib to the deck? This angle should be determined before the boat is built, so that the sheet lead block may have a reinforced place under the deck, where it is fastened. The builder should put in a heavy pad there. This spot must be pinpointed early in the building of a fiberglass boat because of the need to make the deck mold incorporate the reinforcing in the finished one-piece deck.

The deck plan shows this lead block. Through the years it has been found that if you take an angle from where the jibstay or the forestay is located on deck, say around 10°, and extend it aft on the deck plan from those points, you will have a line of position for the jib sheet lead block. Now the important thing is to coordinate this with the sail plan and the angle of the jib sheet in elevation or profile. But there is really no scientific method to locate this angle. Rod does it by eye, and I still do not know exactly how he does it after working with him for 23 years. Rod's experience with 2,300 designs has been the best teacher of all.

Before a boat is delivered to a client, Rod takes her out for a trial. After sailing her long enough to feel confident that she handles nicely, he turns the helm over to someone else in order to make an intensive study of her sails in action. Roaming the deck restlessly, he squints along the edges of each sail, from time to time whacking the Dacron with the flat of his hand. And perhaps he will scramble halfway up the rigging to view things from a different angle

On returning to the deck after one such inspection, he went to see the sailmaker and told him, "The spinnaker's a dandy. Look's just fine. So do the genoa and the mizzen. But the working jib is too drafty. I'd like to see you flatten it a bit near the head. While you're at it, why not reshape the luff to allow for a slight sag in the head stay. The main looks pretty good, but could use a bit of easing along the lower leach, and then we'll really be in fine shape." Coming from Rod, observations of this kind are listened to with the greatest respect by sailmakers, for more than one authority has called him "just about the best sail trimmer alive."

When Rod is at sea he likes to do for himself what less energetic men are perfectly willing to let machinery or gadgets do for them. When he owned *Mustang,* his dislike of automatic gadgets was quite evident. He would not install an automatic or electric bilge pump. Nor an electrical or mechanical refrigeration system. Nor a water pressure system. Nor an automatic pilot. Not even a radio-telephone.

Automatic devices just are not right, he told a friend. "They cost too much, they make noise, they complicate essential maintenance, and they delude you into a false sense of confidence. What's sailing for anyhow? I much prefer to do things by hand. I enjoy pumping out the bilge. It's good for me.

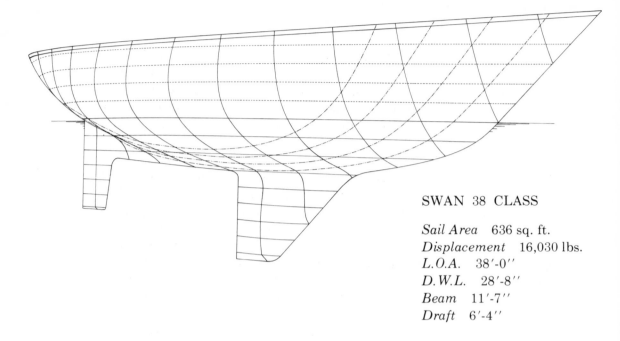

SWAN 38 CLASS

Sail Area 636 sq. ft.
Displacement 16,030 lbs.
L.O.A. 38'-0"
D.W.L. 28'-8"
Beam 11'-7"
Draft 6'-4"

"Electrical or mechanical refrigeration requires running the engine in order to generate electricity or to belt drive the refrigeration compressor. This means often running the engine when you could be sailing. A water pressure system generally means that someone will use too much water. An automatic pilot is dangerous. Many boat collisions, or wrecking of boats on shore, have resulted from people relying on automatic pilots and then falling asleep. As for a radio-telephone, I wouldn't have one on *Mustang.* My idea of getting off in the boat is to get as far away from telephones as possible."

A little story revealing Olin's character was recently told to me by Pete Peterson (William E. Peterson). It happened when he was running his Camden Shipbuilding Company in Camden, Maine, then building a power yacht named *Kinnereth* from S & S designs.

He recalls, "Thirty years somewhat dims memories, but there are recollections that depict scenes of long-forgotten events leaving a feeling of warmth. Olin and I were arguing about the high prices of building yachts in the postwar economy. I told him our costs were related to the price of eggs, and that the price used to be 28 cents per dozen, but now they cost 58 cents. We have to pay the men more money so the cost of yacht building goes up."

Olin answered, "You may be right but... [as only Olin can say that word]... we are talking about the price of this boat, and eggs are not a consideration."

Pete went on to say, "I remember my wife saying this to me after Olin had spent the night with us, during which we had conversed about many things and had received several, 'You may be right, but' from him: 'You know, Olin has the nicest, most pleasing way of disagreeing with you of anyone I ever met. He is one of the real gentlemen.'"

5 *Fourteen Good Clients*

There are many clients of ours who through the years have commissioned S & S to design them several boats during their lifetime. What could be nicer for a designer than to have them return? Some retain the same name for each boat, such as *Palawan* for Mr. Thomas J. Watson, Jr. Or *Morning Cloud* for ex-Prime Minister Mr. Edward Heath.

I can think of at least 14 of these especially good clients for each of whom we have designed three or more boats over the years. They are listed in pp. 82-83.

Some customers keep asking for faster and faster ocean racers, but generally most of these 14 clients specify more and more comfort as their ages increase. Such a man is Mr. Percy Chubb II, a member of the Cruising Club of America and a former commodore of the New York Yacht Club. He is now skipper and owner of S & S's fourth design for him.

The first S & S one that he had was *Topgallant*, one of the Weekender Class. The second, third, and fourth were custom designed by S & S while working with him in carrying out his ideas. *Laughing Gull* was the second boat. She is a pretty and able yawl that must have been easy to handle and great fun to sail. *Antilles* was his third boat. She was a centerboard ketch, larger and with proportionately more beam, being quite comfortable and stiff. I am quite proud of the fourth boat, *Bird of Passage*, having done most of the work on her design. Mr. Chubb's requirements for this design called for a seagoing powerboat with sails to assist and steady her. At first I

PALAWAN III
(Barlow)

Fourteen Clients Who Returned for More S & S Designs

OWNER	NAME OF BOAT	L.O.A.	TYPE	MATERIAL
The late Mr. Harold S. Vanderbilt (4 boats)	*Vagrant*	117'	Motorsailer	Steel
	Ranger	135'	J Class sloop	Steel
	Vim	70'	12-Meter Class sloop	Wood
	Versatile	74'	Motorsailer	Wood
The late Mr. Henry C. Taylor (3 boats)	*Barunita*	38'	Loki Class Yawl	Wood
	Baruna	72'	Yawl	Wood
	Barunita	59'	Motorsailer	Wood
Mr. Edward Greeff (3 boats)	*Puffin*	35'	Pilot Class sloop	Wood
	Puffin	39'	Yawl	Wood
	Puffin	47'	Yawl	Wood
Mr. Arthur Slater (6 boats)	*Saboo*	42'	C. B. yawl	Wood
	Prospect of Whitby	41'	Sloop	Wood
	Prospect of Whitby II	42'	Sloop	Steel
	Prospect of Whitby III	45'	Sloop	Aluminum
	Prospect of Whitby IV	47'	Admiral's Cup sloop	Aluminum
	Prospect of Whitby V	44'	Admiral's Cup sloop	Aluminum
Mr. O. J. Van Der Vorm (3 boats)	*Zwerver I*	60'	Cutter	Wood
	Zwerver II	56'	Cutter	Wood
	Swan 44	44'	Swan 44 sloop	Fiberglass
Dr. Antonio Pierobon (3 boats)	*Alnair II*	36'	Sloop	Wood
	Alnair III	47'	Sloop	Wood
	Alnair IV	41'	One tonner	Wood
Mr. Derek J. Boyer (4 boats)	*Clarion of Wight*	43'	Sloop	Wood
	Clarionet	36'	One tonner	Wood
	Carillion	45'	Sloop	Wood
	Cyclone	38'	One tonner	Fiberglass
Mr. Edward Heath (4 boats)	*Morning Cloud*	34'	S & S 34 sloop	Fiberglass
	Morning Cloud	40'	IOR racer sloop	Wood
	Morning Cloud	44'	Admiral's Cup sloop	Wood
	Morning Cloud	45'	Sloop	Aluminum
Mr. Miles Jaffee (3 boats)	*Leonore III*	36'	One tonner	Wood
	Leonore IV	43'	P. J. 43	Fiberglass
	Leonore	39'	One tonner	Aluminum
Signora Marina Spaccarelli (5 boats)	*Kerkyra*	41'	Sloop	Wood
	Kerkyra II	36'	One tonner	Wood
	Kerkyra III	42'	One tonner	Fiberglass
	Kerkyra IV	38'	One tonner	Wood
	Paxos	35'	One tonner	Wood
Mr. Thomas J. Watson, Jr. (5 boats)	*Palawan I*	47'	Yawl	Wood
	Palawan II	54'	C. B. sloop	Aluminum
	Palawan III	58'	Sloop	Aluminum
	Palawan	67'	Ocean cruiser	Aluminum
	Come On Daddy	37'	Powerboat	Aluminum

OWNER	NAME OF BOAT	L.O.A.	TYPE	MATERIAL
Mr. Percy Chubb II (4 boats)	*Topgallant*	35′	Weekender sloop	Wood
	Laughing Gull	44′	Yawl	Wood
	Antilles	46′	Ketch	Wood
	Bird of Passage	48′	Seagoing power-boat	Fiberglass
Mr. Clayton Ewing (4 boats)	*Dyna*	58′	C. B. yawl	Aluminum
	Dyna	36′	Swan 36*	Fiberglass
	Dyna	52′	Keel sloop	Aluminum
	Dyna	55′	Swan 55	Fiberglass
Prof. Bruno Calandriello (4 boats)	*Dida*	36′	*Gaia* sloop*	Fiberglass
	Dida II	41′	*Alpha* sloop	Fiberglass
	Dida III	41′	Two tonner	Wood
	Dida IV	43′	Two tonner	Wood

sketched up a motorsailer with a short rig. But Percy did not like it. He said, "It looks too much like a motorsailer, Frank." Thereupon I set to thinking what we could do for him.

Then it came to me that there are literally hundreds and hundreds of fishing boat designs that could be used as a seagoing power yacht. I was able to track down a book titled *Fishing Boats of the World*. After going through it, I picked out six different designs that I would like to have, pretending that I was Percy. Then I lent him the book. When he returned it, he had selected the one that I had liked the very best, a double-ended Dutch trawler used a great deal in the North Sea.

So it was that *Bird of Passage* was inspired by this Dutch trawler, and we emulated that design. When the design of *Bird of Passage* was published in the different yachting magazines, S & S received more inquiries about her then almost any other boat the firm had designed. Why? Because she was so unique.

I wrote to Percy and asked him to tell me the various voyages he had made in his four different boats. He answered as follows:

"We have now owned four boats, all of Sparkman & Stephens design. As far as *Topgallant* is concerned, I am afraid we had no adventurous cruises. We bought her just before the war, then laid her up, then sold her a few years after peace returned. The only significant cruise we did was downeast as far as Northeast Harbor, Maine. This was at the very beginning of my cruising experience, and believe it or not going offshore overnight with a landfall in the fog did seem quite an adventure.

"*Laughing Gull* we shipped to Norway in the summer of 1951 and spent a month cruising part of the west coast and part of the south coast on a passage

* A total of 143 of these boats have been built (86 Swan 36's by Nautor in fiberglass, 17 by Benello in fiberglass, and 40 wooden ones by various builders). The design is based on *Hestia*.

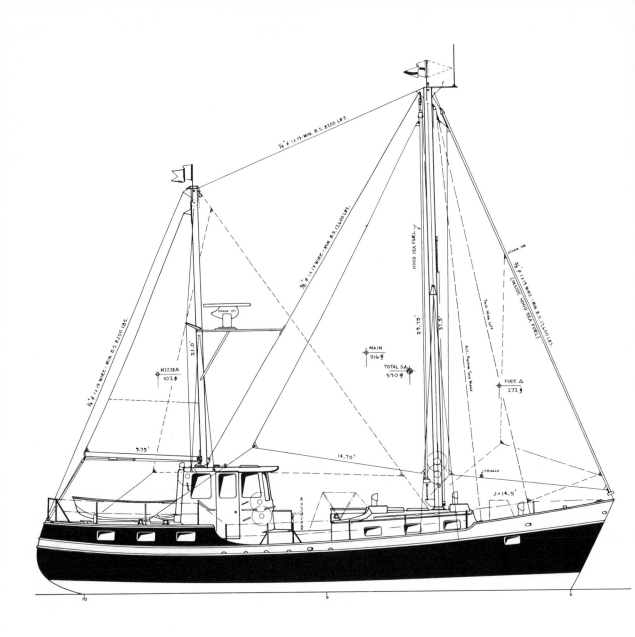

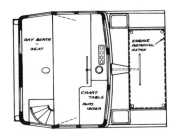

BIRD OF PASSAGE

Sail Area 590 sq. ft.
Displacement 48,500 lbs.
L.O.A. 48′-5″
D.W.L. 41′-5″
Beam 15′-4″
Draft 5′-0″

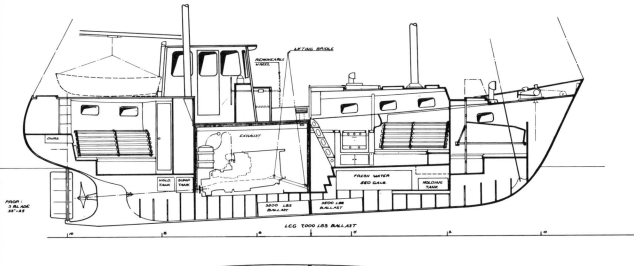

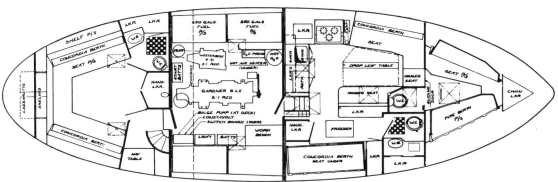

from Bergen to Oslo. Onboard at the time were Corinne and myself and three of our children, the smallest one sleeping in a hammock in the forepeak. Later on we took *Laughing Gull* for a winter cruise in the Bahamas and for a couple of cruises in the Caribbean. The only voyage of note in those years was a passage from Nassau to Savannah in late March and early April, during the course of which we were hove to under bare poles for some time in a northerly gale in the Gulf Stream, about 30 hours before making port in Savannah.

"*Antilles* was a more or less regular commuter between New England and the Caribbean, and also made a couple of passages to the east coast of Nova Scotia, getting as far as the Bras d'Or Lakes. In addition, in 1969 we took part in the joint cruise of the Royal Cruising Club, the Irish Cruising Club, and the CCA on the southwest coast of Ireland, and we sailed her from there to Lisbon and later on in the year from the Canary Islands back to the British Virgin Islands. This last passage was one of the most delightful cruises I have ever taken, and the impressive thing to me was the fact that going downwind in the trade winds with no fore or aft canvas set, and only two twins, she didn't roll at all. I talked to a couple of friends who made similar crossings about the same

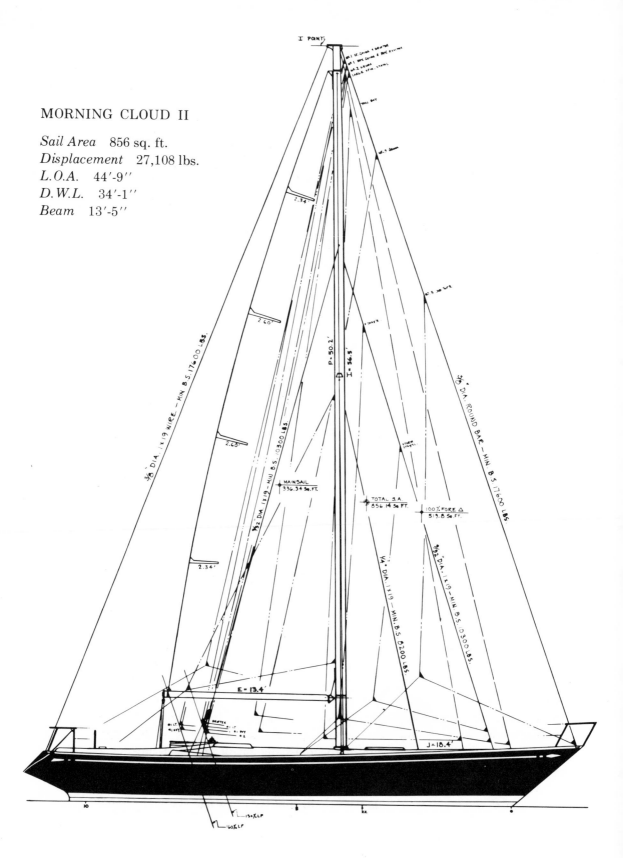

MORNING CLOUD II

Sail Area   856 sq. ft.
Displacement   27,108 lbs.
L.O.A.   44'-9''
D.W.L.   34'-1''
Beam   13'-5''

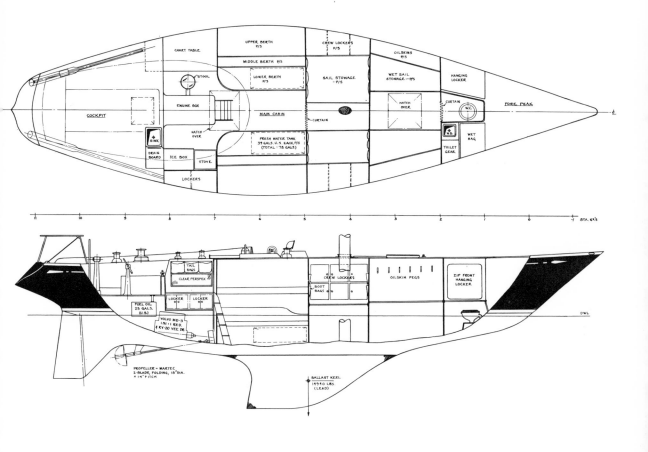

time and were highly uncomfortable, and finally ended up by setting the main to steady themselves.

"As far as *Bird of Passage* is concerned, she has been down and back to the Caribbean twice. In addition, in the summer of 1975 we cruised up to Nova Scotia, the Bras d'Or Lakes, and then along the south coast of Newfoundland. Finally in the summer just past, she sailed from Halifax to Ireland in 12 days, and then carried us on for a delightful and somewhat more leisurely cruise up the coast of Ireland, via the west coast of Scotland and the Caledonian Canal. (A vessel passing through this canal must voyage through Loch Ness. When *Bird of Passage* powered past, 'Nessie' didn't show.) Then she went over the North Sea to Norway. You are aware of some of the constructional bugs that developed when the boat was new, but now that we have these straightened out I may say her performance in the summer of 1976 met our highest expectations."

Mr. Thomas J. Watson, Jr., is another of S & S's fourteen good clients, having come to the firm five different times over the years for five different boats. Except for the powerboat, they have all been named *Palawan*. The first

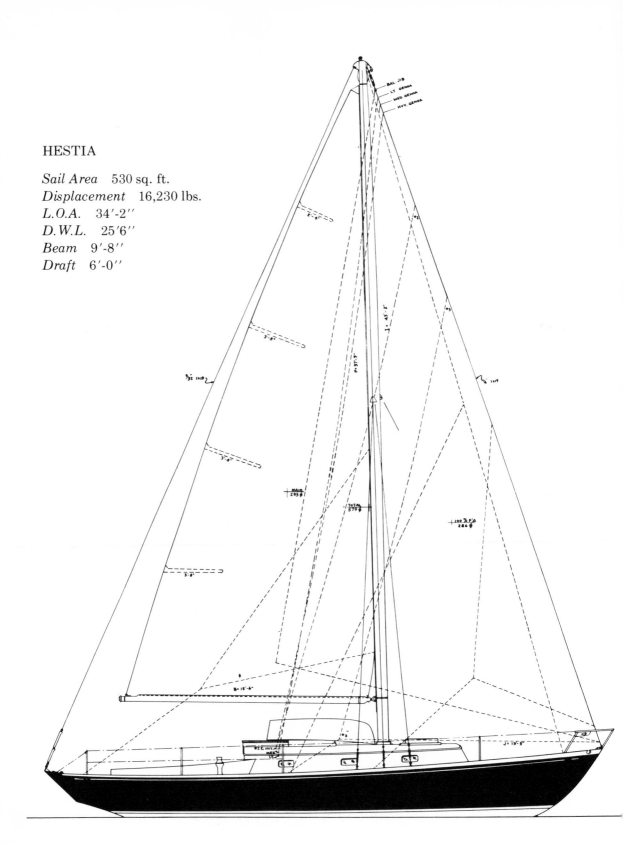

HESTIA

Sail Area   530 sq. ft.
Displacement   16,230 lbs.
L.O.A.   34'-2''
D.W.L.   25'6''
Beam   9'-8''
Draft   6'-0''

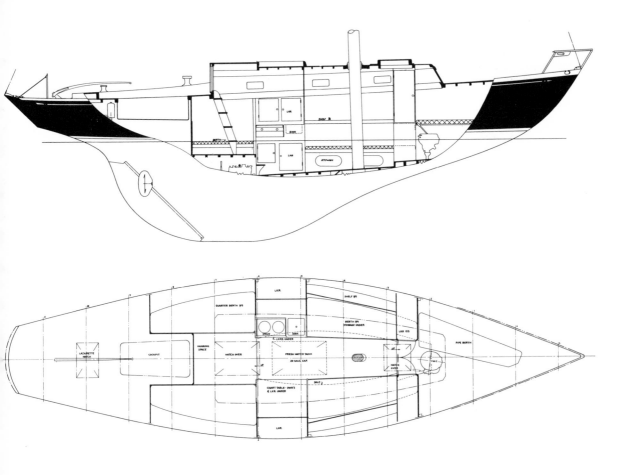

two were wooden yawls built by Aberking & Rasmussen of Germany (one of the very best yards in the world). They were delivered in 1952 and 1958 respectively.

The first *Palawan* was a lovely long-ended yawl 47′ overall with a classic profile and layout, one of the earlier auxiliaries to have a diesel (S & S Design 991). In 1955 she won first in Class B in the Annapolis to New London Race.

Palawan number two won first position in Class B in the 1960 Bermuda Race, then sailed on across the Atlantic to Sweden. She was raced again to Bermuda in 1962 and 1964 and in most of the races on Long Island Sound, and she performed reasonably well.

The third *Palawan* was co-owned by Tom's brother, the late Mr. Arthur K. Watson. She was sloop rigged and constructed of welded aluminum. A model of her hull design was thoroughly studied in tank tests, changed and tested many times at the Davidson Laboratory, to obtain hull resistance and predictions of windward ability, as well as tests for rudder effect and steering ability. An effort was made to develop a hull form that would not only be fast for windward work and light weather, but would steer well going before the wind with the

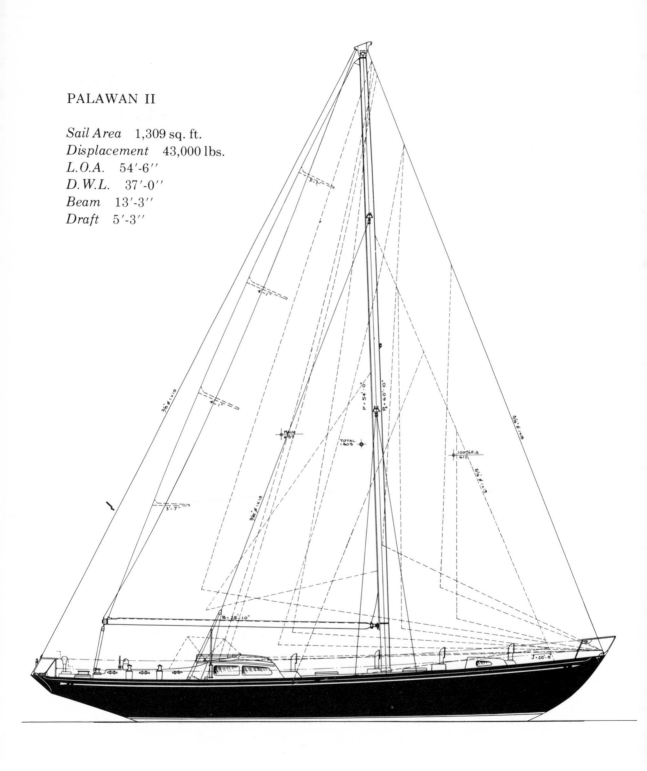

PALAWAN II

Sail Area   1,309 sq. ft.
Displacement   43,000 lbs.
L.O.A.   54'-6''
D.W.L.   37'-0''
Beam   13'-3''
Draft   5'-3''

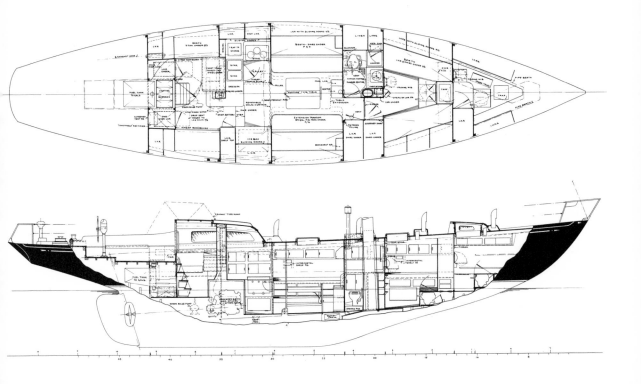

large spinnaker set. She was one of the early boats with a separated skeg and rudder, and some boats of this configuration were having steering problems, so it was good insurance. As it was finally worked out, she had less than the conventional beam and somewhat longer ends than normal. It was perhaps the 12-meter influence that was reflected in her design. She was built by Bob Derecktor in Mamaroneck, New York.

When you look at her racing record, it shows that all this thought and changing of the testing model and thorough planning paid off. From 1966 to 1970 she won first, second, or third 20 times in 29 races, including 7 times first in class and 8 times first in the fleet.

Rod was one of her crew in 1968 while she sailed in the 1,200-mile Buenos Aires to Rio de Janeiro Race; she won second in both class and fleet. She made long passages in some of her races, as well as the Buenos Aires to Rio one: 3,600 miles Bermuda to Denmark, and 2,750 nautical miles Newport to Cork, Ireland. In 1971 she cruised to Newfoundland from Greenwich, Connecticut, via

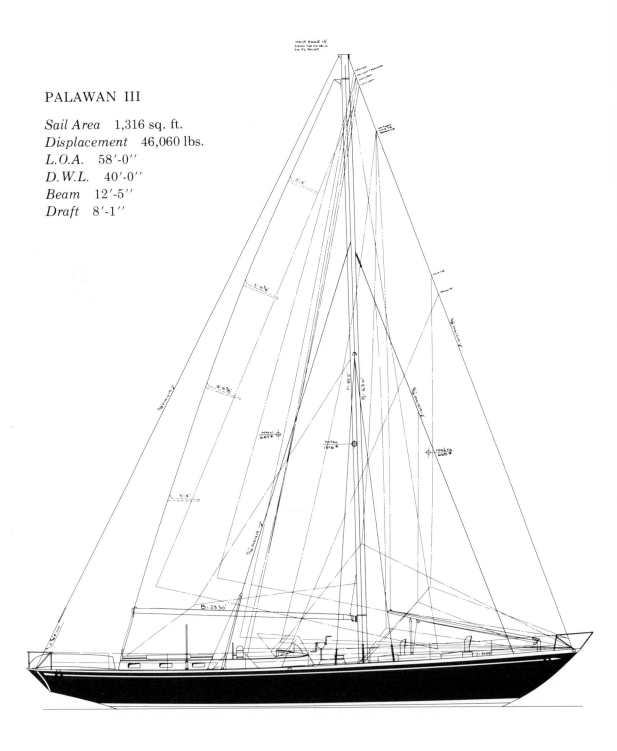

PALAWAN III

Sail Area   1,316 sq. ft.
Displacement   46,060 lbs.
L.O.A.   58'-0''
D.W.L.   40'-0''
Beam   12'-5''
Draft   8'-1''

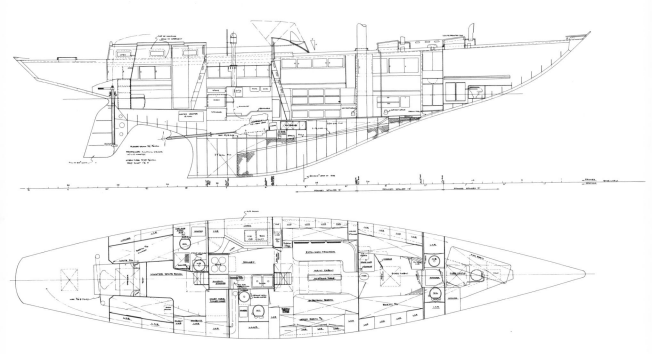

Maine, to Sydney, Nova Scotia, counterclockwise around Newfoundland, returned to Sydney, thence back to Maine.

Because of his health, Tom decided to give up ocean racing, and so when he came to S & S for the fourth *Palawan* he wanted an ocean cruiser. That being my specialty, I got the job. It was really fun working with him. He employed a very good man, Paul Wolter, to take care of the new boat. Paul bought a lot of plywood and soon constructed the interior mock-up of the forward half of our design. When we discovered several mistakes and corrected them, Tom approved. Then Paul tore it down and built a mock-up of the after half of the interior, because Tom's garage in which this was done was not big enough for the whole boat—she was 67' overall. I think I did five different designs before Tom settled on one. (Actually, we did a total of 48 drawings of her.) She too was built by Aberking & Rasmussen of welded aluminum, but this time was ketch rigged. Tandem centerboards used to control balance and steering worked out well. Like the third *Palawan*, she also had a midship cockpit, but this time with an unobtrusive shelter at its forward end.

One of the things Tom asked was how thick the shell plating should be to withstand ice. We did not know, but made it vary in thickness from ¼'' at the deck to ½'' at the keel with frames, web frames, and longitudinals spaced just one foot apart. To give her great range, she carries 1,000 gallons of fresh water and another 1,000 of diesel fuel, doing 9 knots with her General Motors V-6 engine, and faster under sail in a strong breeze.

PALAWAN IV

Sail Area   1,926 sq. ft.
Displacement   98,000 lbs.
L.O.A.   67'-6''
D.W.L.   50'-6''
Beam   17'-6''
Draft   6'-8''

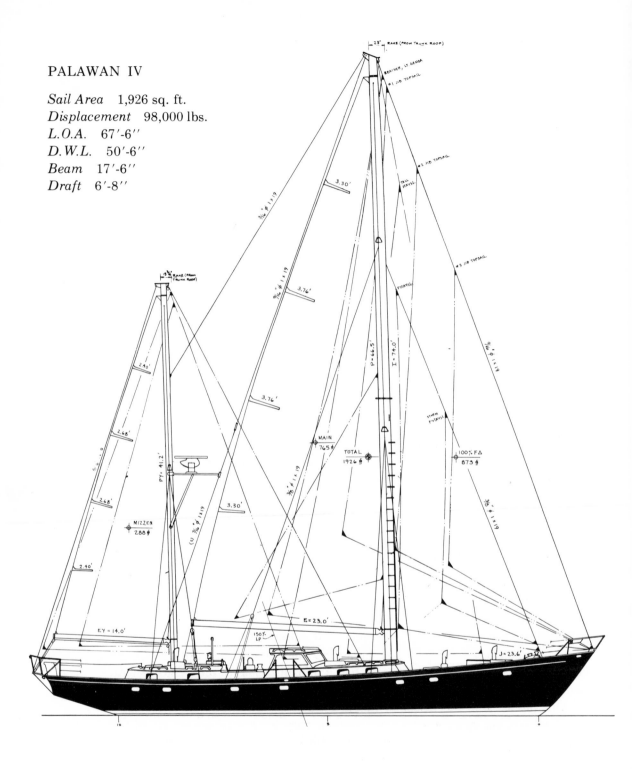

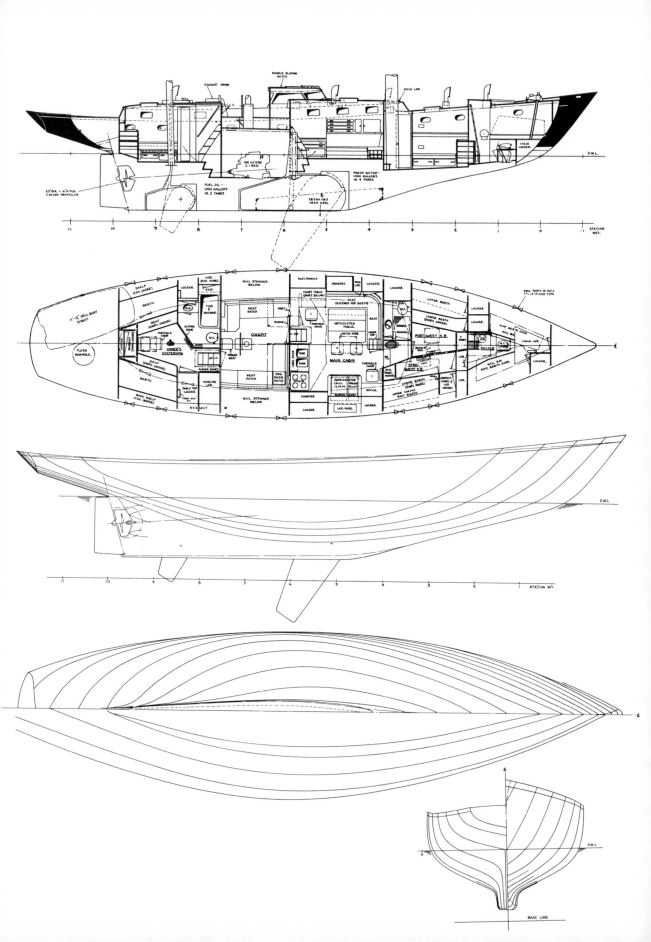

Knowing Tom would probably go far north, we put in a central heating system complete with small oil burner and hot water radiators. Sure enough during the summer of 1974 he went way north along the western coast of Greenland, past glaciers with icebergs breaking off, making growling noises as they moved. There *Palawan* constantly wove between large icebergs.

Since boyhood Tom had read accounts of explorations in this area, so this was a dream fulfilled. In those high latitudes there were 24 hours of daylight each day, with generally clear weather. With Jim Madden navigating, they proceeded past Thule Air Base and headed for Etah, where Peary's base had been; the passage was completely choked with heavy ice. About six miles off Qanaq, with the huts of the town in full view, *Palawan* ran into such heavy ice that she stopped. The temperature of the water was 33°F. Cautiously they backed the boat into an open lead, and after three hours of hard work were able to get her turned around and headed to the open sea.

A note from Tom at that time reads in part: "I thought you might be interested in what it's like to sail to Latitude 74° north. Scenery equal to Norway and almost uninhabited. A total of eleven in our ship's company at different times on this cruise have been comfortable and happy aboard this vessel. Best to all and say thanks to Frank Kinney."

The next summer Tom sailed *Palawan* on a cruise to the South Sea Islands. Once through the Panama Canal she put in at nearby Cocos Island. Next they sailed southwest to the equator and the Galápagos Islands, where Darwin had been in the *Beagle*. The course was the same for Easter Island, where she anchored after a 2,000-mile passage. *Palawan*'s next stop was Pitcairn Island, where her company got to know the descendants of the *Bounty* mutineers. Magna Riva, the fabled Tahiti, Rarotonga, Aitutaki, Samoa, Tonga, Tongataku, Totoya, and finally the Fijis were some of the other South Sea Islands at which she called.

The fifth boat Tom had S & S design was a purely utilitarian 38′ powerboat to serve as a ferry to his summer place on North Haven Island in Penobscot Bay, Maine. She too was welded aluminum and had radar, necessary to get through the thick fogs that occur about half the time in that area. With her deep forefoot she has proven to be a good sea boat and can hold ten passengers in her cabin. (S & S Design 2203, exactly 1,212 designs later than the first *Palawan*.)

Looking over that list of boats for these clients, there was one that is simply lovely. She is fast in light airs, fast in strong breezes, comfortable at sea, and beautiful. She represented the top in yacht design before the war. Her name: *Baruna*. My colleague Bill Stiger has often said, "You ought to get the story of that race from Newport to Annapolis which *Baruna* won. It was almost a tie between *Baruna* and *Bolero*." So it was on one winter's morning I went to talk to Stilly Taylor, her skipper during that race.

"Your mother said that one of the things she contributed to *Baruna*'s design was to make the sheer line an inch deeper," I said.

He answered, "I remember that she insisted on having a prettier stern, so Olin agreed to extend the stern out about 6''. And I think she did have one of the prettiest sterns of any of the Sparkman & Stephens designs."

I agreed, then went on, "Your mother also told me that when you went in this Newport to Annapolis Race, she asked you if there was anything you needed for the boat. And you requested a new mainsail. It was ordered, I believe from Ratsey, but it never arrived in time for the start of the race. What happened?"

Stilly did not remember. It might have been delivered, but it did not fit properly and had to be sent back, he thought. "So we decided to use the ten-year-old cotton main, which was a good-looking sail," he recalled.

The story about the race from *Yachting*, August, 1951, begins with a beautiful picture of the start of that race. I've never seen such a start. There were eight boats almost exactly abeam of one another crossing the line right on the gun. The caption under it reads, "A finer start has seldom been seen in an ocean race." That must have been very exciting.

"Where was *Baruna* in this picture?", I asked Stilly. He quickly pointed to the farthest one to windward.

Stilly began smiling as he recalled, "We started off in a fairly light sou'wester, and I'd say about an hour or so down the way we noticed a little split in our mainsail, and very quickly it split all the way from the leach to the luff about three fourths of the way up the sail. So we had to lower the sail. Bobs Blair, who had been racing with us since 1938, and Captain Lars then proceeded to sew it together."

"Did you have a sewing machine on board?" I asked.

"No, we didn't. We had to do it by hand. During this period we seemed to keep up our speed under the genoa and the mizzen. So we didn't lose very much to *Bolero*, except we fell off to leeward, which later on didn't really make any difference, because the wind shifted favorably so that we were both able to put up spinnakers. And from there to the Chesapeake Lightship it was a rather slow race. We seemed to be gaining on her at night, and particularly in the light air. And if the breeze picked up, she would gain a little bit on us. We felt that the reason was that with our old mainsail of less weight it drew better in the light air than her heavy mainsail did. So the old sail turned out to be an advantage for us. At any rate, we arrived down at the Chesapeake Lightship (now a Texas tower) very close to dawn, gaining on her all that night. We could see by her masthead light that she was getting closer to us. Both boats rounded the lightship absolutely abreast of one another! Then we headed into Chesapeake Bay, and it was the first time during the race that *Baruna* had been ahead of *Bolero*, or even with her."

"But she'd always been within sight since the start?" I asked.

"Yes, always been in sight," he continued. "We had to jibe from port to starboard. And rounded inside of her on the turn, so for the first time we were ahead. Within about 15 to 20 minutes the clew of our cotton spinnaker parted!"

BARUNA

Sail Area 2,342 sq. ft.
Displacement 88,130 lbs.
L.O.A. 72'-0"
D.W.L. 50'-0"
Beam 14'-0"
Draft 9'-6"

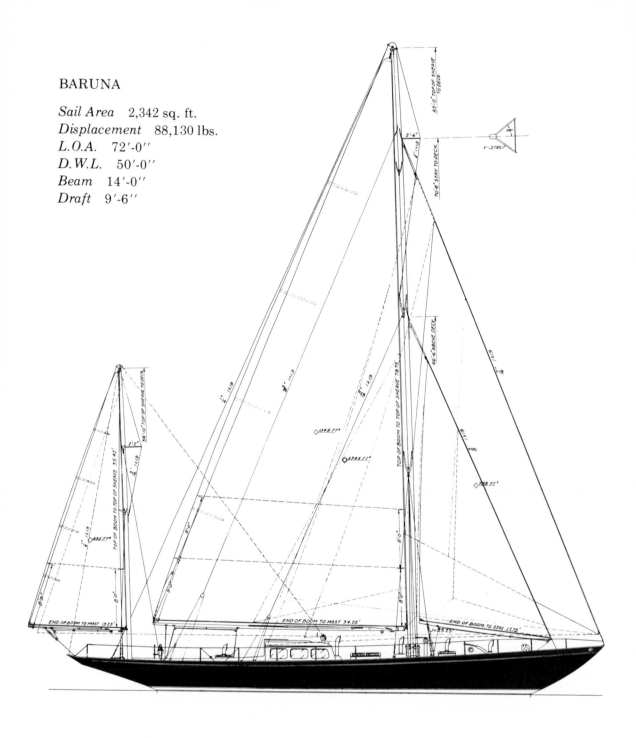

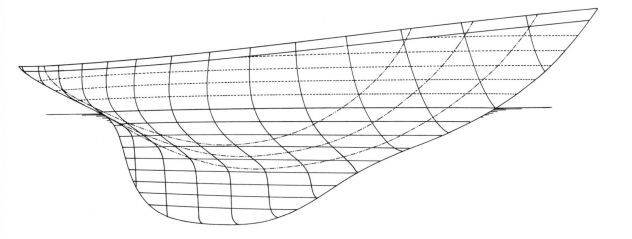

He paused, then said, "By then it had been flying for something over 60 hours. I'm sure the fitting just got tired. While changing spinnakers in the meantime, we lost a few lengths to her. Then once again we got the boat moving, and passed her in light air. For some reason at this point she let us split tacks a little bit, and she dropped far behind us. However, later on that evening the wind strengthened considerably from out of the south and she brought this wind right up to us and went past us."

"That must have been frustrating," I replied. "When a boat picks up a breeze and comes up on you like that, it's not very pleasant."

Stilly went on, "We didn't let her get very far ahead of that new breeze, as we were able to get on her stern and take just enough wind out of her mainsail so that we could blanket her. And we went on that way all night long till we finished, just before dawn.

"A this point none of us on the boat had had any sleep for at least 36 hours, the race had been so exciting. Everytime I would go below I'd hear Bus Hovey, who was the mate on the other watch, say, 'We're gaining a little on her,' or 'She's gaining on us,' and I'd have to get up and see what was going on. I guess this excitement spread to all of us, because I know that nobody was able to sleep during that entire period. As we neared the finish line we were both on the starboard tack, and we were heading slightly east to the finish line. We were either overlapped to leeward of her, or so close that she couldn't jibe. So we drove her (we thought) almost past the finish line and then jibed inside of her. We felt we should have finished ahead of her, but we underestimated the strength of the current, ebbing out of the bay at about 4 knots. Otherwise we were about even with the finish line when we jibed. We thought we'd have her dead astern of us, and unable to get by us, but the current was so strong that we were almost dead before the wind, whereas we'd been on a complete reach going faster before we jibed."

Boat for boat on this 466-mile race it was a matter of only 24 seconds! And the handicap difference was 15 minutes corrected time, so *Baruna* had beaten *Bolero* handsomely. The going was so slow it took five days for the first of that fleet of 32 boats to finish. And as the late William H. Taylor said in *Yachting*, "The two big black B's had such a match race as has rarely been seen in ocean racing."

"It certainly was the most thrilling thing that any of us had ever been through," Stilly went on, "I give lots of credit to our crew, which had been together for a long time, and especially to Bus Hovey, whose experience on the J Class Cup defenders his family owned, *Weetamo* and *Yankee*, was invaluable in working out our strategy. We were always able, even when she was going faster, to take just enough wind out of her mainsail to keep her from breaking away, because she couldn't legally bear off on us."

"Did you get in any luffing matches with her?" I asked.

"No, we really didn't, because we were racing under Offshore Rules, unlike round-the-buoy racing, no luffing is allowed. You've got to maintain your normal course. We chatted back and forth about the rules a number of times across the water with Corny Shields, aboard *Bolero*. Olin and Ken Davidson were aboard her, too. Bill Stiger was with us, and Bob Garland was aboard Porter Schutt's *Egret*."

Stilly looked at a picture of *Baruna*'s crew through a magnifying glass and could recognize Hoyt Ammidon, Bobs Blair, Bus Hovey, Eric Ridder, Evan Thomas, John and Roger Holowell.

Baruna was one of a group called at that time maximum size boats, which were built to the top length permitted by the Cruising Club rule for the Bermuda Race: roughly 72′ overall. She won first overall and in Class A in the 1938 Bermuda Race, and repeated this same victory ten years later in the 1948 Bermuda Race. *Bolero* was a little longer, but part of the length did not count for the rule purposes.

I remember *Baruna* so well. When I worked at Jakobson's Yard, sometimes I would just take my sandwich lunch and sit down underneath where she was stored in the shed and look up at her, getting a fish's-eye view. Every line was absolutely perfect; You could tell by the way the boot top was put on so sweet and fairly; what a lovely curve it was. She is so beautifully proportioned in her entirety, both hull and rig. Her small deckhouse amidships has just the right amount of tumble home to its sides and rake to its front. It seemed to me that she represented the height of the golden years of yachting just before the war. No question about that.

I remember the way Lars maintained *Baruna* with her flush deck, of Port Orford cedar. My, how he had it clean and bright. Stilly added, "We saved, I think, 1,500 pounds by using that instead of teak."

BOLERO and BARUNA
(Rosenfeld)

BOLERO

Sail Area 2,480 sq. ft.
Displacement 93,800 lbs.
L.O.A. 73'-6''
D.W.L. 51'-0''
Beam 15'-1''
Draft 9'-6''

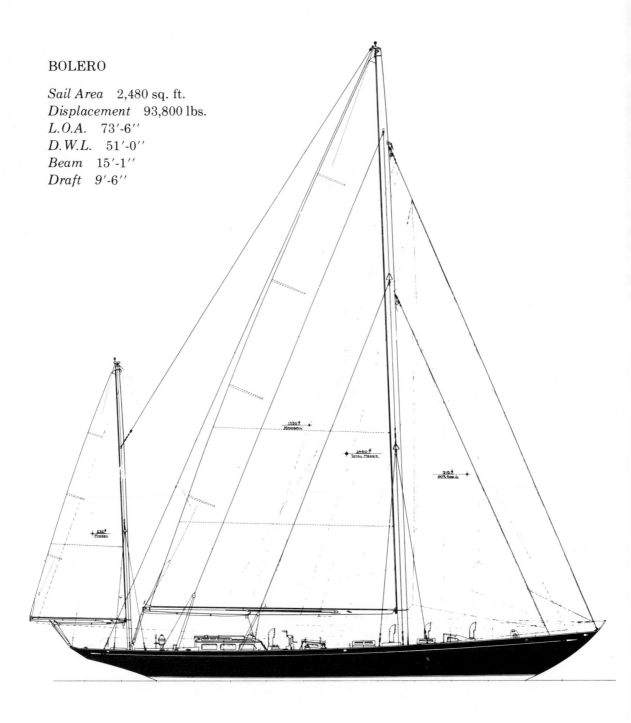

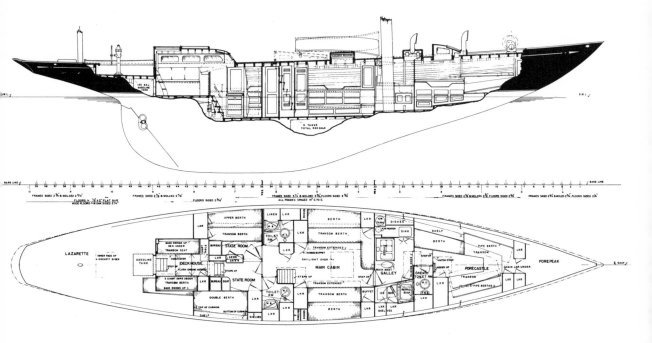

When Lars Myrdal decided to go back to Norway, that finished the boat for Stilly's father. He told me, "I just can't keep her anymore without Lars." He was an excellent man to have on a boat. He took such pride in the way he maintained her. And those black topsides set off by her gilded cove line would just shine, and you'd see the bow wave and the white foam being reflected on the mirror-like finish as she sailed along.

"You know my father sold her to Jimmy Michael in San Francisco, and he was very proud of the boat, kept her in marvelous shape. And she went along for many, many years winning races out there for him. She's a remarkable boat," said Stilly, justly proud.

San Francisco Bay has strong winds. To illustrate two sailing extremes, *Baruna* was good in light airs in the Annapolis Race that she won, after her duel with *Bolero,* and also good in windy San Francisco Bay.

I asked Stilly about the background of why the boat was designed and built, and he replied, "We used to cruise every summer. We'd start off with the American Yacht Club Cruise, then go on the New York Yacht Cruise, from there go down to Maine, winding up in Northeast Harbor, and sailing in the Blue Hill Regatta. Previously we had a New York 50 with a reduced rig that was quite old. When she began to leak, my father decided to build a new boat.

"He went to Olin and talked of our requirements. 'We spend about six weeks a year on the boat,' he said. 'I fly back and forth to business. But the family go off, and they go to Maine, so I want something that will accommodate them, and some friends of theirs, and a boat that will get back and forth to

Maine fast.'" Stilly said his father had no thought whatsoever of ocean racing at the time, and it was not until the plans were well underway that people began suggesting to him that he should consider going in the Bermuda Race. He did, and *Baruna* won it in 1938. "He really wasn't out to have the fastest boat, he just wanted a good, comfortable cruising boat for the family," Stilly pleasantly recalled. "Three of us boys would go, and my father and mother, all of whom were good sailors. So we virtually had our crew ready-made. Sometimes each one of us would invite a friend, and that would give us an ample crew. It was really a family enterprise."

I nodded, saying, "That's my idea of exactly how a boat should be used."

S & S has many foreign clients; half of the 14 good clients listed in this chapter are from abroad. Of these, Mr. Arthur Slater of Yorkshire, England, is one of the leading figures in the competitive world of international offshore racing. He came to S & S six times for six different boats between 1960 and 1974, a remarkable record of faith in the firm. As Lloyd's shipping magazine *100 A1* aptly heads an article in their September, 1976, issue, namely, "Where Every Prospect Pleases," because five of his six boats were named *Prospect of Whitby* and kept winning.

Mr. Slater was, among other things, a sports car driver and for several seasons drove for famous concerns such as Aston Martin, Jaguar, and Armstrong Siddeley. He had raced six times in the Monte Carlo Rally successfully, but the seventh time in 1959 his car crashed into a double telegraph pole. The result was that his left leg had to be amputated above the knee. Being an undaunted sportsman, he decided to get into yacht racing, saying, "In what other active sport could I reach the top with only one leg?"

He was not unlike President Franklin D. Roosevelt, who after his legs were disabled enjoyed sailing his own boat even more.

In 1960 Mr. Slater commissioned S & S for a new design to be named *Saboo*, a centerboard yawl 42'-7" overall built of wood. (All his boats had special helmsman's seats built like padded armchairs.) Returning from the 1961 Fastnet Race, she was overtaken by a Force 9 gale (55 mph or so) off Harwich, which resulted in the main boom fittings and rail tracks being torn off, and the mast and other deck fittings coming adrift. As a result the boat and her crew spent three days drifting a number of miles with neither lights nor radio that worked, gradually being driven toward some shoals. She was reported missing. She stayed afloat, and after the gale blew itself out made home port. Mr. Slater had the rather dubious experience, when coming ashore, of reading his own obituary in the local newspaper!

Saboo was repaired and raced off the Yorkshire coast with some success until being sold in 1964.

His second boat, the first *Prospect of Whitby*, was also wooden, built in Norway, 41'-7" overall and sloop rigged. The first season's racing off the Yorkshire coast was so successful that her happy owner said, "We won everything."

In 1967 she started racing at Cowes and was soon picked for the Admiral's Cup team. This team placed second behind Australia, with the United States third. In 18 starts she came in first once and second 17 times, a remarkably consistent record of success. The next year she raced in America but conditions did not suit her, and at the end of the year she was sold. Despite this, she had within two seasons proved a force to be reckoned with in competitive offshore sailing.

The second *Prospect* (his third S & S design) was to prove beyond all doubt the ability of Mr. Slater and his crew, and place them at the top of the sailing league. She was built of steel, one foot longer than before at 42'-7'' overall, by Frans Maas in Breskens, Holland. "*Prospect II* was built like a battleship," her owner said. For the 1969 season this *Prospect* was once again in the Admiral's Cup team. In the Channel Race she was third Admiral's Cup yacht and third overall in class. Then for the second race for the Britannic Cup she won a fine victory—first Admiral's Cup yacht and first overall.

At the end of the season the Royal Ocean Racing Club decided to send a team to the Southern Cross Championships in Australia, the equivalent of the Admiral's Cup down under. It consisted of a coastal race of 200 miles and two 30-mile inshore races. *Prospect II* was included and showed her usual form. The climax of the series was the final race from Sydney, Australia, to Hobart, Tasmania, a distance of 650 miles. She was the first to finish in the fleet but second on the handicap. Even so, the British team finished second overall. In 1970 she was part of the Onion Patch (a nickname for Bermuda) team. Unfortunately she was damaged when being off-loaded from a ship and never regained her previously highly tuned state. Other than that, *Prospect II* had been even more successful than her predecessor. For the two seasons of 1969 and 1970 she won 23 trophies. By the end of 1970 she was up for sale, and Mr. Slater requested S & S to try again to improve on her good design.

Prospect III was built of welded aluminum, being the first British potential Admiral's Cup yacht of this metal. By June it was obvious to anyone that this *Prospect* was carrying the name and reputation of the other *Prospects* to further fame and glory. Following early season success, she was picked for the Admiral's Cup team along with *Morning Cloud* and *Cervantes IV*. In the series for that cup she gave the British team the best possible start, namely first Admiral's Cup yacht and first overall in Class I in the Channel Race, followed by a second and a fifth. Britain won the cup from Australia, with the United States third. *Prospect III* finished as best British yacht and second Admiral's Cup yacht out of 44. At the end of the 1971 season the Royal Ocean Racing Club again elected to send a team of three yachts to Australia for the Southern Cross series. The team chosen was, naturally enough, the same three yachts that had just won the Admiral's Cup. *Prospect III*, like her predecessor, was shipped out to Australia. Out there the decisive Sydney-Hobart Race was best described by Mr. Slater: "*Prospect* went like a bomb, and at the end of the second day was leading the fleet, *Morning Cloud* second and *Cervantes* third."

In the 1972 season Mr. Slater did not campaign her so hard, sailing with a

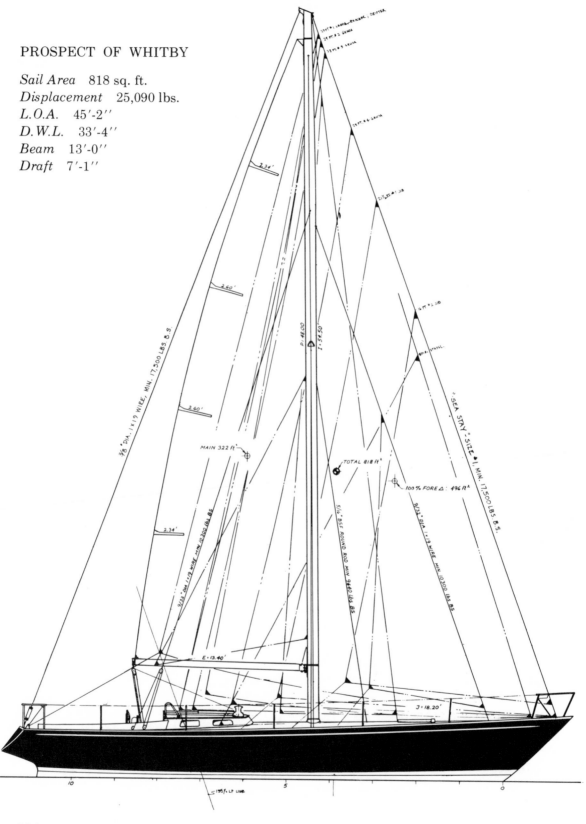

PROSPECT OF WHITBY

Sail Area   818 sq. ft.
Displacement   25,090 lbs.
L.O.A.   45'-2''
D.W.L.   33'-4''
Beam   13'-0''
Draft   7'-1''

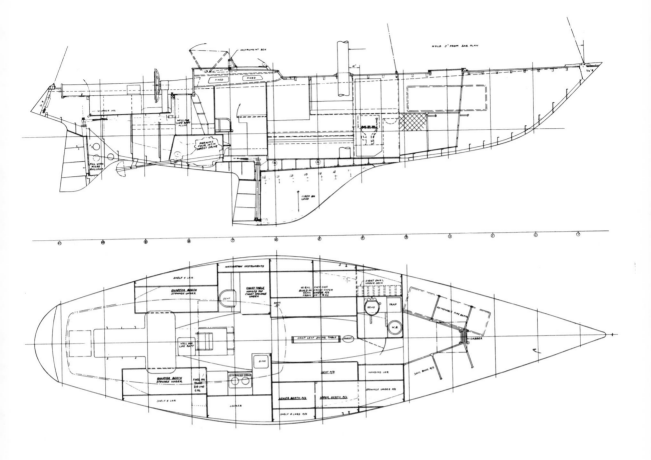

makeshift crew and more for fun. Even so she finished up as Class I champion and won the Somerset Memorial Trophy as yacht of the year. She was sold at the end of the season.

The next year, 1973, saw *Prospect of Whitby IV* as Mr. Slater's fifth S & S design. She was flush decked with only a small cockpit for the the helmsman in her 47′ overall length. On her steeply cambered deck were two aluminum coffee grinder winches, the same type normally found on a twelve meter. She was similar to the twelves in another way, as her jibstay did not go to the masthead but to a point 5′ below it, an effort to reduce the boat's rating. After her unsuccessful early races, which ended in others being selected for the Admiral's Cup team, the decision to change to a masthead rig was made and accomplished.

In her first race after conversion, the Round Isle of Wight, she began to show the sort of performance that people had come to expect from the *Prospects*; she finished second overall and second in Class I. Now with an extra 20 square feet on the genoa and over 100 square feet extra in the spinnaker, and with an hydraulic backstay adjuster to increase tension on it and the jibstay, *Prospect IV* began to outsail the rest of the British yachts. She was best British

PROSPECT OF WHITBY

Sail Area   725 sq. ft.
Displacement   22,080 lbs.
L.O.A.   41'-7''
D.W.L.   30'-0''
Beam   11'-3''
Draft   6'-7''

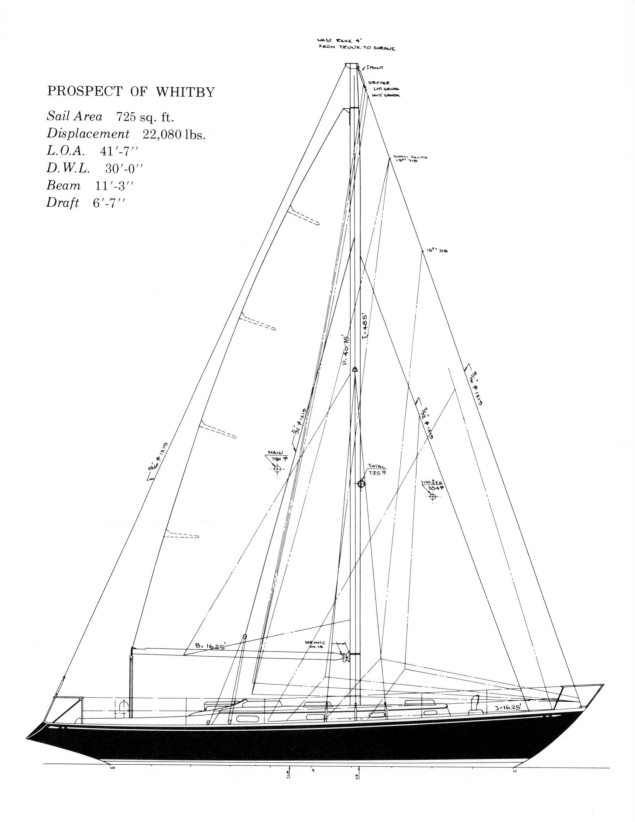

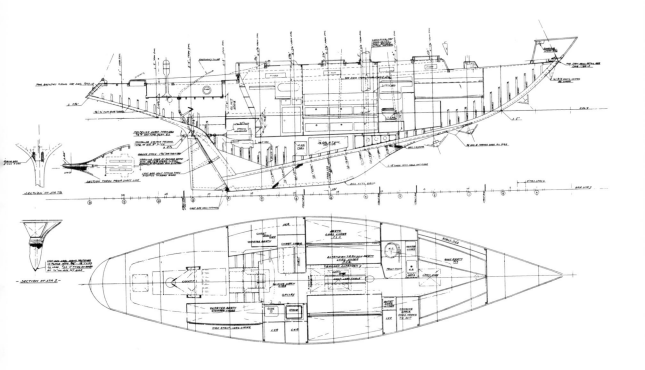

boat (ninth) in the Fastnet, Royal Ocean Racing Club Class I champion. And like *Prospect II* and *III* she went to Australia at the end of the 1973 season. There the British team won the Southern Cross championship, *Prospect IV* being first in fleet and second on corrected time in the Sydney-Hobart Race.

By mid-1974 plans were being made for *Prospect of Whitby V.* Mr. Slater once again went to S & S for another aluminum sloop, 3′ smaller (44′-4″ overall) and considerably lighter. Mr. Slater's determination to succeed remains undiminished. Over the past considerable number of seasons he has established himself as the man to beat in British offshore racing; he intends to keep it that way in the future. His six boats is the record number for S & S's fourteen especially good clients. No one else has had the firm work for them so many times.

One of the traits of character that an oceangoing skipper acquires is, of necessity, self-reliance. When he is out there in the middle of the Atlantic or Pacific with land over 1,000 miles away all around, he must have a self-contained vessel prepared for anything. For something drastic to happen to a well-found boat is very much the exception rather than the rule. But there are two good boats, *Dyna* and *Puffin*, listed in this chapter out of S & S's 2,300 designs that were in such dire straits at sea. It is almost unbelievable that their skippers brought them safely to port on their own. That was self-reliance.

How would you like to lose the rudder of your boat in mid-Atlantic? It happened to one of our 14 good clients, Clayton Ewing on the first of four *Dyna*'s that S & S designed for him.* She was a relatively new 58′ aluminum center-board yawl at the time, in 1963.

Who were the self-reliant men aboard her? The skipper and owner, Clayton Ewing (who casually mentioned over the airwaves in mid-Atlantic that he had lost his rudder, but did not request help), his son Mark, Lynn Williams, William Seger, Richard Killins, Mike Ferry, Stephen Colgate, Dr. Thurston Harrison, Charles Larkin II, as well as the two members of her crew, William W. Robinson, Jr., and Stephens A. Van Dyck, who wrote about it. Their story, which follows, points up how a well-designed yawl can be steered with her sails alone, and that is a great credit to those who created her.

"For the first two-thirds of the 1963 Trans-Atlantic Race events on Clayton Ewing's 58′ aluminum yawl *Dyna* followed the normal pattern of a long ocean race. The main challenge to skipper and crew was getting the most possible speed out of the boat in the varying conditions encountered in the 2,850 miles between Newport, R.I., and the Eddystone Light on England's south coast. This routine was altered sharply on the morning of July 13 when *Dyna* was 980 miles from the finish and 900 miles from the Bishop Rock on the Scilly Islands, her eventual landfall. When running with a spinnaker set in hard going, she experienced a knockdown which was either the cause or result of the loss of her aluminum rudder. The only damage suffered in the two weeks prior to the knockdown was inconsequential and easily repaired. A rudder loss, however, is the one major breakdown, short of dismasting, which is impossible to repair at sea. To complete the race, or even reach land unassisted, *Dyna* would have to sail 1,000 miles without the benefit of conventional steering.

"For the day and night preceding the knockdown we had been running before a freshening southwest breeze at first under spinnaker and then under working jib wung out on a spinnaker pole. By midnight on July 12 the wind was 35–40 knots and *Dyna* was surfing down the building seas in surges which we estimated at up to 13 or 14 knots.

"Shortly after sunrise on July 13 the wind eased slightly, the clouds broke, and our speed dropped consistently below 7 knots. We set our big 2.2-ounce spinnaker in place of the working jib at 0545 and regained speed. The wind started to pipe back in shortly after we had completed the sail change, and steering became increasingly difficult. The seas were big and confused, coming

* Two other S & S boats lost control of their rudders. In the 1958 Bermuda Race *Windigo* was beating up to the Island 30 miles away when the drifts holding the wooden rudder blade to its bronze stock sheared off. Bill Stiger was one of her crew then, and he says they lowered her mainsail and sailed with jib and mizzen only. Leading port and starboard mizzen sheets to cockpit winches, they were able to steer her to windward and tack using the mizzen. They did not lose much time in finishing the race, because it was blowing hard there.

The other boat to lose control of her rudder was *Bird of Passage*. It happened in 1976 when she was coming north in the Inland Waterway. Her helmsman turned the wheel to steer round a bend in the waterway, but she went straight ahead into a sandbank. Her rudder had a flanged coupling welded to the rudder stock just above the blade for its easy removal. The welding on the upper flange let go, and as a result the rudder stock just turned freely inside the flange. A new upper rudder stock was machined down from a solid piece of bronze, eliminating the welding.

from both the port and starboard quarters. This created a ticklish problem for the helmsman. While the boat would shoot straight down the face of each wave once she had started to surf, each sea would send her substantially above or below her desired course. This forced the helmsman to either overcorrect or undercorrect for the boat's natural tendency to ride to windward when a wave would lift her stern and dip her bow into the trough between seas. However, we had experienced a great deal of this type of going in the preceding day and a half, and aside from paying particularly close attention to helmsmanship, we were not overly concerned.

"The speed indicator needle was once again jammed against the endstop at 10 knots coming down the waves and everyone was speculating about our actual speed. We felt we had things pretty well under control, but at approximately 0645 the boat wiped up to weather on a wave. She then went beyond the point of a normal wipe-up. Two other crew members assisted in getting the wheel hard over and she started to come down to course. At this point, with the wheel still hard over, she suddenly drove hard up to weather, collapsing the spinnaker and breaking the pole. The chute was partially filled and heeling the boat well over. The outer third of the main boom buried in the water and put the rail under until approximately a foot of the cabin top was submerged.

"The angle of heel was such that carefully stowed pots, pans, and even a large jar of strawberry jam went crashing to the chart table opposite the galley lockers. Lynn Williams, who was sleeping below, reported that he was thrown out of his bunk on the weather side forward, and fell directly across the cabin into the lee berth.

"We cast off the spinnaker after-guy to spill the chute and right the boat. With the spinnaker flogging and the entire 65' of after-guy blown clear of the water and streaming straight off to leeward, we first set a staysail, and then the working jib in order to get way on and bring her off the wind to blanket the spinnaker. She still would not respond, and we finally winched the spinnaker sheet into the rail, where three of us grabbed it and attempted to pull the sail on board. The strain was still too great, so we eased off the halyard, bringing the head down almost to the wave tops. With the sail streaming out to leeward parallel to the water, we were finally able to horse it aboard.

"The wheel was still hard over, but the boat would not come down to course despite our 6-knot speed. We checked the steering quadrant to see if perhaps a steering cable had jumped the sheave. In the process of turning the wheel, we found all the cables to be led properly and the upper end of the rudder post turning in response to the wheel. But there was still no steerage or load on the steering wheel. That left only one possibility—there was no longer any rudder.

"The mainsail was lowered, and with jib and mizzen we were able to run off before the wind. Skipper Ewing divided the eleven-man crew into three groups: three to sail the boat as near to course as possible, three to put things somewhat in order, and five to construct a jury steering device. Sailing the boat called for a series of experiments in sail combinations, and finally with the working jib trimmed hard and the reefed mizzen eased, we were able to stay near course at 6 knots dead downwind. The spinnaker net had fouled with the forestay and jib halyards and created a tangle of gear, which took some time to clear away.

"The first attempt at a steering device was to put vanes on the repaired spinnaker pole and use it like a tiller. The broken aluminum pole was repaired by sawing out the bent section, then putting inside it a precut wooden dowel the diameter of the inside of the pole. The vanes used were the floorboards from the forecastle floor, and they were then bolted on with pieces of half-inch tie rod. This first attempt failed because there was no adequate way of controlling it in the big seas and no satisfactory method of securing it to the taffrail.

"Our spirits were low after this failure, and the onset of a full gale by nightfall caused concern in more than one of the crew. By late afternoon we had taken off the working jib and mizzen and replaced them with only the staysail, trimmed in hand amidships. All night *Dyna* rode comfortably under this rig, making about 4 knots on the desired course, which was fortunately dead downwind. At times the wind reached Force 10 (55–65) and the seas could only be called huge.

"It was during this stormy night that the second steering device was devised and constructed. The main cabin of *Dyna* became a workshop, and a paravane steerer took shape. It consisted of the sections of the broken spinnaker pole bolted together, open-ended, side by side. This rig was to be towed astern like a box kite on the theory that the water rushing through it could be directed by trimming guys attached to its after end. The paravane would go off to the side and drag the stern around. At 0530 conditions had improved enough to launch the new device. For an hour and a half we tried to make it work. We took it aboard after it lost a steering line shackle and reluctantly abandoned the idea. Response to the mechanism was not sufficient, and the drag created was too great.

"Throughout the morning we tried various sail combinations and finally a satisfactory one was discovered: trimming the staysail to one side and the storm jib to the other. Under this rig the boat made 5 knots somewhat near course. This was satisfactory but slow. We wanted to make the most of fresh following winds, for the next day might bring headwinds or no air at all. At 1430 we tied a double reef in the mainsail and set it opposite to the working jib (set on the spinnaker pole). Setting this combination was quite difficult as both sails had to be hoisted simultaneously to keep the boat on course.

"Once successfully set and drawing, this rig proved to be very effective. The mizzen was lowered and we steered by easing and trimming the mainsail or making adjustments in the trim of the working jib. The speed went up to a steady 7½ knots and often rose above 10 as we surfed helmsmanless down steep quartering seas. The key to the success of this rig was the staysail set on the forestay. As her head came too high, the staysail would push it off, and when she started to jibe the staysail (which was sheeted to weather) would fill from the leeward side and bring her up. *Dyna* would wander about 15° either side of the course and occasionally much higher or lower. Our major fear was that she would jibe when a sea caught the boat by the lee quarter. We experienced some close calls, but never did jibe.

"By the 1900 watch change the wind had shifted enough to require jibing to the port tack. With all hands on deck we lowered the working jib and mainsail simultaneously, leaving the staysail to keep her before the wind. The main boom was jibed over and one reef shaken out. The spinnaker pole and working jib were likewise taken in and set up for the port jibe. When all was ready, the two sails were hoisted together. Time to jib ship, 30 minutes.

"The starboard watch went below after the jibe, and when they came on deck to take the midnight-to-four stint were treated to a real sleigh ride. *Dyna* was charging down large seas before a freshening northwester in conditions much like those which had preceded the knockdown. The difference was that now she had no rudder. We called the man who controlled the mizzen sheet 'helmsman,' but a trick at that position would soon convince anyone that this was wishful thinking. The boat was often pushed off course 20–25° by the seas, but always, thanks to our rig, returned to the vicinity of the course. The stars broke through the overcast occasionally, and it was an exhilarating watch.

"By the morning watch seas calmed slightly and the breeze eased to 20–25 knots. We stuck with the same rig, and at noon we were told that the *Dyna* had logged 179 rudderless miles in the preceding 24 hours. Eddystone Light seemed an awful lot closer than it had only a day and a half before.

"Late in the day the breeze dropped a bit more and came forward of the beam. We struck the staysail and set the working jib to leeward in the conventional manner, continuing to make 4–5 knots through smooth seas.

"The improvement in weather and sea conditions, as well as our reduced speed, encouraged us to think again about some sort of jury steering system. It was a unique experience to everyone on board, and the young winch winders offered their ideas as readily as the seasoned veterans in the crew. After hearing everyone out, the skipper had a conference with Williams and Chick Larkin, *Dyna*'s navigator. The following plan was devised: A sweep was again made from the broken spinnaker pole with vanes at the outboard end. A spinnaker pole bell fitting was taken off the mast and connected to a newly constructed fitting on the end of the boomkin. The spinnaker pole was put in the bell, and two steering lines were connected to the vanes. By winching one line or the other, the sweep acted as a rudder.

"It took nearly 12 hours between the inception of the plan and the actual 'launching' of the rudder at 0815 on July 16, but once it was set up the sweep worked quite well. With it we were able to carry the big spinnaker once again, and we did so all morning. Finally at 1300 it was determined that the drag created by the sweep offset the advantage of the bigger sail, and that speed had not been increased appreciably. We then struck the spinnaker, set our double-head rig of a wung out R.O.R.C. genoa and strapped-in staysail, and brought the sweep aboard. We now had a method of steering accurately in any conditions as long as the seas remained fairly calm.

"We felt that the effort expended on the sweep was well worthwhile, but that it should be preserved for a more critical time. We used the sweep only once more—to steer the last 30 miles to the finish. We never did set the big spinnaker again, although we did carry the storm chute entirely on the weather side of the boat for one watch. We always seemed to return to the wung out jib and staysail rig. It was most effective in the quartering breezes which prevailed for the rest of the race.

"On July 17 we double reefed the mainsail in the face of what one correspondent recorded as 'Gale #4' in his log. We kept a man forward at the mast at all times prepared to let both the jib and main halyards run in the event of an accidental jibe, but again we had no trouble. Our noon-to-noon run for that day was 184 miles, our best rudderless run and our third best day's run of the entire race!

"As we came within 70 miles of the Bishop Rock at twilight on July 18, we began to see a good deal of commercial traffic and had to be especially alert. We knew that any evasive action that might be necessary would have to be taken well in advance.

"We passed the Bishop at about 0230 the next morning. The fog was quite thick, and we never actually saw the light, hearing only the fog cannon. *Dyna* spent all day reaching up the English Channel in a dying southwester, making only about 4 knots. We put our steering-with-balanced-sails ability to the test between two buoys off Lands End, and were able to come within 250 yards of the second marker after a distance of 5 miles in thick fog. The skipper felt that with the increased traffic in the channel we might have to maneuver quickly, so we launched the sweep for the last 30 miles to the Eddystone. We sighted the light through the fog at 2030 about 2½ miles dead ahead. We crossed the finish line carrying main, mizzen, and the same double head rig that had served us so well.

"*Dyna* was hauled at Camper and Nicholson's Yard in Southampton on July 21. It was found that the rudder and rudder post were missing and that the rudder post had sheared off at the point where it protrudes through the hull."

I had a chat with Clayton Ewing and asked him why *Dyna* lost her rudder, because it could have been my own mistake (some of her drawings had come from my board). He told me that since she was one of our earliest welded aluminum boats, the rudder (being hollow) had a tendency to float up against the hull. A couple of years before this transatlantic crossing, her builder on the Great Lakes filled the rudder with oil and put a bushing on the rudder stock above the blade to prevent it from floating up against the hull. Our office specified the saltwater-corrosion-resistant aluminum alloy to be used. But the builder did not adhere to those specifications, and as a result after two years the chemical reaction between dissimilar metals in salt water allowed the rudder to twist off at the top. It angled back, and that broke the single pintle on the heel fitting. (This electrolysis would not have happened if she had remained in fresh water.)

This first *Dyna* had an excellent racing record. After she was launched she won both the Chicago to Mackinac and the Port Huron to Mackinac Races in 1958, then again in 1959. Also she won the Skipper Races in 1959.

Next year, 1960, she won Class A and was second overall in the Bermuda Race, losing first overall by only 20 minutes to *Northern Light*. From there she sailed in a race to Sweden and was fourth out of 20 boats.

In 1961 she was fourth in the Fastnet Race after the rudder was replaced. The next year she was first in Class II in the Astor Cup Race and third in Class A to Bermuda. In 1964 she was fourth in Class A to Bermuda, then Class I winner Annapolis to Newport in 1965.

In 1966 Mr. Ewing built a 50′ aluminum keel sloop of S & S design as his second successful boat. She had many duplicate hulls. *Bay Bea* was a sister boat, plus a class of P.J. 52's, of which *Aura, Scaramouche, Falcon,* and *Bandit* are some.

In 1968 he bought one of the S & S fiberglass stock boats, a Swan 36, for his third *Dyna*. The racing record of this sloop was:

1968: 3rd in Class B (5th in fleet) to Bermuda
1969: 5th in Class I, Annapolis to Newport Race
1970: 2nd in Class I for the Astor Cup

Back he came for his fourth *Dyna* in 1971. She was another fiberglass boat of S & S design, a Swan 55, and won fifth in the Queens Cup Race that year. In 1972 she sailed from Bermuda to Bayone, Spain, in that race. Mr. Ewing owned her until 1973.

Another one of the 14 good clients has had three boats of S & S design, all named *Puffin*. He is Mr. Edward R. Greeff. (I'll tell you about the first and then the third, saving the story about the second for him to relate at the end.)

His first *Puffin* was a 35′ wooden Pilot Class sloop. Rod raced with him aboard this boat along the coast, down East. She was a fast sailboat and won many races.

The third *Puffin*, which he now sails, is a 47′ wooden yawl built by that master of wooden boat construction, Aage Walsted, in Thuro, Denmark. In the summer of 1970 she won second place in every race on the New York Yacht Club cruise. She sailed trans-atlantic in 1972, and Mr. Greeff took her up to Finland.

Rod and Bill Stiger have raced aboard her also, twice to Bermuda as well as in the English Channel Race, during all of Cowes Week, and the Fastnet Race in 1975. In 1972, 1975, and 1976 she placed third each time crossing the

Atlantic. There is an old friendship here that goes back to the days of *Stormy Weather* when Eddie sailed with Rod aboard her.

Most recently in the summer of 1977 the third *Puffin* made her fourth crossing of the Atlantic in that same race. She will winter at her builder's yard in Denmark, after logging quite a lot of nautical miles.

The second *Puffin* had a very eventful happening. It was in the Mediterranean Sea after she had won third in her class in the Bermuda Race in 1966 and had sailed from the island on across and through the Straits of Gibraltar. She almost foundered in that sea. But again self-reliance came to the fore. This time it was Eddie Greeff, her skipper, and his crew that managed to avert disaster.

You will see the reason why in his story to follow, but that incident made me think that most trunk cabins on wooden sailboats are not strong enough. This influenced me to strengthen the cabin sides on my own boat by adding four laminated knees inside it, one between each port as well as the existing ones in way of the mast, and the vertical rods through the trunk sides, one each side of each port.

The story of this close call is best told by Eddie Greeff himself.

"For some time I had been planning after the 1966 Bermuda Race to sail to the Azores, thence to Gibraltar and on through the Mediterranean to Genoa. This tale primarily concerns our passage from Port Mahon on the Isle of Minorca, easternmost of the Balearic Islands, to Reale Bay on Asinara Island, Sardinia, a distance of 200 miles. During this passage, on the evening of August 15, *Puffin* was unexpectedly caught in a mistral, a fierce northerly gale peculiar to the Med, which usually occurs only during the winter months. We were 60 miles out of Port Mahon when the mistral started, and 36 storm-tossed hours later we were hit by a huge cresting sea, the biggest I had ever seen.

"Here's how it happened.

"We had left the Onion Patch June 27, arriving 13 days later in the Azores. It was a fine passage except for persistent head winds and one severe, but short, gale five days out. From the Azores to Gibraltar we had a nice but uneventful sail. *Puffin* behaved beautifully, and we were reasonably comfortable despite punching to weather in big seas with winds of 25–35 knots.

"From Gibraltar we proceeded along the coast of Spain to Palma in the Balearics. The sailing was very pleasant, but light breezes prevailed and much of it was ahead. At Gibraltar, two of my original crew left for home, and we were joined by my wife, Betty. At Palma, Braman and Marjorie Adams came aboard for the balance of our cruise. David Smith and Kim Coit had been aboard from the beginning.

"We arrived at Port Mahon on August 13 and prepared for the long hop to Bonifacio on the Island of Corsica—about 240 miles. We planned to leave at noon on a Monday, which would allow us time to take on ice and last-minute supplies, and also get a weather report. I always have made it a habit to obtain weather forecasts before passages of any distance. I contacted the local port authorities, but they were of no help, so Kim Coit went out to the airport to try the fly-boys. They were very cooperative and said the weather would be fair, visibility good, with winds 10–12 knots from the NNE and that approaching the coasts of Corsica and Sardinia they would become variable. This sounded favorable enough, and we left on schedule.

"We had a fine breeze standing out of the harbor and found that we could just lay our course of 077. We had on the big #1 genoa and were moving along at about 5½–6 knots. During the evening the breeze died down and we started our old faithful Westerbeke, again making good our course at 5-plus knots.

"At sundown I had noticed a rather heavy cover of clouds appearing in the west with some high cirrus preceding them. It looked like trouble, but the barometer still remained at 30.05, where it had been for weeks with only slight variations. In view of the weather report, I thought there was no point in alarming anybody by mentioning ominous clouds.

"By 2050 the breeze returned and started to freshen. We also began to get a big swell from the NNW. By midnight we had gone from the #1 genoa to the #3 and then to the working jib, then soon decided to put a single reef in the main and lower the mizzen. We were still making good our course with sheets eased a bit, wind N × E, at about 30 knots. By 0200 we had a double reef in the main and ran into some rain. Sleep was rather difficult as I was worried about the change in weather, but since there was still no change in the glass, I felt it probably would not last very long. At 0400 I decided to take off the main and proceed under working jib and mizzen. The wind was now abeam at 35–40. By this time we realized we were in for trouble, and a French broadcast from Monaco confirmed the existence of a very severe storm. All this time waves had been building quite rapidly. One of the peculiarities of Med seas is their shortness and steepness.

"By sunrise *Puffin* was again going too fast with the working jib and mizzen, so we shifted to the storm jib. We found that by keeping speed down to 5–5½ knots, she did not labor. With two girls aboard I did not want to make it any more uncomfortable than necessary. After dawn the skies cleared and the wind (now west of north) increased to a good 40–45 and perhaps more in the puffs. It seemed to increase as the morning wore on. It was a magnificent sight to see the crests of waves blown off in the sunshine. I had been rereading the 'Sailing Directions' about mistrals, which can last for 25 days with winds as high as 60 or 70. In summer, however, they do not occur very often, and their duration on the average is not over three to six days. At a time like this, one always wonders what to do—whether to take everything off and run before it or heave to. With the wind abeam we had Africa to leeward, and I therefore decided to continue. At noon we set the storm trysail and lowered the mizzen. We continued on this way, fortunately with only one case of seasickness and everybody else in good spirits, safety belts being worn on deck. *Puffin* dry below.

"During the afternoon the wind increased still more and it seemed that it was blowing a steady 50 and certainly higher in the gusts. By 1800 the storm jib was taken off and we kept on under storm trysail alone. The wind continued to back more northwest and by early evening was about WNW. Rather than continue on course for the night, I decided to trim the storm trysail flat and heave to with a man at the tiller. *Puffin* rode comfortably while taking the seas about a point on the port bow and making perhaps 2 knots through the water, but certainly not over the bottom. The seas, as mentioned, were very steep, and occasionally a crest would break on deck, partially filling the cockpit.

"I was now quite tired and got my first four hours of sleep. Dave Smith and Kim Coit were standing one watch, Braman and I the other. Tuesday night passed without incident, except for a heavy cloud cover and some rain which followed a tremendous display of lightning to the north. The Monaco radio at 0400 said the storm had stalled over the Gulf of Genoa and done great damage along the French and Italian coasts.

"When Braman and I came on deck for the 0400–0800 watch, the wind had moderated somewhat, but gusts still were quite severe. We both felt, as time passed, that gusts were lessening, and during lulls the wind dropped to possibly 20 knots. At 0600 the seas seemed to be down and we could hold off on course again. It had been almost impossible to take sights Tuesday, as there are no radio beacons on the west side of Sardinia, our position was only an estimate—about 40 miles WNW of Punta Scorno.

"The breeze was on our port quarter and with just storm trysail our speed only about 3 knots, we set the storm jib with the hope of getting up to 5 knots. Things shortly looked so encouraging that we set the mizzen rather than wake one of the boys to set a larger jib. About 0645 I went below to improve my estimated position, and felt that the wind had increased slightly, but still was no more than 30 in the puffs. Braman, who had the tiller, said she was all right.

"About 0715 I was standing on the lee side of the main boom when I heard a roar astern and turned to see an enormous wave with a broken crest tumbling down its face. The width of it must have been about 75 yards and the height of the crest 8 to 10 feet. I yelled to Braman, 'This is coming aboard, hold her off and steady.' Actually, I was not worried, because everything was battened down.

"As this sea broke over our stern I put my arms around the main boom. The sea went over both of us, and the next thing I know there was a force of water around my waist so great that I was torn from the boom. Seconds later I was underwater being pulled along by my safety line. *Puffin* had broached, starboard side down, and was carried in the breaking sea on her beam ends, her masts in the water. By the time I had climbed aboard, the boat had righted herself. Braman was still at the tiller, but we were lying in the trough.

"Dave Smith came up to lend a hand and I yelled to hold her off again. She paid off on course without difficulty though a bit sluggishly. Betty, who had been thrown out of her bunk, smashing her nose, informed me that water was about 1½ feet over the floorboards. I could not believe my eyes when I saw that 8 feet of trunk cabin on the starboard side was broken in. Water had apparently rushed through this hole with such force that the plexiglass slides in the companionway were torn out.

"Puffin was in a dangerous condition. We had to work fast. We took off the mizzen and lashed a gangplank, used for stern-to-mooring in the Med, alongside the holed starboard trunk. I hoped this might keep out another sea until we could get water out of the boat. Puffin has two hand-operated bilge pumps, one that can be worked on deck and one below. However, gear had gone down into the bilge and the suctions of both pumps were clogged. Dave and I bailed with a bucket until we removed enough water to get at the suction. With Dave's long arms down in the bilge to keep it clear, I pumped and soon we were free of water.

"The next job was to properly secure the 14′ gangplank to the deckhouse. We took off the treads, bored holes through the plank, put the reads on the inside of the trunk cabin in a vertical position, and then passed lines through the holes and around the treads. This arrangement held the plank very securely. Because it was heavy and could not conform to the side of the cabin, we had to stuff towels in the open spaces. This was accomplished by about 0900. As Betty was bleeding badly and we could not seem to stop the flow, I sent out a 'May Day.' After about an hour and a half an Italian yacht answered and offered to relay our message. By this time things were under control, and I informed them that we were in no immediate danger, were proceeding to Bonifacio, would like a vessel to stand by, and would need medical assistance on arrival.

"Kim Coit, who had been sleeping in the main cabin's lower port bunk, was thrown out and landed in the starboard upper. He received a bang on the head and shoulder, fortunately without permanent injury. Dave Smith, who had been in the port upper, was not hurt at all because the Dacron bunk boards prevented him from being thrown out. Marjorie Adams had been in the starboard bunk in the forward cabin and had nothing more serious than bruises. Betty, who had been in the port bunk in the forward cabin, had hit her face on something—she doesn't know what.

"Puffin was moving along at about 4 knots on course, and I estimated our position to be about 20 miles west-northwest of Asinara Island (the northwestern tip of Sardinia).

"After a quick breakfast I went on deck to take a careful look at the damage. Our survey showed that when Puffin broached, the spinnaker pole lashed atop the starboard trunk cabin was torn off; a Dorade-type ventilator on the starboard side of the mast was sheared off at the deck level, box and all; a Dorade vent on the lazarette hatch also was broken off; stanchions were bent; a horseshoe-type life ring, strobe light, and float were gone from the starboard side aft.

"The mizzen rigging was slack, and we found that the mast had crushed the step, a bronze plate, and was resting on the horn timber. Crushing of the mizzen step was probably the result of the sea breaking onto the mizzen sail and main boom, which was hanging on a wire strap from the mizzen mast, creating

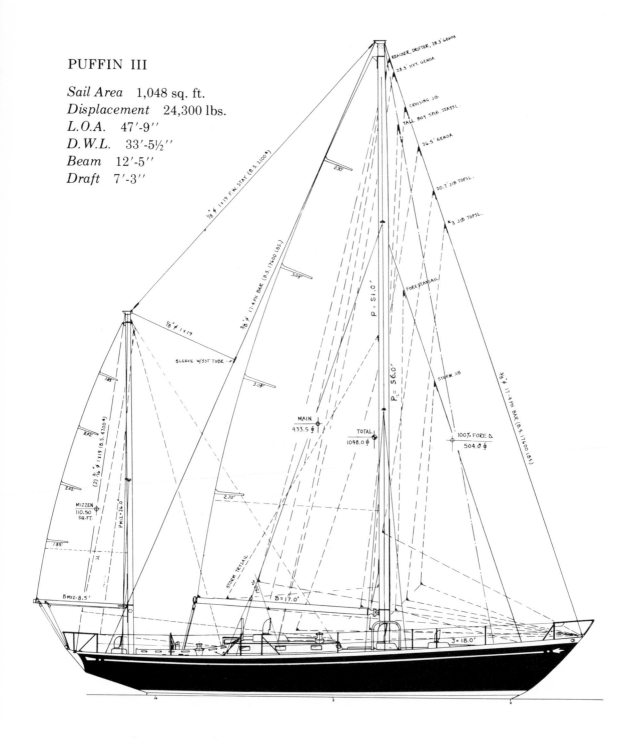

PUFFIN III

Sail Area   1,048 sq. ft.
Displacement   24,300 lbs.
L.O.A.   47'-9''
D.W.L.   33'-5½''
Beam   12'-5''
Draft   7'-3''

120

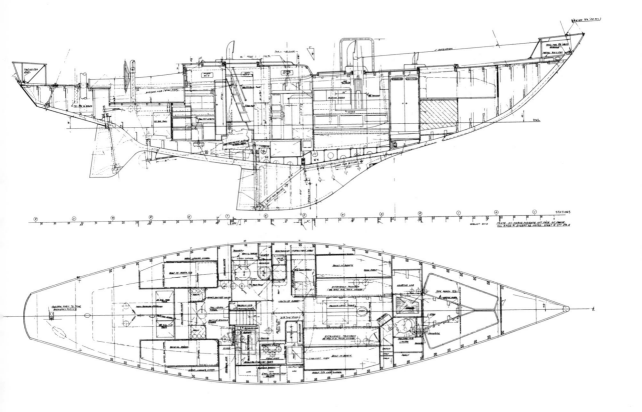

tremendous compression load. Fortunately the mizzen did not break, partly due to a mizzen backstay always being set.

"The dinghy, a Dyer Dink sailing type, was secured in chocks atop the cabin. These chocks were through-bolted and the securing line went through the chocks and over the dinghy several times. The painter was secured around the mainmast. The dinghy did not move in its chocks, but both sides were crushed inward so that the thwarts punctured the fiberglass. This gives an idea of the force exerted on the dinghy.

"By 1100 our progress was slow and Dave said, 'Why don't you try the engine?' It never occurred to me to try it, as I knew water had been over the battery. But miracles do happen—the engine started. It was probably fortunate that the battery terminals were heavily greased. But even more important, the engine was a diesel.

"With the engine our speed increased to over 5 knots. We picked up the coast and identified the northern tip of Asinara. Shortly after noon the Italian yacht called again asking for our latest position. She directed us to Reale Bay on Asinara Island to meet a tug which would have a doctor aboard. We anchored there about 1430. The tug came alongside and put aboard a doctor who did not have the equipment necessary to make an examination. He asked us to go to Porto Torres—13 miles away—so that Betty could reach his office and a hospital. We then asked the tug to give us a tow and thus save time. We arrived at Porto Torres about 1730, and Betty was under medical care shortly thereafter.

"*Conclusions:* We all would like to know how it happened, what to do at such times, and how to avoid a similar situation. Normally when the going gets really tough, one is apt to take everything off, run before it, and sometimes tow things astern to slow down the vessel. In our situation we were sailing, because it was not blowing hard and we had good steering control. There were moments, as wave crests passed under us, that *Puffin* did not respond quickly, but at all other times we had excellent control.

"In my opinion there were two reasons for our broach. The first is that the sea was so high and steep that it broke into the mizzen sail exerting great thrust, which spun *Puffin* around. The other is that Braman Adams was hit so hard by the sea coming aboard that he was thrown over the tiller, and to starboard. Although he never lost his grip on the tiller, it went down to leeward, and we broached to port. Fortunately he had his safety line attached, but perhaps if he had had less slack in it he would not have been thrown as far.

"I have no doubt that this could happen only in the Mediterranean where the waves are extremely short and steep. We had been through a severe gale in the Atlantic and at no time were there any seas that could have done this to us. I would guess that the seas in the Med are half the length of those we experienced in the Atlantic and twice as steep.

"One other reason for our trouble was that *Puffin*'s trunk cabin sides did not have the vertical through-bolts called for in Sparkman & Stephens' specifications. These bolts were supposed to go down through the sill into the header below the trunk cabin. They would have added considerable strength, but the builder had left them out.

"Reviewing our experience, here are a few observations that might be worth remembering:

"In the future, in a similar situation, I would try to take steep seas on the bow until there was absolutely no chance of them coming aboard. When running off in a big sea, never carry any sail aft.

"If *Puffin* had been a centerboard boat, I doubt very much that she could have come back from a knockdown with as much water below as we had. I strongly recommend a keel to anyone planning an ocean cruise in a small boat.

"Sheets of ⅜″ plywood, as wide as trunk cabin is high, should be carried. Plenty of screws and bolts of all sizes, along with nails if you have a wooden ship, are invaluable. The same goes for a full set of tools to be used working metal or wood, including three types of drill—electric, hand "eggbeater" type, brace and bit.

"Safety belts should be the harness type with drop-forged galvanized snap hooks. Run a ⅜″ nylon line on both sides of the deck to allow fore and aft movement without unhooking.

"The area surrounding bilge pump suctions should be screened to prevent clogging. On wood boats it is particularly important to have strong limber chains running through compartments where suction intakes are located.

"Plenty of spare Dacron should be carried. Besides repairing sails, it can be used to cover holes, cracks, etc. Strong wood lath is also handy to hold down cloth, and it has many other uses."

What did this good client, Eddie Greeff, do next? He came back to Sparkman & Stephens for his third wooden boat design. This time he had her built in a boatyard of the highest integrity, Aage Walsted's, in Denmark. The third *Puffin* is an excellent boat in every respect, the very best from the concept of her design to the execution with particular care of all details in her construction.

OLIN   (Rosenfeld)

6 Olin's Thinking on Design

I asked Olin how he characterized Sparkman & Stephens' role in yacht design and naval architecture.

He said that was a little hard to answer, because the idea was so general. "Our role has changed and developed over the years," he said. "So I'd have to think in terms of certain periods of time. We started out on a very small scale in the late 1920's and had a pretty successful period of 10 years before the war. During that time we had a small and active group in our drawing room, and worked on mainly sailing boats, but not exclusively so, and again largely, but not exclusively, racing boats. We did have pretty good success with the racing boats. You might say that was our specialty during that period."

"Indeed the firm has been answering the requirements of different clients in what they want in the way of yachts," I summarized. "And when war comes along we pitch in and do naval vessels. Some people want luxurious powerboats, and we work with them on those kind of boats. Also commercial craft, tugboats, and to some extent fishing boats. Even barges as well."

"You've emphasized the variety, which I like," he continued. "I didn't bring that out in my first comments, but here in the office I have been interested in boats of all kinds. Rod and I started with cruising experience, and have always been interested in both cruising and racing. Gil Wyland came with us toward the end of the period I'm speaking of, but Gil has been very much interested in all kinds of boats, and is largely responsible for our activity in the powerboat in naval and commercial fields. Before Gil was with us we had a chap named Al George, whom I had known when we worked together at Gielow's, which was the first job I had had. And Al George came with us and was experienced in powerboat design and interested in it, and helped a lot on that phase of the work. To me the variety of the work that we've been able to do has kept us thinking, and I think that one kind of design contributes to another. I also think it's fair to say I've tried to be rather open-minded about meeting a client's requirements. I've tried to accept what the client wants, rather than telling him what he should have, or what he should want. I hope that's resulted in a certain amount of flexibility. In the end the suitability of the boat that has been designed for each man will be what he wants."

"Continuing about clients," I reflected, "my thoughts are that nowadays it seems we get a lot of clients in the form of builders, who want to produce stock boats, mostly of fiberglass, and then it's rather difficult to size up what the prospective buyer really wants."

Olin allowed that in some ways it is less interesting and in other ways more of a challenge. It certainly is not easier. It is not always quite as interesting, but it is a new phase of our work, which was quite different from anything in the prewar period. It has really transformed activity in the office, because it has become the big thing both in terms of drawing time and in terms of income, rather than the "one-off" boat.

"We just scratched the surface of the series-built and production boat before we got into the war," he recollected. "We did have one or two quite successful early series classes, of which the best known is probably the Weekender, which was built by Lawley and came out in 1937 or 1938. But we went through that period with good performances in racing, culminating in an association and the design of *Ranger* with her success in 1937. Then in 1938 we got out *Baruna* and *Blitzen,* which were both class winners in the Bermuda Race. *Baruna* won overall and *Blitzen* was second overall that year.

"Then by 1939 we had *Vim.* But everybody I think saw the war coming, and it put a very different picture before us about the work in the office. We went into some design competitions that the Navy organized, and it so happened that we won the competition that they set up for motor torpedo boats. Although we entered a submarine chaser that we designed in the competition, it didn't get a prize. However, later when the Navy wanted some plans for boats to be built, they gave us an order to design some submarine chasers, and gave the motor torpedo boat to a couple of other firms, including Cox and Stevens. We were by that time involved in small boat work for the Navy, and we went through the war in quite a different situation from that which we had experienced before, and I had to provide for the management of a much larger office. It went up to about 100 people, which means finding space enough and people enough. Somehow I got it done. We carried it on in that way through the period of 1939 to 1946. That was, I'd say, a completely different ballgame than we had been playing before. It was interesting in its way. I didn't enjoy the necessity for it, nor did I find the types of boats as interesting. Nevertheless I think there is something about the total commitment that you get in wartime that has a good side to it. So it wasn't all that uninteresting or difficult."

I asked him if he preferred working with a small group, such as the firm has now, better than having a hundred people.

"Oh, I prefer the small group," he replied, "although sometimes I think the size of our office as it is now is a little unhandy, in the sense that it's a little too big for one person to see, and it's too small to compartmentalize efficiently. It's just a problem that we have to face, and accept and handle, as we go about the kind of work we're doing today. It's rather different. It's a bigger office than we had before the war, a smaller office than we had during the war. And I feel some problems about just the size which we are running now."

My next question was about a particular project because I was curious to know what the polar diagrams that S & S does are used for.

"I think they have a dual use, Frank," he began, "and that the people who are sailing on boats buy them for guidance, even though I hope they are not convinced of their perfect accuracy. The diagrams themselves are based on what you might say is incomplete and to some degree untested data, and the instruments that they have to look at in applying this data are not 100% accurate either. So we're not getting down a fine line with these estimates, but they do give people on a boat a good idea of what she should be able to do under certain conditions. We find that having a target is useful. More specifically, to the extent that they have been tested out. So I strongly would urge any owner or skipper who is using these diagrams to test them.

"They are useful in getting onto a certain course, either upwind or downwind, which approximates the most efficient point of sailing. They help to avoid the danger of pinching a boat and pointing too high, or sailing off too wide, and in racing they help a great deal in determining what sail might be set on the next leg. With a plotting board or with a small calculator you can figure out what the apparent wind will be if you know the true wind speed and direction. You also need the course and speed of the boat, and a polar diagram gives you a pretty good check on the speed of a boat on a forthcoming course. I think further, and perhaps most specifically, that while a good sailor can beat the polar diagram going to windward at any time, I'm a great believer in tacking downwind, and I think it's very hard for the best man in the world to judge by the feel of the boat going downwind with the spinnaker whether or not he's sailing on the best course. In so far as it's possible to check out and accept the data presented on the polar diagrams, you can do a good job in tacking downwind, which is where some pretty good sailors are beyond their depth, without something of that sort to help them. Now the other side of it is, again so far as it's accurate (I'm somewhat hesitant about putting too much faith in them), is that it gives us the basis to compare rather extremely different designs. I think

BLITZEN

Sail Area 1,302 sq. ft.
Displacement 46,900 lbs.
L.O.A. 55'-9''
D.W.L. 40'-0''
Beam 12'-5''
Draft 7'-9''

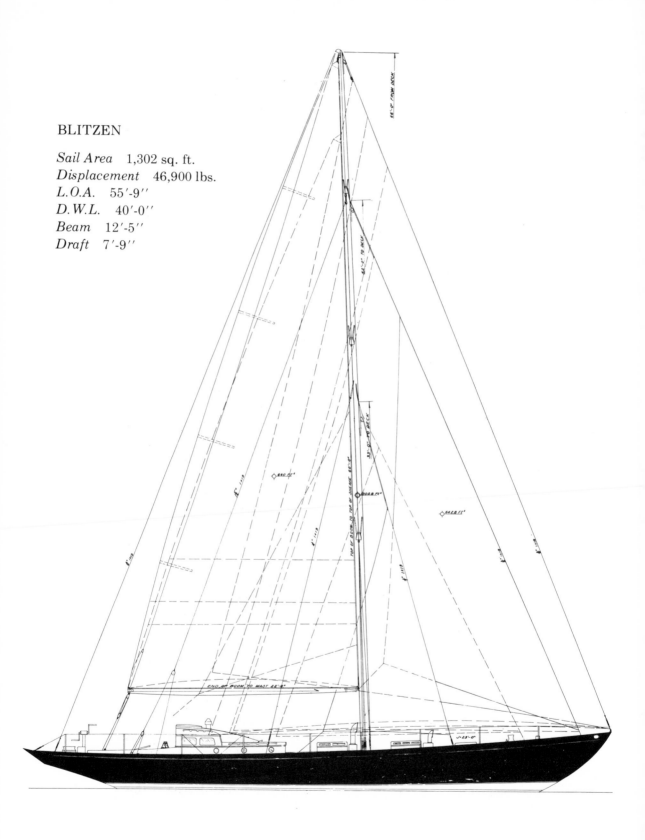

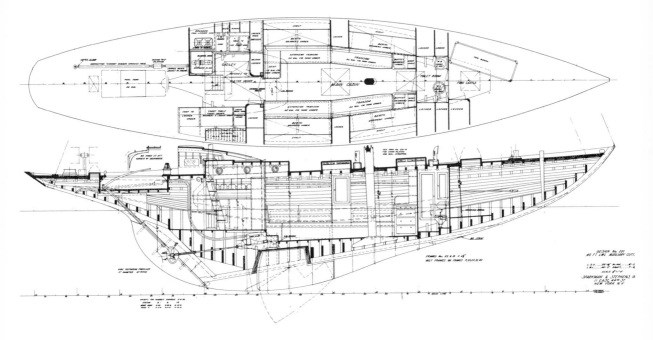

this is what we're working toward, what I'd call the analytical approach as compared with the intuitive one. I think our change of method over the years has been really from what we could call the intuitive toward the analytical. Personally, I don't think you can produce good work without a combination of the two. And I think that if you're trying to compare boats that are radically different, that the polar diagram, or at least the speed calculation, which does not have to be presented in a polar diagram but is perhaps the most convenient way to show it, that this is almost the only way that you can compare radically different boats. Taking all the different conditions that apply into account, you get a reasonable answer as to which is likely to be the faster boat."

"That sounds like a pretty scientific way of winning a race," I replied.

"Well," he went on, "some people kid about it and say you can do it now with a radio-controlled boat, and as you know people do race such models. It's been said that you don't even have to make the model, you can just take the characteristics and put them in a computer. While this may be fun for people, where they wish to do yacht designs, I think it's quite important to raise now the point that almost anything, I suppose, can be divided into two parts, so you can look at the question of designing a boat as being for one factor a selection of characteristics, which I think can be helped by both the computer and the polar diagram. And the other factor is simply the geometrical shape of the boat, and the sweetness of her lines and shape, whether it's a good shape or a bad shape. This is far less accessible to any kind of computation. I certainly don't feel that even the considerable faith I have in the analytical method provides an answer

OLIN EXPLAINS A POLAR DIAGRAM

The true wind polar diagram here is simply a convenient way to show either predicted or recorded performance of a sailing boat under varying conditions of wind strength and angle of course to wind. In the case illustrated, the performance of a 25 ft. D.W.L. Half Ton racing boat has been calculated according to a specialized computer program. The numbers running up and down from the pole indicate boat speed in knots and apply right around the semicircles, so that the distance along a radius from the center to any point on the plot represents boat speed. The heavy contour lines represent true wind speed (V_t). Numbers around the semicircular perimeter indicate the true wind angle in degrees between the boat's course and the true wind direction.

The simplest case is probably that of a boat running dead downwind, i.e., at 180° true wind angle, in which case the speed is measured from the pole vertically downward to the intersection of the vertical margin and the appropriate true wind speed, or if necessary from estimated wind speed points between two of the heavy contours. In a six knot breeze, the respective boat speed will be read as 3.6 knots. However, note further that in a six knot breeze, the best speed made good downwind occurs at a true wind angle of between 145° and 150° where the boat will actually be sailing approximately 4.4 knots through the water but making good approximately 3.8 knots downwind.

Similarly, the best speed made good to windward can be read from the projection to the left hand border of the highest point on the wind speed contours. In this case, in a breeze of 18 knots, the best windward speed made good will be at just under 40° true wind angle slightly over 4.7 knots made good. However, the boat will be sailing at approximately 5.9 knots.

Between the running and the windward conditions will be found the various reaching courses, and according to the true wind angle and the true wind strength, the actual boat speed can be read from the plot by following the appropriate semicircular line around to the left hand margin, or simply measuring off the distance from the intersection of the true wind angle line with the boat speed line, and then measuring into the pole.

These are theoretical optimum performance curves for smooth water and take into account the boat's estimated leeway. They answer the question of how fast a boat should be able to sail in any given breeze. The potential speed of any boat for which appropriate data is available can be predicted and compared with boats having different characteristics. Such knowledge is useful in terms of design, and has become an important element in the study of rating rules. This is also useful to an owner who is able to judge at any time whether his boat is performing as expected. While piloting or navigating, it is often helpful to be able to correctly forecast the boat speed under expected future conditions.

Although such forecasts are becoming increasingly available through the widening use of computers, a word of caution may be advisable, because such forecasts should not be considered in any sense precise. Increasing knowledge and experience will improve the accuracy of the forecasts. But even at best, the condition of an individual boat will not be taken into account, so that good or bad helmsmanship, good or bad sails, the difference between a clean and a foul bottom, as well as differences in the efficiency of the design will produce variations which the computation cannot take into account.

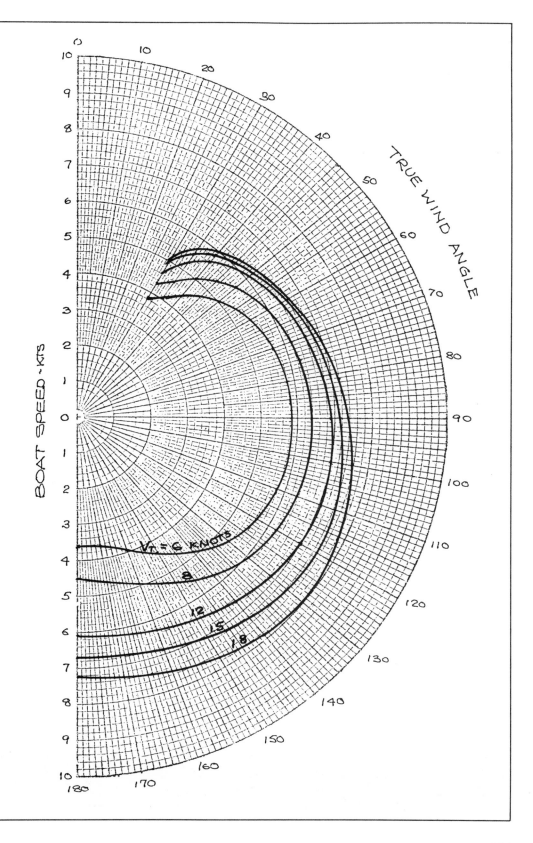

TRUE WIND ANGLE

BOAT SPEED ~ KTS

$V_T = 6$ KNOTS

8

12

15

18

WEEKENDER CLASS

Sail Area   596 sq. ft.
Displacement   16,240 lbs.
L.O.A.   35'-0''
D.W.L.   27'-0''
Beam   9'-6''
Draft   5'-7''

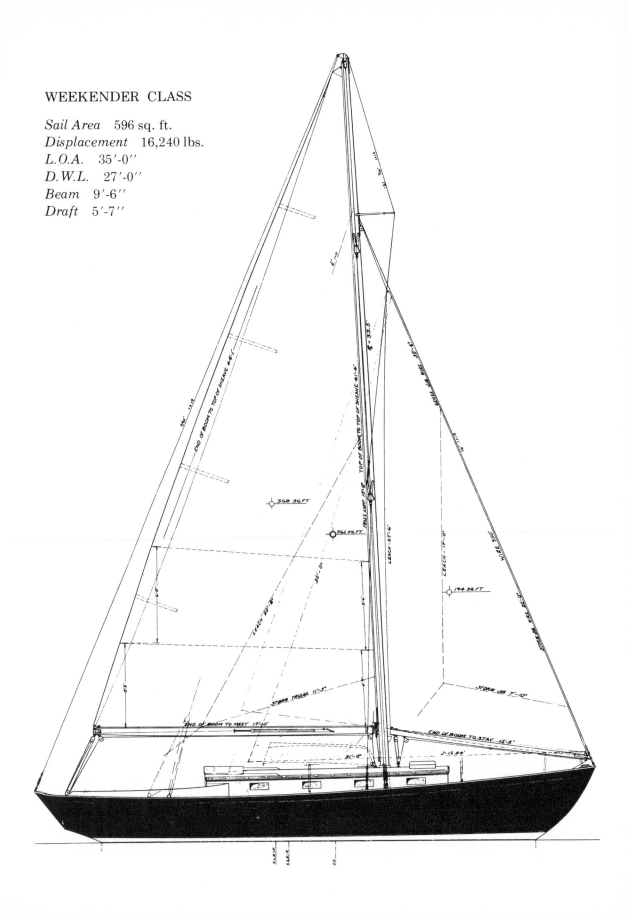

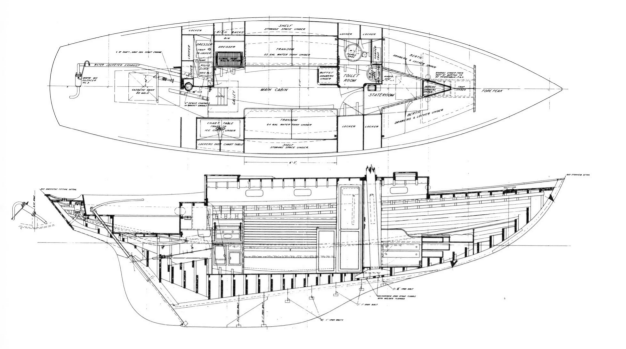

to the second part of the design project, which is equally important. Somebody who has a sense of proportion and a feeling for shape and so on must be responsible for a nice clean set of lines and the resulting appearance and character of the boat. That is quite a different thing to get out, and a different thing from anything you can get out of a computer."

"That makes me feel better," I mused. "Maybe I won't be displaced by a computer.

"I've noticed, Olin, that the optimum streamlined waterlines for underwater appendages, such as fin keels or skegs with rudders on sailboats, seem to be changing. Specifically, years ago the streamline shape used to have its maximum width about ⅓ or 33% aft from the leading edge. Then when we did *Yankee Girl* we were interested in the helicopter blade foil, and that maximum width was 45% aft of the leading edge, and now since 1975 we're back to the widest part being 35% aft of the leading edge. Why so?"

"The answer is, we've been trying to feel our way to something that would be better," he replied. "During the period which you point out with *Yankee Girl* we were working on a keel section taken from an aircraft wing section, which was intended to produce and maintain laminar flow. This is in distinction to turbulent flow. It is a condition we think largely about, and have to take into account in the towing of smaller models. As you know, it's a kind of technical matter, and the transition results largely from differences in what is known as the Reynolds number, which is again, not exactly but approximately, a number that's reduced by multiplying the length and velocity of a surface, so that when

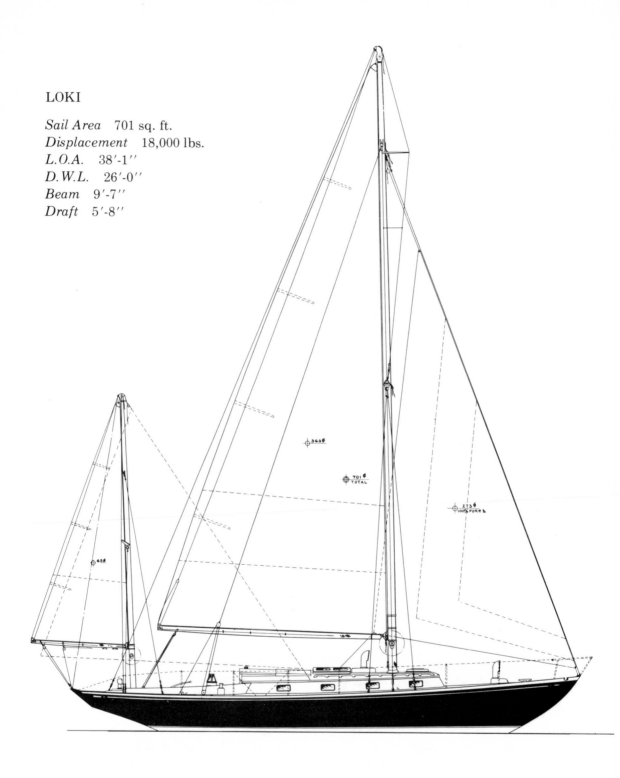

LOKI

Sail Area   701 sq. ft.
Displacement   18,000 lbs.
L.O.A.   38'-1''
D.W.L.   26'-0''
Beam   9'-7''
Draft   5'-8''

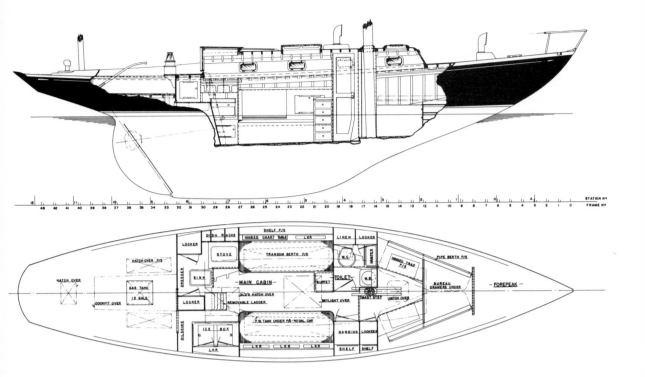

you test the model or sail a boat slowly you have a low Reynolds number. You can, at very low Reynolds numbers, be in the region of laminar flow, where resistance is very much less than with the turbulent flow. As the speed or velocity increases, you move over into the turbulent flow area and the resistance goes up. Certain shapes will hold the laminar flow longer than others, and the type of section we used in *Yankee Girl* and a number of succeeding boats is based on a special wing section. It was intended to prolong the period of laminar flow and postpone the transition of turbulent flow, and thereby keep resistance down. The section that we are using now is a more efficient section in terms of lift and drag, and I think our experience would bear out the theory that it results in boats with better windward performance. I think we were making an unjustified assumption or hopes in the benefit from laminar flow in accepting a lower lift-drag ratio in the hope of cutting down the boat's resistance, because it seems the background turbulence, which exists in seawater most of the time, virtually eliminates the possibility of laminar flow. We probably gained very little or maybe nothing at all from the laminar flow section, and sacrificed some of the higher lift-drag ratio you can get with other sections."

"When you look at it," I interjected, "there's a hollow in the after part that is unbelievable. You'd think it would be better if it were just a straight line. It's just hard to believe that shape is so good."

"Well, it is maybe, I really don't know the answer," said Olin. "I think we in the office have compromised that very frequently. The textbooks and the

FUJI 40 CLASS

Sail Area   776 sq. ft.
Displacement   27,065 lbs.
L.O.A.   39'-2''
D.W.L.   30'-0''
Beam   12'-8''
Draft   6'-0''

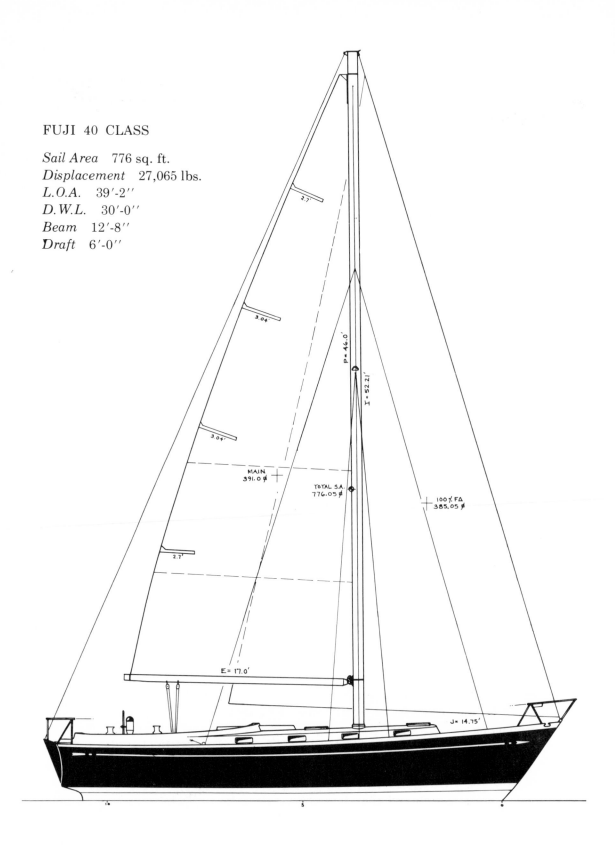

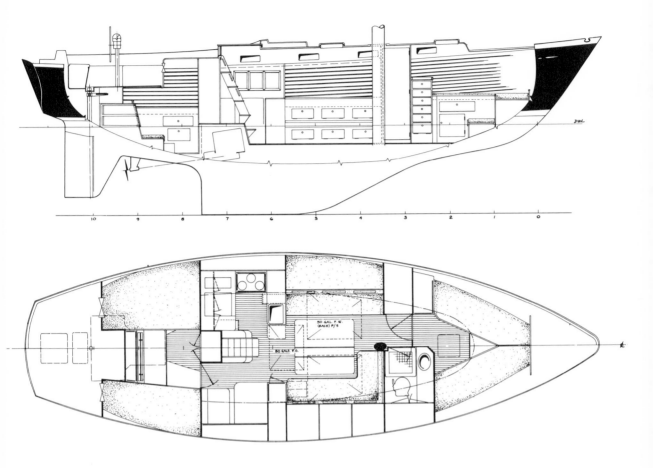

tests, which are behind the textbook data, indicate the hollow has some advantage, but not very much, when one considers the difficulty in casting a keel which has the shape we want it to be. Especially the difficulty of making a very, very fine trailing edge. We often compromise that section by using a straight tangent over the after part of the trailing edge."

"Yes, it's really interesting to see how much thought and testing goes into one single line which is what this is, a waterline," I noted.

"It's supposed to be the most efficient section for this purpose," Olin said, "but you do have to compromise."

"Well now, switching to another topic, Olin. What about the future of rating rules and handicap systems? Do you think the emphasis should be analytical, or statistical, or political? And what measurements would you think should be emphasized?"

"This is something I've considered a great deal, Frank, without coming to any perfect conclusion. I don't think there is any perfect conclusion, but there are many, many possibilities. As you know, I'm supposed to be back as chairman of the ITC (International Technical Committee), which is the com-

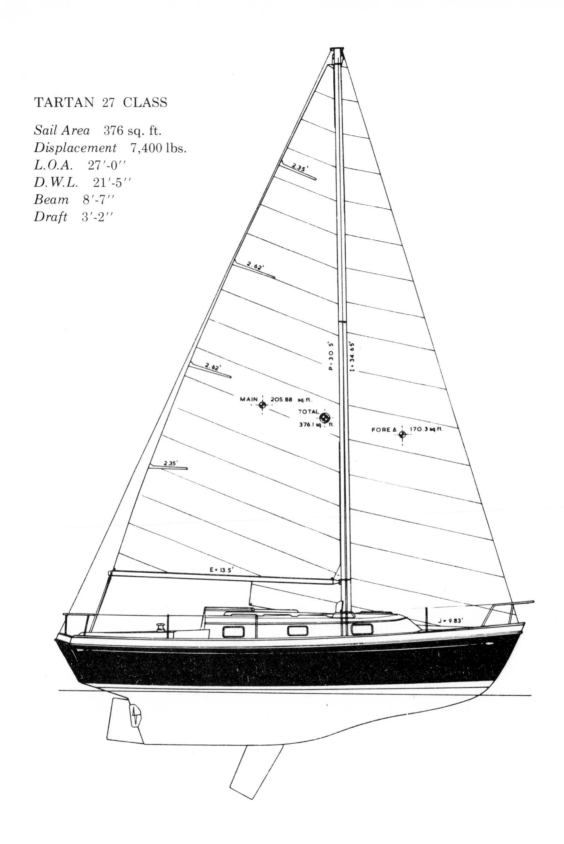

TARTAN 27 CLASS

Sail Area 376 sq. ft.
Displacement 7,400 lbs.
L.O.A. 27'-0''
D.W.L. 21'-5''
Beam 8'-7''
Draft 3'-2''

MAIN 205.88 sq. ft.
TOTAL 376.1 sq. ft.
FORE Δ 170.3 sq. ft.

P = 30.5'
I = 34.65'
E = 13.5'
J = 9.83'

2.35'
2.62'
2.62'
2.35'

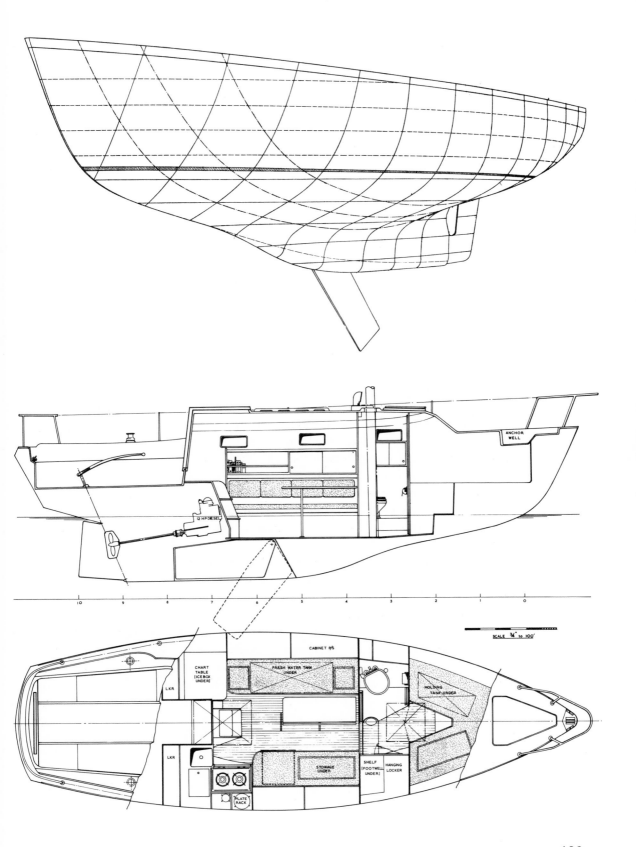

ANCHOR
WELL

12 H.P. DIESEL

SCALE ¾" to 1'0'

CABINET OVER

CHART
TABLE
[ICEBOX
UNDER]

FRESH WATER TANK
UNDER

HOLDING
TANK UNDER

LKR

LKR

STOWAGE
UNDER

SHELF
[FOOTWELL
UNDER]

HANGING
LOCKER

PLATE
RACK

10   9   8   7   6   5   4   3   2   1   0

139

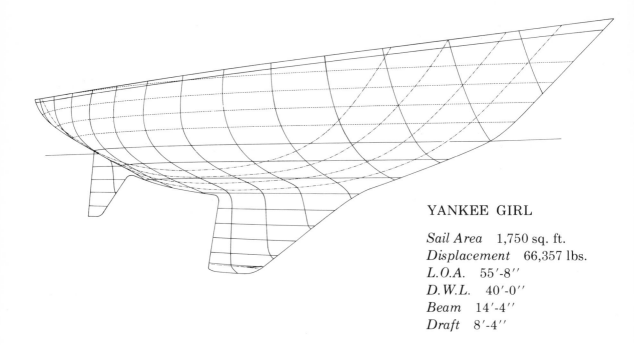

YANKEE GIRL

Sail Area   1,750 sq. ft.
Displacement   66,357 lbs.
L.O.A.   55'-8''
D.W.L.   40'-0''
Beam   14'-4''
Draft   8'-4''

mittee controlling the development of the IOR (International Offshore Rule). Also, I'm a member of the USYRU (United States Yacht Racing Union) Handicap Rule Committee, of which Lynn Williams is the chairman, and I might say that this second committee is doing its best to develop a good rule on the basis of a primarily analytical approach, resulting from the presence as advisors to the committee of Nick Newman and J. Kerwin of MIT. The purpose of this committee is to develop the most equitable possible rule, and the method will be to try to the fullest extent to emphasize the work which has been done at MIT.

"As chairman of the ITC," continued Olin, "I think I have to take a little more pragmatic view for several reasons, one of which is I think we have to be prepared to work more quickly to have a rule in being. We don't want to change it any more than we have to. We have certain measurements that are taken, and we don't want to change the way those measurements are taken and put a lot of people to the difficulty and expense of remeasurement. You might say, in that rule we are committed to the statistical approach. I try in theory to minimize the political aspect. I suppose I do feel that to be realistic, and to get things done, that you have to consider the political implications, which really means the conflicting interests and wishes of the two committees have to be ultimately reconciled. So I think every move on the rule is based on those three considerations, but in the case of the USYRU rule the analytical predominates. And without overlooking analysis, we are more committed to a statistical approach as an alternative."

"It must be quite a problem, Olin, with all these different skippers and owners pulling in different directions and trying to have a fair handicap rule for all," I noted.

"It is a very difficult problem, because it's probably in realistic terms really an impossible one. It certainly is impossible to suit everybody, and that would mean having everybody win. That would be self-defeating. Nevertheless, there are many avenues for improvement, which at least look very promising. One of these is a type of rule which is called variable rating, which would be based to some extent at least on the speed of a race. It's clear that the speed-producing characteristics of any given design vary greatly according to the speed at which the boat is going. Sail area is obviously important in light weather at low speeds; displacement is much more important at high speeds. If a rule can evaluate these factors, and do it on the basis of the actual boat speed so that there is no subjective rise, this seems rather promising to me. At any rate, it's receiving a lot of attention right now."

"Throughout the years, Olin, it seems different rules have produced different types of boats, some of them rather undesirable as far as seagoing ability is concerned. Do you attach any importance to what kind of a boat is produced by a rule?"

"I definitely do, Frank. I think any rule should produce a boat which is safe and practical. I suppose I give a rather considerable latitude to what I consider safe in terms of a rule, because I do truly believe that what is safe depends more on the structure than the rule-induced shape. I think it's very important to have a boat strong. I take the opinion perhaps to defend a little bit the IOR against the feeling that it doesn't produce a very seagoing boat, and I think myself there have been few problems with these boats, and those few that have been were due to structure rather than to shape. I agree, however, that the tendency is probably going too far toward light displacement, and these boats that go fast and hit seas hard. True, the typical IOR boat lacks little or nothing in space, and frequently lacks a great deal in terms of actual accommodations, because it's been found that the boat goes faster if the hull weight and accommodations are kept very light, and probably lack a good deal in comfort. I think the older boats were nicer cruising boats, and in the sense that they were evenly matched, were just as good for racing. We really have achieved considerable progress in terms of actual speed from here to there, with the more recent designs. I think it's very largely this speed that makes the boats uncomfortable."

"Olin, I don't want you to have to give away any secrets about the book that you intend to write, but can you give me a hint about the analytical design ideas that will be in it?"

"It's pretty hard to say, not having gotten to it, and not really knowing whether I ever will. I like to think I could make something that was interesting, which would be the only justification for doing it. I do believe there have been many books on the technical phases of naval architecture, and there's your own

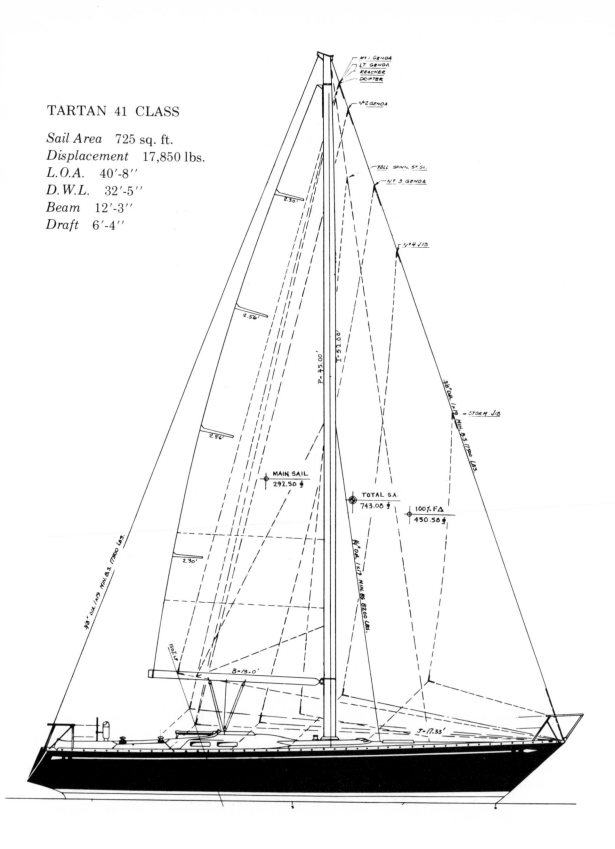

TARTAN 41 CLASS

Sail Area 725 sq. ft.
Displacement 17,850 lbs.
L.O.A. 40'-8''
D.W.L. 32'-5''
Beam 12'-3''
Draft 6'-4''

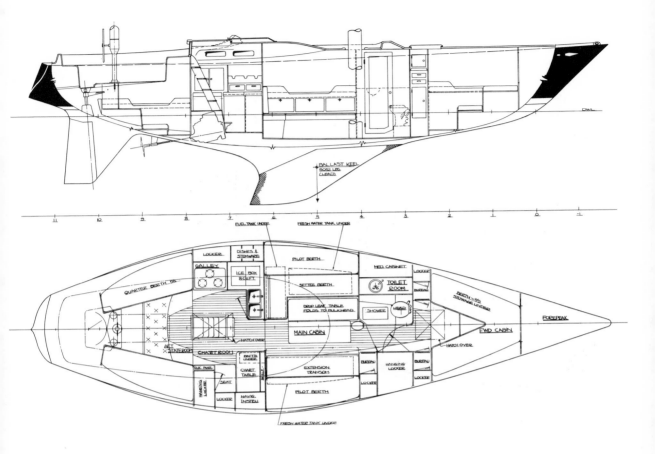

very good and very practical book which was based on Skene's original work on yacht design, which is probably the most helpful book that's been broadly available to the yacht designer. But I would like to try to put things together to a certain extent to explain, as I've done very briefly here, something about the background of the analytical approach in terms of performance prediction, and the planning and performance of the polar diagram, or similar presentation. Then also, maybe go into some of the theoretical side of the strength of things. I think it's something I think about every now and then, but I've never gotten to the point of really outlining it, and working it all out. I do think I have the background of experience with a good variety of yacht designs which I might be able to put together into something worthwhile."

"There is a need for it, Olin. I for one would be most interested in having it to use," I said eagerly.

This chapter about "Olin's Thinking on Design" would not be complete without including his thoughts on tank tests in yacht designing, so it should be interesting to yachtsmen and designers alike to read the following text he wrote in 1937 on that subject. It is as apropos now as it was then.

TARTAN 37 CLASS

Sail Area   625 sq. ft.
Displacement   15,500 lbs.
L.O.A.   37'-3''
D.W.L.   28'-6''
Beam   11'-9''
Draft   4'-2''

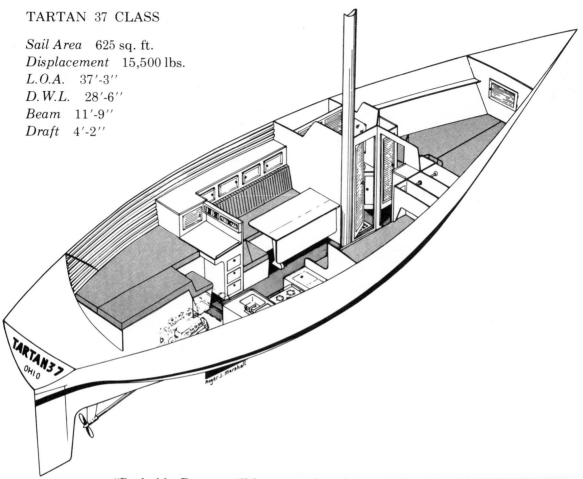

"Probably *Ranger* will be remembered in yachting history as the boat that proved the value of testing yacht models in the towing tank. At least her success has done more than anything else to call attention to the usefulness of the towing tank to the yachtsman and the designer. Until the middle of last summer, there has been a great deal of skepticism and the opinion was often expressed that models were more likely to be misleading than helpful; now there is complete acceptance of the fact that model testing is an important part of the design of any racing yacht.

"This wide interest makes it worthwhile to review what has been done and to explain the how and why of yacht model testing as carried out under the direction of Professor Kenneth S. M. Davidson at the Stevens Institute of Technology. It is he who has developed the methods and the equipment used in the work on *Ranger* and other yachts that, after testing, have by their performance shown the value of the tank.

"When the first model towing work was started at Stevens Institute in the fall of 1931, it was not surprising that there was a good deal of doubt as to whether anything worthwhile could be worked out; the testing of yacht models was not new and the performance of yachts built after model tests had not been noticeably above the average. Also, on account of the high cost of towing models, such work had been done only on large and important boats. It is said that G. L. Watson designed *Shamrock II* after testing her model against others, and that, following her defeat by *Columbia* in 1901, he expressed the wish that 'Nat' Herreshoff might also have had a towing tank. Although model tests were used in the design of other America's Cup boats, among them *Vanitie*, Watson's expression was typical of the general opinion of towing tank tests. On the other hand, the general method of model testing had played an important part in the development of the steamship and the airplane, and to Professor Davidson there seemed to be a good chance of success in new methods of applying well-known principles to yacht testing.

"When the work at Stevens first started, there was little money available. This in the long run has helped, at least from the yachting standpoint. The first testing was done in the swimming pool, where it was necessary to use much smaller models than those made for the usual steamship tests. Twenty-foot waterline models were being used in Washington because, though smaller models had been tried, the predicted resistances had been pretty far away from the actual resistances found in practice. So, in the older tanks, large models were used as a matter of course. The expense of using them was not a severe drawback when working on the plans of a naval vessel, a merchant ship, or a large power yacht.

"Many full-sized yachts, such as six meters, are not much larger than these models. Therefore the relatively high cost of working with models put tests out of the question in the case of ordinary design. The opportunity of using a small model with its low cost made the whole problem practical and interesting to the yacht designer, and I have done everything I could to cooperate with Professor Davidson since he first talked with me about the work.

"This problem of getting accurate predictions with a small model was the first one which had to be solved. To obtain the resistance of the full-scale boat from the model, it is not possible to multiply by a single factor. The model resistance must be divided into two parts, one representing principally frictional resistance (that caused by the friction of the water against the hull surface) and the other residual or wavemaking resistance. At speeds high enough to cause waves, it is impossible to separate these two factors by a direct test of the model. However, because they must be multiplied by different amounts before they can be added together to give the final resistance of the full-sized boat, the division must be made fairly accurately. To do this, it is necessary to calculate one or the other part. The success of resistance predictions based on large models has lain in the accuracy with which the frictional resistance could be calculated, both for the large model and the ship. When the model was small, this calculation for frictional resistance seemed to become unreliable.

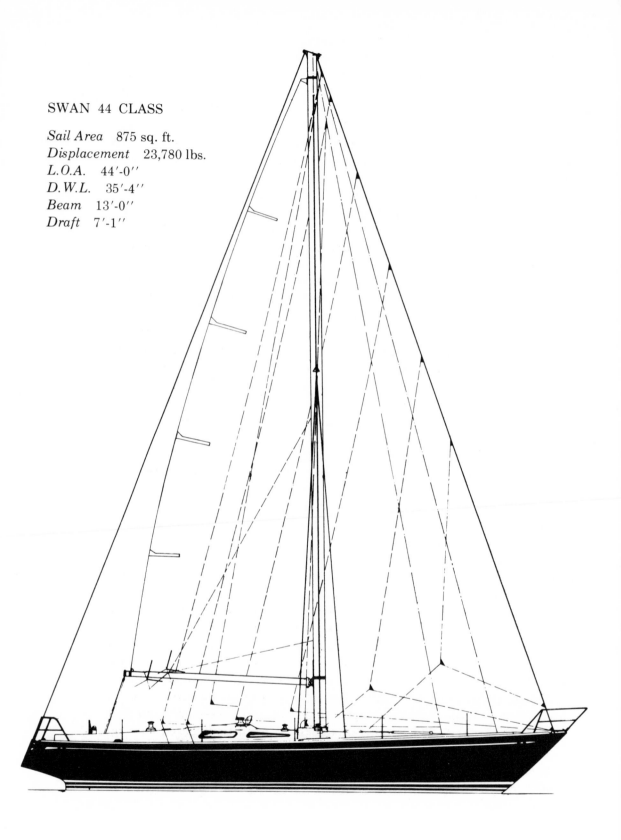

SWAN 44 CLASS

Sail Area   875 sq. ft.
Displacement   23,780 lbs.
L.O.A.   44'-0''
D.W.L.   35'-4''
Beam   13'-0''
Draft   7'-1''

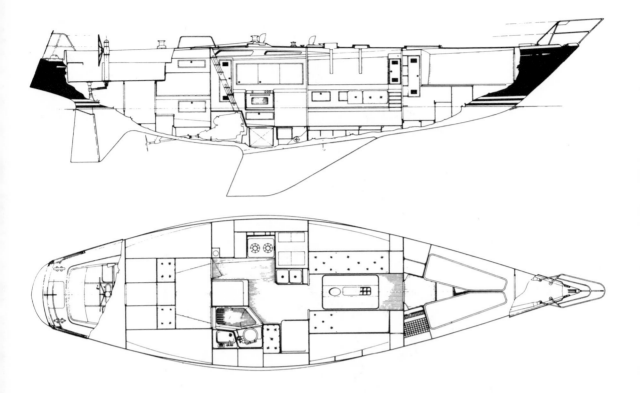

"However, at about the time this question came up at Stevens, new development in the theory of frictional resistance had been worked out and, although they were at that time connected chiefly with aeronautical research, it was possible to apply them to small yacht models. It is unnecessary to go into these theories, but it was discovered that, by roughing the forward edge of the keel and then applying the right correction factor, accurate correlation could be made between models as small as 3′ on the waterline and the full-sized boat.

"This ability to work with small models cut down the cost of experimental work to a point where it could be carried on with real hope of success.

"The purpose of earlier tests with large models of sailing yachts had been, as in the case of power-driven vessels, to determine the resistance to forward motion with the boat in an upright position and moving along her own center line. Perhaps in some cases the models had been heeled and possibly even skewed a little to simulate leeway, but if this had been done it was evidently done with small models and without any knowledge of how to deduce their full-sized resistances accurately. With the question of the small model cleared up, the next step was to determine the forces actually applied to a full-sized boat by the wind acting on her sails, and to scale these down properly from ship to model and up again from model to ship. To do this, sailing tests were made on the 23-foot waterline *Gimcrack*, a small boat with a fairly conventional rig.

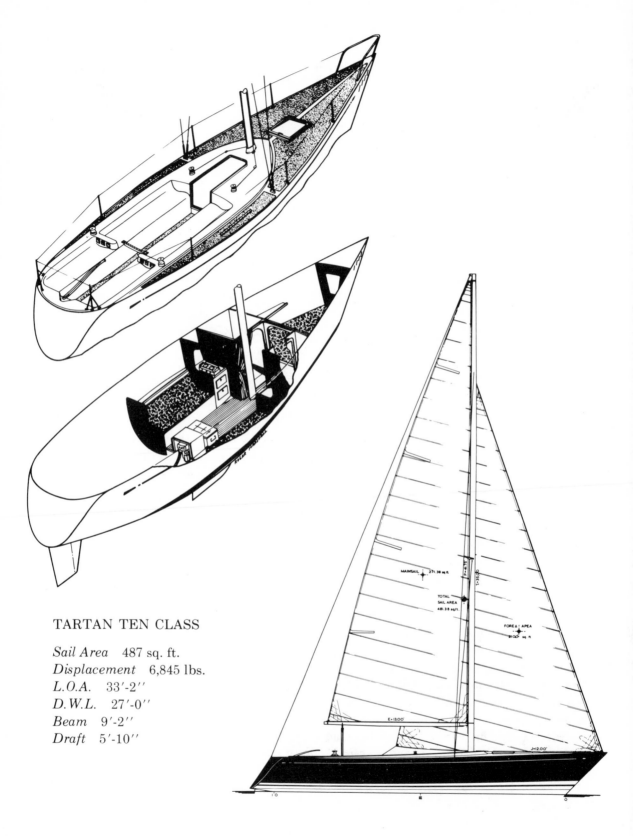

TARTAN TEN CLASS

Sail Area   487 sq. ft.
Displacement   6,845 lbs.
L.O.A.   33'-2''
D.W.L.   27'-0''
Beam   9'-2''
Draft   5'-10''

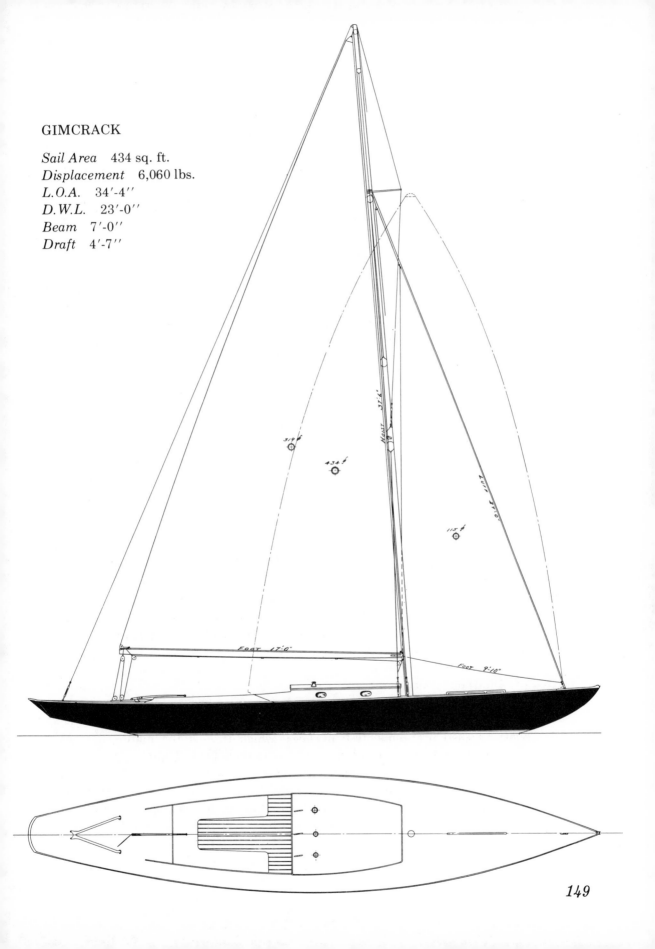

GIMCRACK

Sail Area 434 sq. ft.
Displacement 6,060 lbs.
L.O.A. 34'-4''
D.W.L. 23'-0''
Beam 7'-0''
Draft 4'-7''

149

These tests consisted of taking simultaneous readings of wind speed, boat speed, and heel angle while *Gimcrack* was being sailed close-hauled in winds of various strengths. *Gimcrack*'s resistance was checked both by towing the actual boat and by towing a model. Her stability was also checked both ways. From these tests, curves of the driving and heeling forces exerted by the sails at various heel angles and wind strengths were determined. Appropriate values taken from these curves can be applied to other boats, making it possible to calculate the probable speed for a boat built to a model that has been tried out.

"For a given design which has a certain characteristic sail area, height of rig, and height of center of gravity, we can determine what the heel angle will be for a wind of any given strength and, at that heel angle, what the driving and heeling forces applied by the sails of the hull must be. From a model test of the hull, the speed through the water and the number of points away from the wind the boat should be at her best can be determined. From this, her speed made good to windward can be easily calculated.

"The emphasis has been placed on speed made good to windward because that is generally considered the most important point of sailing and is probably the most difficult to determine from tests. At the same time, other valuable data can be obtained from the model test. Running and reaching speeds can be worked out and leeway determined, as well as the position of the true center of lateral resistance and the stability of the hull in motion, which usually differs from the stability at rest.

"This has all been worked out over a period of six or seven years. I have not dwelt on the technical features of the work, but those who are interested are referred to a recent paper by Professor Davidson." ["Some Experimental Studies of the Sailing Yacht," published in 1936 by the Society of Naval Architects, Vol. 44 Transactions.]

The accompanying photograph showed the carriage in the Stevens Institute Tank with a model in position for a test run at a heel angle of 30°. Sensitive scales on this carriage measured the resistance of the model as well as the 'thwartships force at each end of the model. Actually, this total 'thwartships force must be just sufficient to support the opposing force of the rig as scaled down in magnitude. As the picture showed, the model is slightly twisted from the direction of its motion, and its motion through the water in that position creates the necessary force.

Olin's text continued:

"The accuracy of these tests is really amazing. Their value has been indicated not only by the success of *Ranger* but also by the outstanding success of boats designed after model tests in classes which, through the building of a great number of boats, have been built up close to their peak. I think it is generally recognized that this type of model testing has earned its place as an important step in the design of many yachts. It should be emphasized, however, that a great deal of care and thought must be used to get the greatest advantage from these tests and to avoid being led astray by the results. The speed predictions are remarkably close, but our racing boats are close as well, and small differences in design data will spread points on either side of the probable range of speed.

"The tank will not design a boat; it will answer a question. To get a useful answer, the right question must be asked. And to have the answer mean much, there must be some basis of comparison. In the actual practice of using the tank to work out a new design, there must be considerable flexibility. Sometimes only one model is made, while at other times several are needed. This, of course, depends on the speed of the model which has to be beaten and on the designer's ability to produce a faster model.

"However, while successive improvements in design in a class or type of boat make it gradually more difficult to beat any particular boat, the definite quantitative information supplied by model tests can build up a background of understanding of the influence of various shapes, and changes in shape, which distinctly help the designer in attempting to improve an existing design. The method of calculating speed also emphasizes the relationship of the various factors, such as resistance, stability, leeway, sail area, etc., and helps to give the designer a clear picture.

"So far with racing boats, a number of models, perhaps two or three, sometimes more, each with variations in shape, have been made before settling on a final design. However, even when the last bit of speed is not important, the model test is valuable for the information it gives about stability and balance under sail, and the action of the model in waves. The relation of these data to the speed curve is extremely important and may well affect a decision between boats fairly close in speed.

"It is too early to predict just what the effect of the tank will be on the yacht designer and his design. I have heard some people express the fear, others the hope, that the element of chance has been eliminated from yacht design. I am sure that is not the case. It will be a long time before all the possible variations in yacht form, great enough to make a real difference in performance, have been tried out. In the meantime, the ability to turn out an easily driven, stable, well-balanced hull will be as important as ever and, to take full advantage of the tank, the ability to work out the hull and rig structure and their weights accurately and efficiently will be even more so."

7 *Highlights of Rod's Sailing Experiences*

Years ago young Phil Le Boutillier, Jr., told me that when Rod skippered *Stormy Weather* across the Atlantic and cruised the northern European coast, the boat had no engine, so Rod sailed her into a berth backwards by using her mizzen alone. I believe Phil said it was in Denmark. I asked Rod just how he did it.

"Well, I've been quite an enthusiast for the yawl rig, because you can use the mizzen to control the heading of the boat. It enables you to tack when you've really lost steerageway, and we made use of that frequently, particularly in this type sailing around the Norwegian coast, where there are some very narrow waterways. We did the same thing with *Dorade* in 1933. I think what Phil Le Boutillier was particularly talking about was a very small basin in Copenhagen, a little circular place where the boats moor stern-to, around in a circle, and there's not a whole lot of room right in the center. We came into that very small place under sail very slowly, and we wanted to go astern in between two boats. We were able to more or less lose way in front of them, and then by backing the mizzen first on one side and then the other, we kind of forced the stern to go into this small opening in between the two adjacent boats, and as we literally did back in, we picked up the buoy over the side on the way and held lines on that, and when we got far enough back got a line to the dock astern. So I guess that's what he was thinking of, and it works okay."

You must be a good sailor when you do not have an engine. It is a tribute to the Stephens brothers' skill that both *Dorade* and *Stormy Weather* sailed such long passages without power.

"I think it's unfortunate today that engines are taken so much for granted," Rod continued, "because people do lose some of the ability to handle boats, which all of us had in days when engines were not so generally used."

"It makes a boat a lot sweeter inside, too, doesn't it?" I said.

"No question," he replied. "We took the engine out of *Stormy Weather* for the transatlantic, because we wanted to have considerable storage, and we didn't want to make the boat too heavy, or get her out of trim. We had done a similar trip before in *Dorade* and didn't suffer from not having the engine. So that was more or less the first thing we did after it was arranged between Mr. Le Boutillier, Sr., and myself that we would use *Stormy Weather* instead of *Dorade* in this 1935 transatlantic race and cruise."

"It's a fact," I said, "that nowadays people want their frozen food and all the amenities of home on their boats, so they've got to have an engine for powering the refrigeration unit and generating electricity for lights and electronics, etc."

"Unfortunately, it also has to be run pretty often, and I've noticed on the trips I've taken recently on boats," said Rod, "that if it isn't the batteries getting down, it's the icebox getting warm, so either for refrigeration or for electricity. I really think it's just a shame to go along with the motor running when you have a nice sailing breeze, whether you're cruising or racing. And I think that people have gone altogether too far in tying themselves up. After all, the energy isn't going to be available forever, anybody can see that coming. So I think it would be a good chance for the sailors to begin to take the lead there, and save energy, and learn how to sail better."

"Another story you told at lunch a little while ago, Rod, was that you were quite apprehensive in one of the Cup races on a twelve meter when a helicopter came so close, and you were racing aboard in an America's Cup Race. Why was that?" I asked.

"Actually, it was in the 1967 match, and I wasn't on board, I was watching the race," he replied. "It was *Intrepid* when she was new and doing very well. In this instance a Coast Guard helicopter was trying to pull out crew members from a small catboat that had first of all gotten in the way of the twelve meters, where it shouldn't have been. Because of the downdraft made by the helicopter trying to shoo her away, the little catboat capsized and swamped, so the people had to be rescued. They were directly in her path, so *Intrepid* had no choice, because I believe they had already gone up to the point where they were virtually fetching the mark. There was only one thing to do, go ahead. Now they wouldn't have had the slightest difficulty in avoiding this small catboat if the Coast Guard had left it alone. It was a small, slow boat, but the Coast Guard trying to get the boat out of the way really created a problem. You asked why I was concerned. Because there was a very strong draft. When a big helicopter is hovering, there's a direct downwind wind force. When you sail in a fresh breeze, as the boat heels it relieves itself, and you also have a chance to luff and spill the wind. When the wind is being blown right down on top of you, I'm not sure I know just exactly what option you have. In any case, *Intrepid* took a rather severe knockdown at a time when she was being beautifully sailed by Bus Mosbacher. The thing we were all noticing and admiring was that he maintained an absolute uniform heel angle at what was apparently the optimum point. The boat seldom heeled noticeably more or less, whereas his competitor was alternately being put down and coming up, down and up, but Bus was just going along steadily. The strength of the rig on a twelve meter has not much margin, and it was equivalent to sailing in a much stronger wind. That's why it did worry me."

"You were telling us quite awhile back," I went on, "that it was very beneficial when you rigged two jibs with alternate hanks on the same jibstay 'wung' outgoing before the wind, cruising in the Caribbean."

"This was along the north coast of Puerto Rico," Rod recalled with a smile, "and a time when there was a normal trade wind quite fresh, say 25 plus, maybe a little more in the puffs, a few squalls, and it was aboard *Revonoc* in 1950. We had a good crew, but we were not in any way interested in carrying a spinnaker in such heavy conditions, and so we decided to try these two jibs. At the time there was no system for more than one jib on a stay, although the racing boats today more or less take it for granted. In this case the boat had a single headstay, and we picked two genoas, the biggest one and the next biggest one, and interhooked them on the single stay and hoisted them up and winged them out. It was a very satisfactory arrangement. We had only a single spinnaker pole, so on one side it was lead to the spinnaker pole, and on the other side it was lead to the main boom, which we topped up a little extra and let well out. We didn't set the mainsail at all, and we did run very fast. It was a pleasure to steer; the rolling was very minimal. We did pass through a few squalls with the breeze fresh, but you felt absolutely no pressure or no difficulty, and it didn't require careful or skillful steering. It was just a matter of being there and keeping her more or less on course."

"Would you say if you were just interested in cruising and making passages at sea that it would be better to use this twin jib arrangement than using a spinnaker?" I asked.

"Very much better, Frank. I'm not an enthusiast for a spinnaker, as I think that it requires a good deal of horsepower, particularly to get it in when the breeze is very gradually but steadily increasing. Boats do roll undesirably and yaw around, and with this two-jib system rolling was minimized, and the boat was easy to steer. And I'd say it was very definitely a desirable arrangement and furthermore, when we got to the end of the island, and we had 5 or 6 miles to go to the place where we were going to lay for the night, the wind was abeam

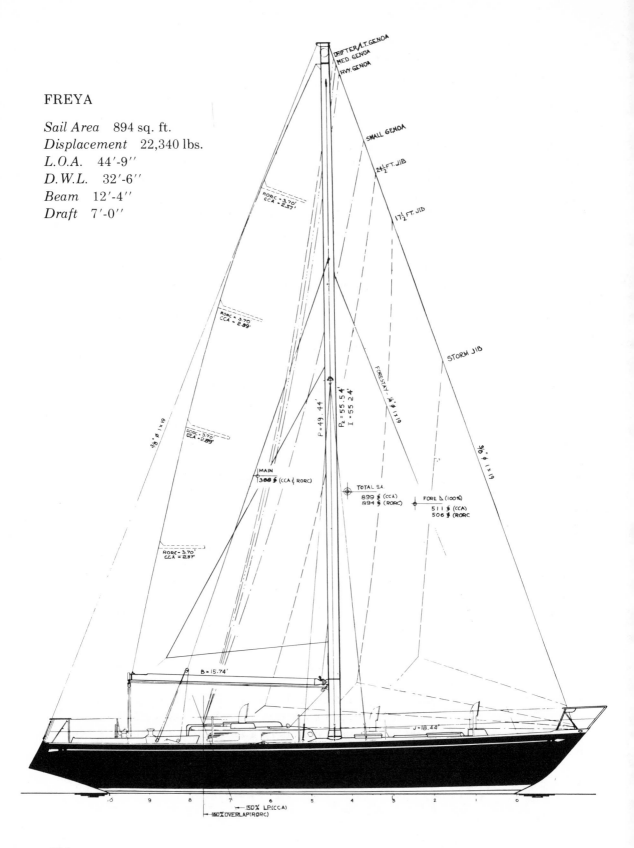

FREYA

Sail Area 894 sq. ft.
Displacement 22,340 lbs.
L.O.A. 44'-9''
D.W.L. 32'-6''
Beam 12'-4''
Draft 7'-0''

DRIFTER/LT. GENOA
MED. GENOA
HVY. GENOA

SMALL GENOA

24½ FT. JIB

17½ FT. JIB

STORM JIB

RORC · 3.70'
CCA · 2.57'

RORC · 3.70
CCA · 2.89'

RORC · 3.70
CCA · 2.89'

RORC · 3.70'
CCA · 2.57'

3/8" ⌀ 1 x 19

FORESTAY-¼"⌀ 1 x 19

9/16" ⌀ 1 x 19

P = 49.44'

P₂ = 55.5 4'
I = 55.2 4'

MAIN
388 § (CCA & RORC)

TOTAL S.A.
899 § (CCA)
894 § (RORC)

FORE △ (100%)
511 § (CCA)
506 § (RORC)

B = 15.74'

J = 18.44'

150% LP (CCA)
150% OVERLAP (RORC)

10 9 8 7 6 5 4 3 2 1 0

156

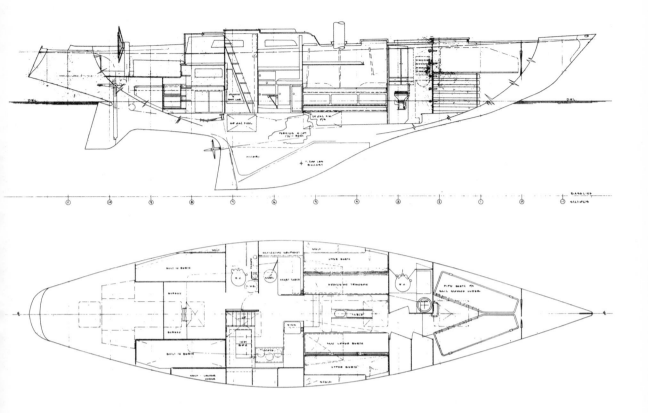

and ultimately we had to come on the wind to get up to the anchorage, so we just jibed the weather sail over on top of the lee one. It was very satisfactory, no problem at all, and it was a nice feeling."

"But I was going to say," Rod continued, "that it gave us the feeling that in an emergency—as, for example, recovering somebody that had fallen overboard—you could still maneuver the boat and sail on the wind. There's nothing at all wrong with having two sails of generally similar size and shape laying one on top of the other, because they behave very much like a single sail. Actually, in one easy simplification: If the sheet is used on the lee sail of the two, there being one sheet on each sail and one on each side of the boat, you can tack and sail on the wind as you could with just a single sail."

"Then you think, Rod, it would be easier to pick someone up who fell overboard from a boat running before the wind with a rig with the twin jibs like that, than if that boat had a spinnaker set?"

"That's very definitely my opinion, because with a spinnaker set the best you can do is kind of come up and bring the wind about abeam. It's not easy then to get the spinnaker off, and the spinnaker has to be down on deck before you can get higher on the wind, or perhaps go back on the other tack as necessary to keep close to the person who is in the water. Whereas with this rig you can immediately bring the boat up, let this weather sail jibe on top of the lee sail, and you could sail the boat just as high as it could be with a genoa jib of that size. You could tack in a few seconds, if it was desirable. That's a great safety feature. In that case it has an advantage over other possible arrangements."

"Rod, I remember a couple of years ago Halsey Herreshoff gave a talk at the New York Yacht Club, and one of the pictures he showed was from a movie of a wind tunnel test, where they had set up a small mast and a small-size spinnaker. And the mast of course was fixed to the floor of the tunnel, but the spinnaker just simply began oscillating all by itself, which shows you what happens on a boat going before the wind with a spinnaker. It gets oscillating so much, especially with these very tall rigs, it's rolling the boat so much that pretty soon it rolls the rudder out of water and she broaches, and is 'wiped out' as they say, then you have a hell of a time. Don't you think that something ought to be put into the handicap or racing rules that would limit the size of spinnakers, so that this wouldn't happen at sea?" I asked.

"Frank, it's long overdue. And I think back some years, when most of the better ocean racers had the, perhaps today old-fashioned, smaller fore triangle, although I will say there is some tendency to get back to them at least in the smaller classes. In any case, with the smaller fore triangle the spinnakers were smaller, and also the spinnaker technique was not as effective and the spinnakers were a little more triangular, and a little less rectangular, so that they were smaller and their leverage was less, because they attached to the mast lower down. Also their own center of effort was relatively lower. The whole thing snowballed. But the old rig gave you a very stable situation.

"I think back on the years with *Mustang*," Rod went on. "We never hesitated about setting a spinnaker under running conditions in some pretty fresh breezes, and never was there any idea of broaching—the boat never broached, never in any condition. You had to steer hard sometimes, and it would roll sometimes, but never any feeling that it was just going to lay over on its side. And yet today we almost take that for granted, and I agree with you that it's dangerous, it's undesirable, unseamanlike, very easy to lose people in rough water offshore, and it's very easy to have a serious collision in close quarters with another boat. If all of a sudden your boat starts to oscillate and you realize it's apt to broach, there's not a whole lot you can do about it. I think it's overdue. I think the spinnakers are too big, and I don't like the current tendency to raise up the fore triangle and increase the rig size, because it's favored the way the rules work. It's very unfortunate for downwind sailing. Upwind you can shorten down. I don't mind how much sail area a boat is designed with for sailing to windward. If you have the right sails with you, you can have a pleasant and perfectly safe and interesting time in very heavy weather. But downwind it's another story. With the spinnakers attaching so far up from the deck and the normal spinnaker so large, it becomes a very unpleasant situation," Rod emphasized.

"I'm glad you feel the way I do about that," I said. "Now to change the subject a bit. You were describing when you were in charge of the foredeck on one of the J Class boats in the America's Cup races. When you rounded the windward mark you described how perfect the timing had to be with the changing of sails to go from the windward to the downwind leg around the windward mark."

"Yes, there was obviously a good deal to do," he replied, "because the sails were large and it took longer even with the competent crew to make the appropriate changes, so that you did have to move pretty fast. However, there was one thing that worked a little bit in the other direction. It was that if the wind was not going to be almost dead astern, especially in light air, then the boat was going through the water pretty fast. Although you went around the weather mark in what was ostensibly a windward and a leeward race, there were times when there was no hurry at all, because of the speed she carried, even though the breeze was light sailing against it. The boat just went very fast in relation to wind speed. So in this instance as you rounded the mark in going downwind, there was no big hurry with the spinnaker because, as you carried your way around, the wind was still well forward of the beam. If you were able to hold the speed, you ended up going back on a reach. But no thought of just quickly getting the spinnaker on, the way, for example, the twelve meters do today. There wasn't that same pressure in a light breeze. In a fresh breeze it was perfectly normal, you would then not change the wind direction very much. And then there was the hurry to get this large spinnaker on, which had to go up 150 or whatever feet in the air, just to plain hoist it that far. The sail we had on *Ranger*," he reminisced, "was about 150′ across the foot, and the spinnaker pole was pretty large. It was all quite an operation."

"It must have been something, sailing on *Ranger*." Then I mentioned another of Rod's activities. "My friend, Jane Page, tells me that you made a great contribution in training the crew on her father's six-meter *Goose*. What are some of the other boats aboard which you have trained the crews?"

"Well, first in regard to *Goose,* I think that perhaps Jane is overstating it a little bit. We had a lot of very successful racing, and I was with them a great deal of the time. I think we had a good group, but it was more because of individual competency. There was also an extremely good hand. His name was Ole, a Scandinavian hand, and he was one of the best professionals racing on a small boat. I would like to bow out a little bit from that one, and simply say that we did have a good crew, and we did sail together quite a lot. I might have occasionally made some small suggestions, but in general we worked together, and we did race a good deal. That was perhaps equivalent to crew training."

"As far as some of the other boats, I have a couple of times done that aboard Italian boats, spending several days, which might fairly be called crew training. There the people were not as familiar, as the crew of *Goose* was, with exactly the way he wanted to do things. For example, as a lot of European boats did, and some still do, use a double spinnaker pole jibe. I believe that, except in extreme heavy weather, it's really a lot simpler and quicker just to get over the one pole you've already got up there in the rig. In the case of these Italian boats, three boats by name *Alnair II, III,* and *IV* owned by a personal friend, Dr. Antonio Pierobon. We really did practice aboard her. Not extensively, but quite a little. We went out with the crew, changed sails, jibed the spinnaker, shifted from a spinnaker to a genoa, rounded hypothetical lee marks, and so forth. Quite extensively did we practice at Le Havre for the One Ton Cup. It was the year that *Alnair IV* was delivered.

"And then another example was the Italian boat, *Mabelle*," Rod went on. "She was made available just a little before Genoa Week in 1969. In her case I combined normal builder's trials with crew practice. There again it's somewhat like *Goose,* because this particular boat had two paid hands, who were extremely competent. They were willing to do things more or less the American way, or the way I thought things would work well. We did go out and shift sails, check sheet leads, and check the speed of jibing with a single pole, and such maneuvers. I'd say that would probably rate as crew training, and was pretty effective. If I remember rightly, in that Genoa Week of 1969 *Mabelle* won every race in the cruising or ocean-racing class, and it was reasonably competitive. So it was probably a good result.

"Another example: in the case of *Ranger*, in 1937, we certainly did a whole lot of practice sailing, but I wouldn't say I was the one who was training the crew. Here it was probably more Mr. Vanderbilt. I was learning. Olin and myself were under the very clear direction of Mike Vanderbilt, although he left the mechanical matters to us. First of all, he believed in going sailing every day, even though we had a boat that seemed to be faster than our competitors, and we thought would probably be faster than the challenging boat for the America's Cup. There was never a day when the wind and weather made it all feasible to sail that he didn't say, 'Okay, boys, we're going to go out at 9 o'clock,' or whatever, and there we certainly did practice a whole lot.

"The same thing carried on through the twelve meters in the postwar period starting with *Columbia* in 1958, and right on down to the present. There, there was a whole lot of crew training. I was somewhat involved with *Columbia* in 1958 and a little bit involved with *Constellation* in 1964, and certainly perhaps I was some assistance in the crew training, but again it was more a matter of the crew working together. Simply repeating operations, then trying to iron out any difficult spots by reorganizing the relevant rigging or position of a cleat or something like that.

"Perhaps one other example, *Blitzen*," Rod recalled. "In 1938 when she was a new boat, prior to the Bermuda Race, we did a good deal of sailing particularly off Newport, but before the Bermuda Race started, in which we went out and practiced reefing. In this case the mainsail was very high and narrow for that period, so instead of reefing we shifted to another mainsail that was the same length on the boom but came down 7' or 8' on the mast, and that sail in turn had a couple of reefs. We practiced and got it down so that we could

RANGER   (Rosenfeld)

change the mainsail in a couple of minutes, and of course we did a lot of jib changing for practice. So that might again have been an example of crew trainings, and I had a little bit to do with it.

"The same thing again on *Mustang* in the postwar Bermuda Race years. At least we sailed more than most of the other boats, right off Newport the day before the race, when people are always finding plenty to do ashore. We generally made it a point of getting underway early, even though the crew was always very competent, and most of us had sailed together a great deal. When we got the actual crew aboard for that particular race, there was always a change of one or two people. We did go out and we speeded up our technique of reefing, changing headsails, handling the spinnaker, and so forth. And in that case also there was certainly some crew training, again perhaps under my direction. Most of the crew knew just about as much as I did, so it shouldn't be overemphasized," Rod said modestly.

"What about *Finisterre,* Rod. Did you have a hand in her success winning the Bermuda Race three times?" I asked him.

"I'd say very little," he replied. "I sailed with Carl Mitchell on his previous boat, *Caribee,* at a time when he was just getting interested in ocean racing. Perhaps I made some small contributions by suggesting that things should be pretty well organized and not just stowed in a pile. The first time we sailed on *Caribee* I was surprised at how casual detail and mechanical arrangements were. Also prior to *Finisterre,* Carl Mitchell sailed in several races on *Mustang* in the Block Island Race. Particularly one I think of. After the finish of the race he asked if he could stay on board for a while and take some pictures and make notes. In that case it probably contributed just a little bit to *Finisterre*'s success, because she was totally different from *Caribee* in that there was a clear place for everything and it was kept there most of the time. That must help any boat, but again *Finisterre* had an extremely competent crew. While I raced in several races, I was not involved in any of the Bermuda Races which she won. I'd say there it was a case of having a very good crew, and they were individually competent. They did work at it, and they had things well organized."

"Rod, what were your most pleasant sailing experiences?"

"Well, that would be a hard question to answer. I would say that we have to consider the transatlantic race of 1931 in *Dorade* as a very enjoyable one, because things went very smoothly and we were highly successful in the race. We weren't really expecting to have it the way it came out. It was very thrilling and enjoyable to come up to the English coast and communicate by flag with the Lizard lighthouse, asking when the boats had finished the race, expecting that several of the much larger boats were several days ahead of us, and to be told that nobody had finished, and that we were the first boat—very, very exciting moment. A few hours later, when we actually sailed into Plymouth quite unexpected, the commodore of the Royal Ocean Racing Club came out hurriedly in a small boat and was very pleased to see us and said, 'Nobody's finished at all.' We were one of the lowest rating boats in the race. Here were several very large boats, which we thought would be several days ahead of us. So that was a very thrilling and satisfactory experience. The entire summer was, too. Later in a race around the Isle of Wight we actually lost by 30 seconds, having finished 2 hours ahead of a small boat that beat us. We won second. And in the Fastnet Race, which was a relatively hard race, we were kind of on our mettle, because we figured everybody would say perhaps we were just lucky in the transatlantic race, and we thought, 'No the boat was good,' and therefore we really went at it hard. We again had a very good result and won by a considerable margin, although in that instance we didn't finish first. There were several large boats a little ahead of us, boat for boat, but not saving their time.

"Then coming up to the postwar period," he continued, "I think the two cruises we made on *Mustang* to Nova Scotia, one in 1947 which started with a cruise to Marblehead, then in the Halifax Race the next part of the program. After that we went on to Cape Breton Island, then came back all along the coast. It was six weeks, as I remember, and a very pleasant time. Everything went nicely, and we enjoyed all of it.

"We had a generally similar experience in 1959 one year after *Columbia* defended the America's Cup. In that case we didn't race from Marblehead to Halifax, but we sailed from Larchmont directly to Lunenberg, where many boats are built, in the southern part of Nova Scotia. Then cruised along the Nova Scotia coast including a couple of crew changes. Next again to Cape Breton Island, and back from Lunenberg to Nantucket, and so down the remaining bit of coast, because we were a little ahead of time. This, however, was a three-week excursion. It was extremely pleasant, and we had good shipmates, good weather, and things went nicely. I'd say those three would be hard to choose among, the *Dorade* 1931, or *Mustang* 1947, or 1959 to Nova Scotia—all very enjoyable."

"Well now, Rod," I asked for a final question, "if you were going to build yourself a new boat, what do you think you would like to use for the material—aluminum, steel, fiberglass, or wood? Certainly not ferro cement."

"I think I'd be very tempted to go in the direction of fiberglass, because I have seen enough in our own professional experience to see that, when it's well done, it produces a very strong boat. It appeals to me particularly because it does reduce maintenance. I would find that was a very important consideration, because the first cost is really bad, but the continuing maintenance on a wooden boat is perhaps almost worse. It has increased so much from previous times that I'd be very anxious to build something that was minimal, at least on necessary maintenance, and a boat that didn't deteriorate if, for financial, health, or whatever reason, was neglected a little bit. I think that fiberglass has a very good plus in that respect. We know wood boats can last more or less forever, but not if you stop taking care of them. The same goes for aluminum. I've never been particularly interested in steel, because I think it's hard to get a good compass, and I think that's very important. So I think I'll opt for fiberglass from a practical standpoint. From a sentimental standpoint I'd certainly go for wood, because it produces a more beautiful boat, and for technical reasons I might go for aluminum alloy, because it's quite easy to determine exact strength and reinforce any heavily stressed areas," Rod concluded.

8 Finisterre

There's no question about it, men love their boats. How do we know that? Just listen to them talking. They don't describe "it," but "her." They say "she" steers two points closer to the wind than a man could expect of his wife (as Robert Louis Stevenson wrote). Except of course when they are talking about fighting ships, which are referred to as "men-of-war." It must be beauty, especially in a sailboat, that conjures up the ideal of a lovely lady to a sailor.

Such a man, who still loves his old boat, is Carleton Mitchell. And no wonder. Remember *Finisterre*'s record of winning so many races twenty years or so ago? That record has never been excelled. And making so many passages to foreign ports. And cruising in the Caribbean and through the Bahamas? Her first owner, justly proud, remembers her well.

And so I believe you will understand his feelings about this yawl, later referred to as "my old girl," as he writes about her so well:

"It is 20 years since a fat centerboard yawl named *Finisterre* came to the starting line for her first Bermuda Race. As a competitor, she represented a presumptuous—but still valid—idea: that in a small package could be combined speed, seaworthiness, and comfort, in something like equal proportions. Before she was launched in the fall of 1954, I had written in *Yachting*: 'Not forgetting the maxim you can't have everything in any one hull, and that every boat must be a compromise, I must confess wanting to try to build a boat

FINISTERRE
(Rosenfeld)

that has everything: fast enough to be interesting to race 'round the buoys, yet rugged enough to face the possibility of a hurricane off the Azores; small enough to be easily taken for an afternoon sail by one person, yet comfortable enough to live aboard for weeks at a time, even in areas remote from stores; draft shoal enough to poke into the byways of the Chesapeake, or the Bahamas, or the Baltic, or the Mediterranean, yet possessing the ability to cross an ocean en route to the next gunkhole.'

"On that distant June day off Brenton Reef Lightship, *Finisterre* had already lived up to many of my hopes. During her very first ocean race, a pre-S.O.R.C. (Southern Ocean Racing Circuit) warm-up from Fort Lauderdale to Bimini, a chance remark so well encapsulated her performance that it was to become a slogan throughout her racing career. As we slammed through boisterous Gulf Stream seas before dawn, Bobby Symonette asked, 'What do you suppose the little boats are doing?' He had to be reminded that *Finisterre* was the smallest boat in the fleet. At the start, we had pointed so much higher than *Hoot Mon,* the reigning S.O.R.C. champion, Dick Bertram had thought our chief rivals were deliberately holding low to stay out of the current, and when we finished, only the masts of mighty *Ticonderoga,* the 72′ scratch boat, showed above the palms. We were second across the line in a windward thrash which saw three boats withdraw, one dismasted. That winter—1955—*Finisterre* was second to *Hoot Mon* in light downwind Miami–Nassau and St. Pete–Havana races, and thereby was runner-up for the S.O.R.C. title, but the following spring she came out on top.

"Yet it was as a cruising boat I felt *Finisterre* was truly a success. We had not only poked into gunkholes of the Chesapeake and throughout the Bahamas, but on returning from Out Island Regattas in Georgetown had threaded our way through previously taboo areas of the Exumas, including much of Pipe Creek, where the water is spread thin, indeed. During the design and building phases, as much thought had been given to convenience and comfort as to efficiency. When single-handed I could set the mizzen and sheet it flat, hoist the main, and stroll forward to get in the anchor with an electric windlass; back in the cockpit, a yank on a sheet broke out a roller-furling jib, used only for cruising. Filled away, the auto-pilot could be flipped on to hold course while I tidied ship, or went below for brief periods. A belt-driven compressor made ice, that manna of the tropics, and hold-plates kept the refrigerator chilled for the next 24 hours. If caught in high latitudes late fall or early spring, a coal-burning stove in the main cabin could be stoked to a cheery glow. Fond memories include dining by the light of candles and a gimbaled lamp gleaming against rubbed mahogany paneling, while epicurean feasts flowed from the compact galley, both at anchor and underway. Swinging relaxed in placid harbors, we listened to music that truly deserved the oft-misused title of hi-fi, yet which underscores the technological advances of the past 20 years. Battery-powered cassette decks still in the future, a Swiss hand-cranked turntable capable of playing LP records was combined with a German FM portable radio and four English Wharfdale speakers.

"Withal, *Finisterre* has been called 'the first of the modern boats.' As Doug Peterson commented recently: 'Proportionally she was very close to a one tonner.' On an overall length of 38'-7½'' and designed waterline of 27'-6'', her beam of 11'-3'' was considered astronomic, and still is within design parameters. Bronze centerboard up, she drew 3'-11'', down 7'-7''. She had a measured sail area of 713 square feet. She was strongly built by a magnificent craftsman, Seth Persson of Saybrook, Connecticut, in a one-man shop. The hull was double-planked of cedar and mahogany; cabin trunk and other deck structures were of teak, as was the cabin sole; although the mast was wood, a monel mast step and bronze floors permitted heavy tension on the headstay. Yet, as unorthodox as was her beam when she appeared, her displacement would be equally so today. Doug Peterson rolled his eyes heavenward when told that by actual measurement on Maryland Highway Department scales she tipped the scales at 22,330 pounds—this loaded in accordance with the CCA (Cruising Club of America) rule permitting only three 'working sails' aboard, water tanks empty, and stores enough for a weekend. When actually racing, sail and food lockers crammed, tanks filled, an eight-man crew aboard with no restrictions on their gear, plus spares and equipment I deemed essential to any vessel making an offshore passage, *Finisterre*'s total displacement staggers the imagination.

"Almost equally, *Finisterre* represented a departure in equipment," continued Mr. Mitchell. "Wheel steering for a boat of her size simply did not exist; the binnacle and steering column had to be custom fabricated by the Aluminum Company of America, and H. B. Nevins on City Island machined the gears. Roller furling on the main was so untried that Rod Stephens persuaded me to have reef grommets sewn into our first mainsail, and Ernest Ratsey felt it essential to back it up with a handsewn cotton main having conventional reef points in case the newfangled cloth called Dacron didn't work. Kenny Watts from the West Coast supplied a prototype cockpit wind direction indicator which so far as I know was the first to have the wire run inside the mast while a boat was building. Double foot blocks permitting a genoa to be set and sheeted while the spinnaker was being dropped, or vice versa, had to be specially made. The list was long, even without such gadgets as the automatic pilot and ice-making compressor, causing barnacle-encrusted shellbacks to sneer into their beer.

"But when *Finisterre* came to the starting line for Bermuda in 1956 she was a well-tried and well-loved little ship, at least by her crew. Honesty compels me to record the affection was not shared by many of her competitors. Looking back, I am reminded of an old advertisement for a course teaching music by mail: 'They laughed when I sat down at the piano to play . . .' went the blurb, with the implication amusement turned to jealousy as the formerly tone-deaf slob ripped off the opening chords of Beethoven's Fifth. Similarly, visitors would either snicker or shake their heads and mutter, 'Poor Mitch!' on entering Seth Persson's small shop and looking up at *Finisterre*'s broad behind during building. Less than 2½ times as long on the waterline as she was wide, my dream ship did remarkably resemble a plump watermelon in a day when go-fast vessels were supposed to be narrow and deep. But then when *Finisterre* began to win races, up went the perennial cry of rule-beater. It was true, in the sense that the then-Cruising Club of America rule assumed a wide, shallow boat needed help to be competitive, but not intentionally so. Never once during design discussions with Olin Stephens was the rule considered, nor was a rating calculated by Bob Blumenstock until long after launching. Then, before reading it to me over the telephone, he asked if I was sitting down, in case of shock. There had been no tank tests, only a half model of the hull I lugged around studying before lines were finalized. *Finisterre* was simply a vision brought into focus during night watches through the years, a compendium of experience and theory, and Olin transmuted my thoughts into reality. The result turned out to be fast, to the consternation of many, including the framers of the rule.

"It blew hard with big seas during the Bermuda Race of 1956, 'big-boat weather' in the language of the time. The smallest vessel in a fleet of 89 stormed through to finish over eight hours ahead of the second boat in her class, which wound up thirty-fifth on corrected time. As I wrote in *Yachting*: '*Finisterre* in every detail was planned as a sea-going and sea-keeping vessel. So far as I know, there is not one fitting missing, or one item lacking, which would be provided on a 72-footer. From the first I determined that she would differ from the largest ocean racer only in size, not in equipment or design. Part of this stems from my own respect for the sea, and the belief that whenever a boat clears the shore she must be an independent unit, ready for anything.' Thus we could drive *Finisterre* without worry. I had specified extreme beam to guarantee a stable sail-carrying platform, but after my previous centerboarder, *Caribee,* a 58-footer with masthead rig and comparably large foretriangle, had declared there would be no sails which could not be carried forward with one hand. This had partially determined *Finisterre*'s dimensions. Winches were four Nevins No. 6's, the most powerful available, grouped around the cockpit to allow any combination of double teaming. Combined with carefully engineered roller furling on the main—the boom-to-mast fitting rode on roller bearings to prevent binding under strain—sail changes could be made as required to conform with my single ocean-racing maxim: At all times keep the boat moving at her maximum potential speed in the conditions of the moment.

"After a brief pause in Bermuda to celebrate, Mr. Hyde—dubbed The Monster by S.O.R.C. competitors—turned into the homey Dr. Jekyll and took off to cruise the Mediterranean. At first seas were calm as we ghosted under spinnaker, stopping occasionally for a swim, but then it freshened. Yet we still carried the 'chute, although provisions had been made for booming out twin headsails on long passages. *Finisterre* was so docile and easily handled two-man watches always felt in complete control. When overtaken by a depression which piped up gradually, we came down all the way to a #2 jib without intermediate changes. And, although happily there was no hurricane in the Azores to prove how much *Finisterre* could take, between Fayal and San Miguel we swooped over immense seas from a Force 10 gale centered to the north without missing sleep or a meal. The reach to Gibraltar across the Portuguese Trades was an exhilarating sleighride, but it was with surprise we heard our navigator report we had sailed almost 3,700 miles from Newport—only 635 of them racing—averaging over 150 miles per day, perhaps something of a record for a 27½′ waterline boat with wine bottles standing upright on the swing table at lunch and dinner—and chilled, if the menu called for a white. Undoubtedly the sincerest compliment *Finisterre* ever received on the score of comfort came the morning following our arrival in Gibraltar, after nearly 24 days at sea. Looking over the shimmering Straits from the terrace of The Rock Hotel as we breakfasted, Frank MacLear murmured, 'What a nice day for a sail!' With no demurrers, we paid our check, went down to the quay, and left for an unscheduled crossing to Africa.

"When *Finisterre* got home after poking along the Spanish, French, and Italian coasts, an indolent summer of anchoring stern-to in front of waterfront bistro or trattoria, the rule makers had been busy. I had expected—nay, believe it or not, welcomed—a rise in our rating to lessen the chorus of woe, but hardly anticipated the form it would take. Even now it seems odd that while *Finisterre* took the maximum penalty under the revision, the boat which came down most in rating was *Vim,* a twelve-meter yacht made eligible for racing in the cruising class by virtue of installing an engine and a few interior changes. Two years later, engine removed and again stripped, *Vim* came within a whisker of defending the America's Cup. Throughout the fleet, boats seemed to be penalized exactly in proportion to how close they came to the supposed ideal of the CCA rule, true cruiser/racers. The increased rating didn't make much difference to *Finisterre.* Mr. Hyde went on carving up the competition in 1957 and 1958, winning the Miami–Nassau Race both years, but not entering enough other S.O.R.C. events to qualify for another championship, as Dr. Jekyll had partially retired to enjoy more fully the cruising life. In 1958 *Finisterre* again won the Bermuda Race, and once more the characteristics which made her so ideal for cruising were penalized. Then, after several thousand more carefree miles had flowed astern, racing sails were taken out of storage for the first start in two years.

"The 1960 race to Bermuda has been well-chronicled," continues Mr. Mitchell, "and also undoubtedly lingers in the memory of anyone who sailed it. After light reaching and running breezes beyond the Gulf Stream, a real buster swept the fleet. There were knockdowns and a dismasting. Some boats hove-to under trysail, others lay a-hull with bare poles, a few even ran off dragging lines astern. Hurricane-strength gusts were recorded aboard one large vessel carrying an anemometer, and most experienced seamen agreed there was a sustained gale of Force 8/9. Through it all *Finisterre* carried sail. During the early stages

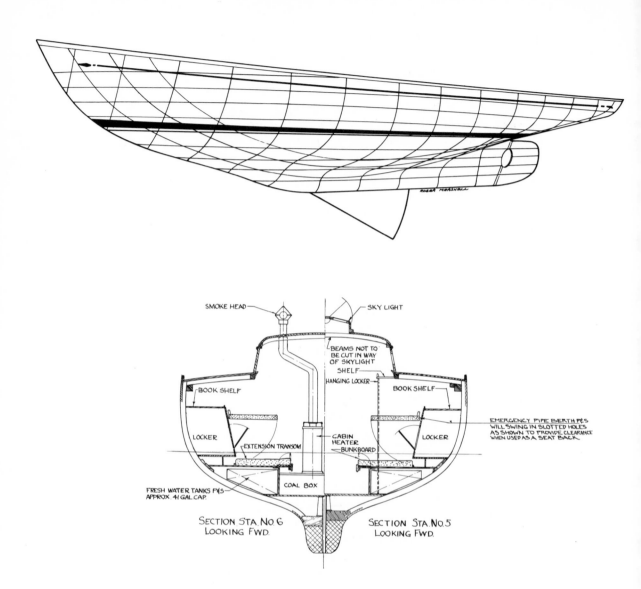

SMOKE HEAD

SKY LIGHT

BEAMS NOT TO
BE CUT IN WAY
OF SKYLIGHT
SHELF

HANGING LOCKER

BOOK SHELF

BOOK SHELF

EMERGENCY PIPE BERTH P&S
WILL SWING IN SLOTTED HOLES
AS SHOWN TO PROVIDE CLEARANCE
WHEN USED AS A SEAT BACK

LOCKER

CABIN
HEATER

LOCKER

EXTENSION TRANSOM

BUNKBOARD

FRESH WATER TANKS P&S
APPROX. 41 GAL.CAP.

COAL BOX

SECTION STA. NO. 6
LOOKING FWD.

SECTION STA. NO. 5
LOOKING FWD.

when there were variations in strength and direction, the main went up and down like a window shade as reefs were rolled in and out and headsails were changed. After settling down to the body of the blow, *Finisterre* kept plugging to windward under #3 jib, deeply-reefed main, and full mizzen, sheets eased only enough not to be stopped by the heavy seas. When results were posted, it turned out she had beaten 109 of 135 starters boat-for-boat, without calling on handicap. Although for the first time in three Bermuda Races she had been led across the line by one of her own class, *Finisterre* had sailed the course faster than all of the Class D, all but 2 of Class C, 18 of 28 B's, and 9 A's.

"For any boat to win the Bermuda Race she must possess certain virtues, the most important of which is the luck of being in the right place at the right

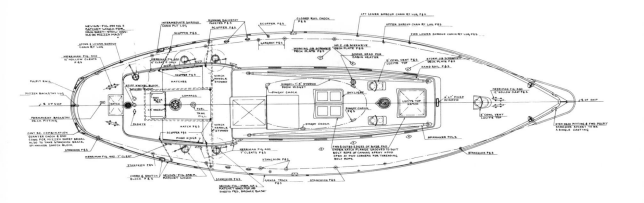

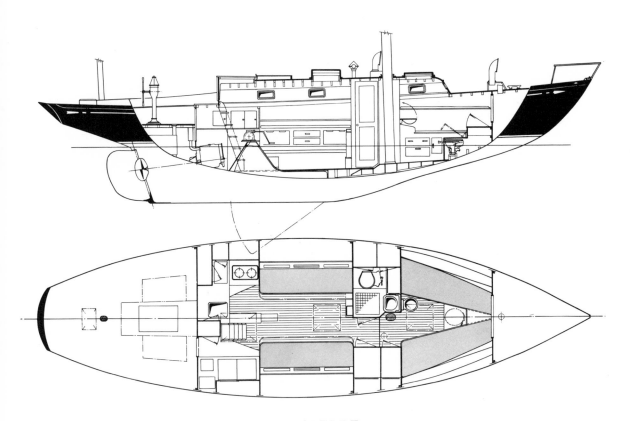

FINISTERRE

Sail Area 713 sq. ft.
Displacement 22,330 lbs.
L.O.A. 38'-7''
D.W.L. 27'6''
Beam 11'-3''
Draft 3'-11''

time. For a boat to win three times in a row is simply proof that luck, like lightning, can indeed strike more than once. Yet for every mile *Finisterre* raced during my ownership, she cruised at least ten, thus my emphasis on her competitive achievements is principally to make the point that a husky and comfortable cruising boat can also be fast.

"The question is, how fast is fast? Rating aside, *Finisterre* almost always finished in the top third of a fleet, especially to windward in open water. Evaluating her potential against the current crop is like trying to compare Tilden with Jimmy Connors, or speculating on the outcome of a Joe Louis–Muhammad Ali bout. Downwind, *Finisterre* would undoubtedly be murdered by light displacement, minimum wetted surface hulls, just as she was beaten by the light displacement *Hoot Mon* 20 years ago. But to windward? I wonder. Her weight and stability gave her a feeling of power in getting through head seas I have never felt in another hull, and performance could undoubtedly be improved by updating the rig and deck equipment. And, lest it be assumed by a new generation of sailors that gung-ho tactics have been recently introduced, in *Finisterre*'s heyday we were small boat sailing ocean races 24 hours a day; hand tending rather than cleating headsails, including spinnakers; controlling sails and rig with kicking straps and backstay adjusters; riding the weather rail like a row of crows on a fence. New gear has made many operations more convenient and effective, but I have seen no new techniques.

"There may be a lesson for the rule makers in *Finisterre*. The revolt against what modern ocean racers have become now extends from disgusted skippers to race committees searching for a solution to overnight obsolescence, miserable accommodations, and vile sea characteristics. Much is blamed on the IOR rule, but undoubtedly the pressures of the last decade by a new group of owners, builders, and designers, many unhampered by thinking of a boat as a way of life or knowledge of what the ocean can be like, would have found loopholes in any rule. Yet surely some factor could have been cranked in which would have produced boats capable of being cruised comfortably as well as being raced competitively. Perhaps a percentage of total weight should have been forced into accommodations, to ensure sleepable bunks, places to sit relaxed, adequate galleys, dining tables, drawers and lockers for storage, and above all enclosed heads. When *Finisterre*'s rating first went up while the skinned-out narrow vessels profited, it would seem the door was opened to many excesses. It is hard to argue that displacement—plus beam—is not the key to comfort and sea-kindliness. And even if a fractional advantage in speed is lost, helmsmanship, sail handling, and the other factors adding up to competitive success would remain equally important.

"And what of *Finisterre* two decades later? For the past five years Victor Smith, his wife, and children, have made their home in southern waters. After losing touch for some time, my old girl herself wrote me a letter at Christmas, dictated to her new owner: 'I now have a permanent sun awning and weather clothes for cruising. My galley stove has been remodeled to use propane, and the aroma of fresh bread, cakes, and pies frequently fills the cabin. This past year my family has set me free to sail them through the Bahamas, the Caicos, along the coasts of Hispaniola and Puerto Rico, and through my beloved Virgin Islands. We are now heading down through the Windward and Leeward Islands, those same waters you and I explored years ago. . . . I've done some racing, too, this year. After being measured for the West Indies Yachting Association, I came in first both days on elapsed and corrected time in Tortola's Annual Autumnal Equinox two-day series. I placed first in cruising class in the Virgin Islands Rolex Races; third in the Around Tortola Race, and got a fourth, second, and first in the Petit St. Vincent Thanksgiving Races. I still like to be out ahead of the pack. I am a truly happy racing-cruising yacht again, and I thought you'd like to know.'"

Following these reminiscences of such a good boat, I would like to tell you how I, as a designer, have been baffled many times after studying *Finisterre*'s plans, especially her lines drawing. I've asked myself so often how a boat with a hull shaped like hers could sail so well. Frankly, she appears to be a bit tubby to my eye.

The answer to that question came to be obvious one day while sailing in our second *Santa Maria* beating to the west'ard near Point Judith. Off that point we intercepted the New York Yacht Club cruise. The fleet was on a squadron run headed east. This is always a race from port to port, although they may call it a cruise. Boat after boat, went by "with billowing sails" as the club's Latin motto reads in part. All spinnakers were set to catch the moderate sou'wester, which makes up in that area almost every day. As we were close-hauled and they were running, they passed us quickly, one after another. The last one, by no means the smallest, had a familiar look about her. I looked harder and let out a gasp, "My gosh, that's *Finisterre*, and she's last." I took a look through the binoculars, and then I saw what was to be the answer to my question.

There, flying from her starboard main spreader, was that small dark blue rectangular flag that means just one thing, "Owner ashore." She was under charter. Mitch was not sailing his boat, and so she was last.

I have come to the conclusion that 60% of *Finisterre*'s victories have been because of her owner's ability as a racing skipper to keep her moving at top speed under all conditions with the crew he trained so well, and 40% because of good luck that everything about her design, her sails, and her construction with its weight in just the right place, all these luckily came together so well to produce optimum performance. Some rare boats, only a few, turn out like that, and this well-handled boat, S & S Design 1054, certainly did. But in my opinion she could not have done all that winning without Mitch in command.

AVOCA   (Rosenfeld)

9 Naval Architecture and Marine Engineering

Because the Stephens brothers are best known for the sailboats their firm creates, it may surprise a good many people to learn that some very fast and excellent powerboats as well as commercial craft have been designed at the same time in the same shop. The man who heads the team of designers behind Olin and Rod is the chief engineer, Gil Wyland. It is under his supervision that all S & S designs are engineered and built.

He became acquainted with Drake Sparkman, Rod, and Olin in 1936 when they formed the association with Starling Burgess to design *Ranger*. The project engineer, Henry Gruber, who formerly worked with Burgess on the J Class *Enterprise* and *Rainbow,* was in Germany and was not available, so Gil got the job. The need was there for just such a man at that time, and he fulfilled it. His responsibility was to be in charge of the design office that did her working plans at the Bath Iron Works, and to inspect her construction. When she was launched and towed to Newport, he went with her as project engineer through the racing season. After the successful conclusion of the 1937 America's Cup Races, he stayed with Olin and Rod and became their chief engineer a few years later.

Two of the many powerboats designed under his eagle eye are: the first *Avoca,* a wooden cruiser about 68′ long, which did about 32 knots; and *Aurora,* a 114′-footer, of aluminum construction, built in Italy, with a speed of 20 knots.

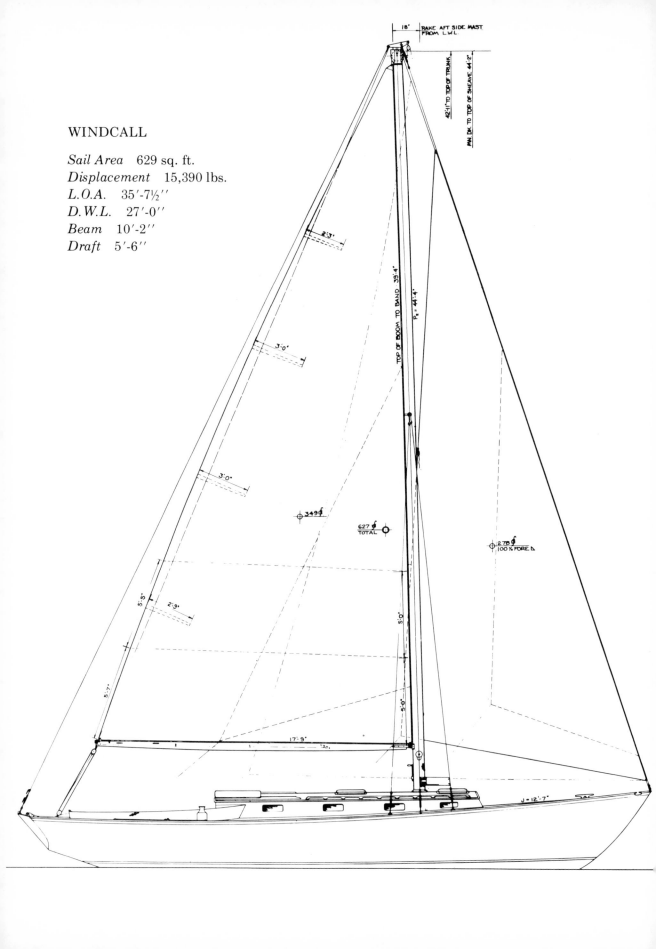

WINDCALL

Sail Area 629 sq. ft.
Displacement 15,390 lbs.
L.O.A. 35'-7½''
D.W.L. 27'-0''
Beam 10'-2''
Draft 5'-6''

0-12 M.P.H.

12-20 M.P.H.

20-27 M.P.H.

27-35 M.P.H.

35-45 M.P.H

45-55 M.P.H.

ABOVE 55 MPH.

SAIL COMBINATIONS

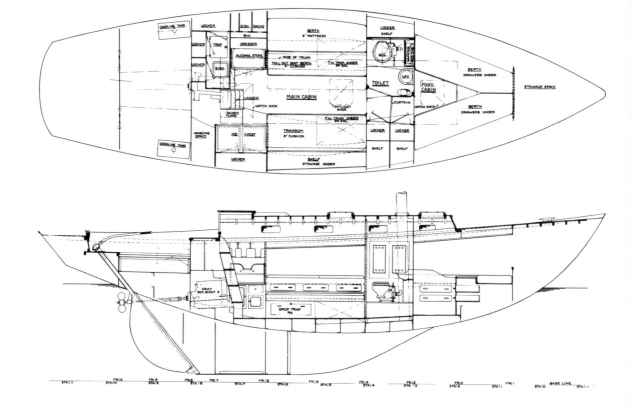

There were a number of Burger-built boats whose lines were done by S & S designers.

Hank Uhle is the designer who works closely with Gil Wyland. It is from his drawing board that most of these powerboats have come. *Alva* was designed for Ev Dickenson. Then *Kalamoun* for His Highness the Aga Khan was a very interesting boat, whose lines and arrangement plans were done by John Angeli, a designer from Detroit; Gil and Hank had complete charge of the boat's design beyond that. She was 93′ long and, like an aluminum PT boat (but most luxurious), she did 46 knots.

The boat that went a fabulous 56 knots was the *Double Eagle*. This fastest speed of any was made possible by the use of gas turbine engines. She was 71½′ on the waterline, designed by S & S as the prototype of some aluminum crew boats for United Aircraft. An interesting feature of her design was the articulated deck she had to absorb the bumps of waves for her crew.

A client who came to S & S twice for powerboats was Mr. Nicholas Goulandris. His first design was *Discoverer*, a 61′ wooden boat of 13 knots. Recently S & S designed his second boat, *Mania Two*, a very interesting aluminum boat 92′ long, whose speed is 21 knots. He still has both boats. The latter, *Mania Two*, is most interesting; not only is she a three-deck luxurious yacht, but she is fitted

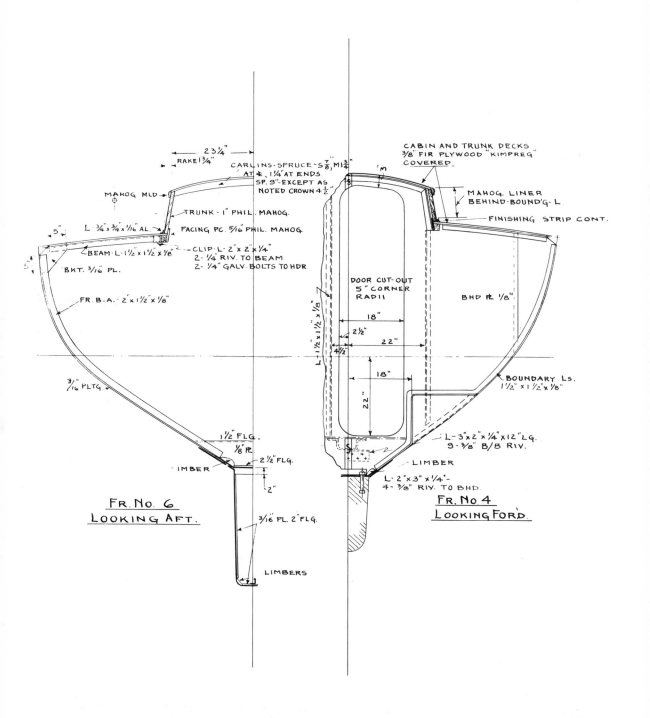

CABIN AND TRUNK DECKS
3/8" FIR PLYWOOD "KIMPREG"
COVERED.

MAHOG. LINER
BEHIND·BOUND'G· L.

FINISHING STRIP CONT.

CARLINS·SPRUCE·S 7/8", M 1 3/4"
AT ℄, 1 1/4" AT ENDS.
SP. 9"·EXCEPT AS
NOTED CROWN 4 1/2"

23 1/4"

RAKE 1 3/4"

MAHOG. MLD

TRUNK·1" PHIL. MAHOG.

FACING PC. 5/16" PHIL. MAHOG

L· 3/4" x 3/4" x 1/16" AL.

5"

CLIP·L· 2" x 2" x 1/4"
2·1/4" RIV. TO BEAM
2·1/4" GALV. BOLTS TO HDR.

BEAM·L· 1 1/2" x 1 1/2" x 1/8"

BKT. 3/16 PL.

FR. B.A.·2" x 1 1/2" x 1/8"

3/16" PLTG.

1 1/2" FLG.

1/8" PL.

LIMBER

2 1/2" FLG.

2"

3/16" PL. 2" FLG.

LIMBERS

FR. No. 6
LOOKING AFT.

DOOR CUT-OUT
5" CORNER
RADII

18"

2 1/2"

4 1/2"

18"

22"

22"

L· 1 1/2" x 1 1/2" x 1/8"

BHD PL. 1/8"

BOUNDARY Ls.
1 1/2" x 1 1/2" x 1/8"

L· 3" x 2" x 1/4" x 12" LG.
9· 3/8" B/B RIV.

LIMBER

L· 2" x 3" x 1/4"·
4· 3/8" RIV. TO BHD.

FR. No. 4
LOOKING FOR'D.

BLACK JACK

Sail Area 880 sq. ft.
Displacement 21,500 lbs.
L.O.A. 44'-10''
D.W.L. 31'-0''
Beam 11'-6''
Draft 6'-6''

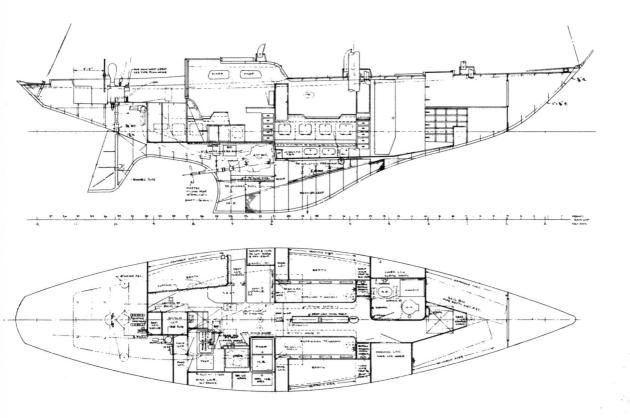

out for fishing with nets, and has ice-making and a big fish hold forward. Mr. Goulandris likes to fish this way, sometimes bringing as much as 1½ tons to market.

This boat is designed to pay out 4 or 5 miles of gill netting from her stern. These have lead weights on the bottom and floats on the top. After this much netting is paid out and a certain time elapses, the boat is turned around and picks up the netting over hydraulic rollers from the port side of the bow. Because it is gill netting, the fish come up with their gills caught in the net, and those that are kept are tossed into the fish hold under the foredeck. These rollers were especially designed by Gil Wyland for both *Discoverer* and *Mania Two*. They work somewhat like the film in a movie projector, making a U-turn with what they haul over the center of three rollers in order to get friction needed to haul in the net heavy with its catch.

Like some big ships, *Mania Two* has a bow thruster to assist in maneuvering during docking and fishing operations. The main engines, which are V-12 cylinder diesels of 1,100 horsepower each, give her a 21 knot top speed.

There is an interesting financial fact about building *Mania Two*. Two American yards underbid two Dutch yards when S & S sent out her plans and specifications to obtain the best price. She was finally built at Stephens Marine

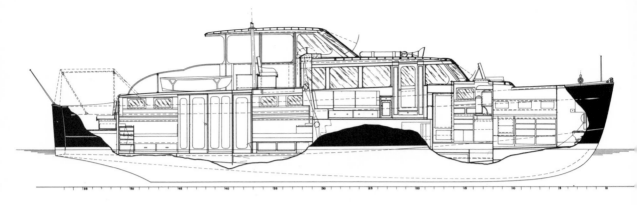

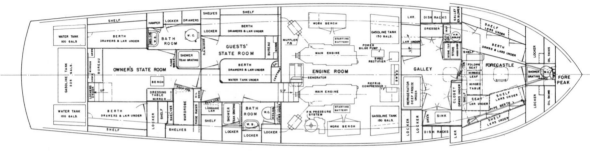

ALVA

Displacement   50,625 lbs.
Speed   14 knots
L.O.A.   60′-0′′
D.W.L.   57′-9′′
Beam   16′-1′′
Draft   4′-1′′

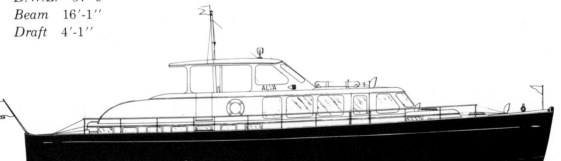

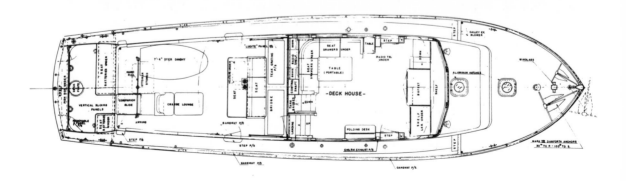

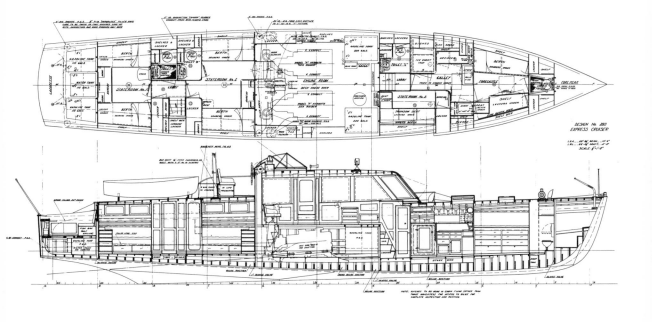

AVOCA

Displacement   47,470 lbs.
Power   2 Kermath 500 H.P. gasoline engines
Speed   32 knots
L.O.A.   68'-9''
D.W.L.   66'-4''
Beam   13'-6''
Draft   4'-0''

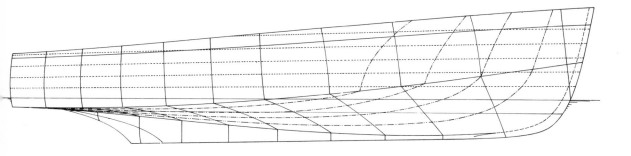

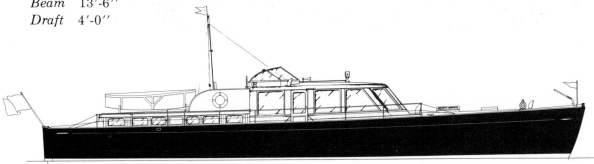

CRUZAN

Sail Area   1,747 sq. ft.
Displacement   74,400 lbs.
L.O.A.   65'-6''
D.W.L.   47'-0''
Beam   16'-0''
Draft   6'-6''

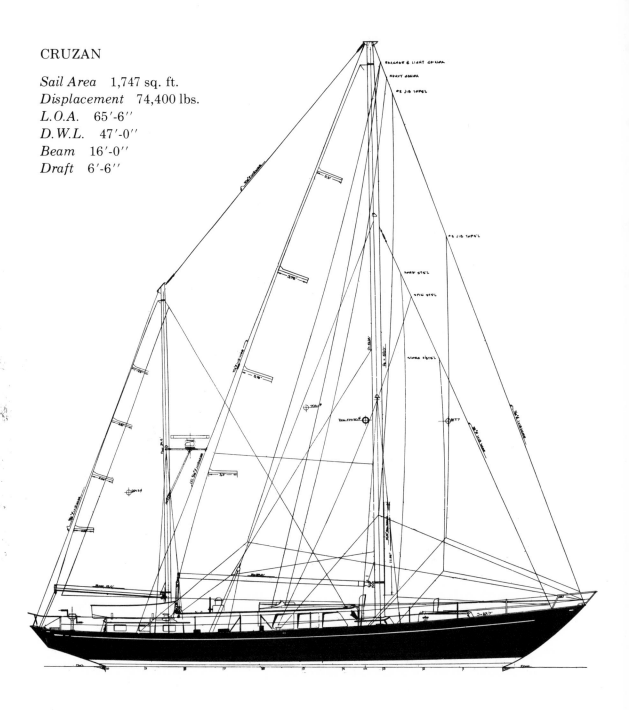

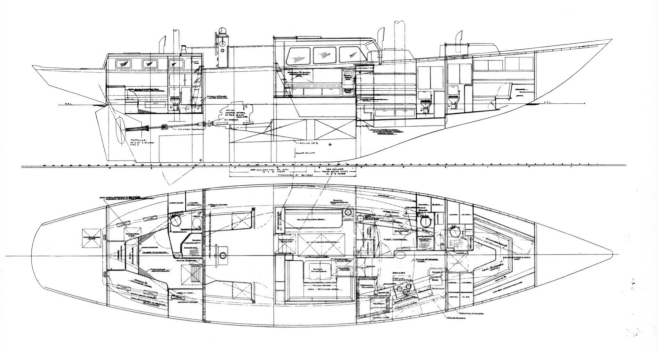

(no relation to Olin and Rod) in Stockton, California. Thus a European client came all the way to California to build his boat at a much lower cost.

When they took her home they went 3,700 miles south, through the Panama Canal, along the northern coast of South America, past Trinidad, then across to the Cape Verde Islands. Next stop was the Canaries and then on to Greece—9,500 nautical miles in all.

One of the faster powerboats that came from the boards at Sparkman & Stephens was *Scarlett O'Hara*, for Dick Reynolds. She was a wooden 50-footer with a speed of 35 knots. There was also another 50′ wooden powerboat named *Whirlwind*, of 39 knots, that S & S did for Laurance Rockefeller. *Dauntless* was the first of the V-bottom aluminum type S & S designed, and she made 41 knots. *Avoca* was one of the loveliest V-bottom craft, being 66′ and making a speed of 32 knots for her owner, Ev Dickenson; she was the second powerboat S & S did for him. A few others are: the 12½-knot, 64′ *Clovelly II* for Charles Ballot of St. Johns, Newfoundland; *Witch of the Wave*, a 42′ sports fisherman type of wood that made 19 knots; *Electron* for R.C.A., 77′ and 13 knots, also wooden. My own favorite powerboat design is the round-bottom *Escort,* an interesting wooden launch done for Briggs Cunningham, 39′ and with a speed of 24 knots; she is still in fine condition.

In thinking about some of these powerboats, the speed of 56 knots, which is 64.4 mph, kept coming back to mind as something quite outstanding. I cornered Gil to talk about just how *Double Eagle* could do it. I asked him how the gas turbines worked out. "Quite well," he said. He told me that S & S has made

MANIA TWO

Displacement   175,220 lbs.
Power   2 MTU 12 cyl. diesels
Speed   18 knots
L.O.A.   92'-0''
D.W.L.   84'-0''
Beam   21'-3''
Draft   7'-1''

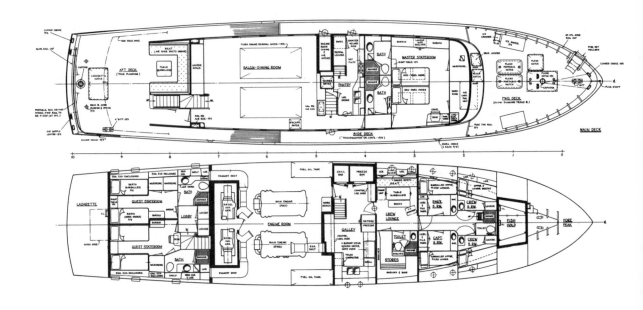

DISCOVERER

Displacement 79,750 lbs.
Power   2 GM 6-71 Diesels
Speed   13 knots
L.O.A.   65'-0''
D.W.L.   61'-4''
Beam   16'-6''
Draft   5'-0''

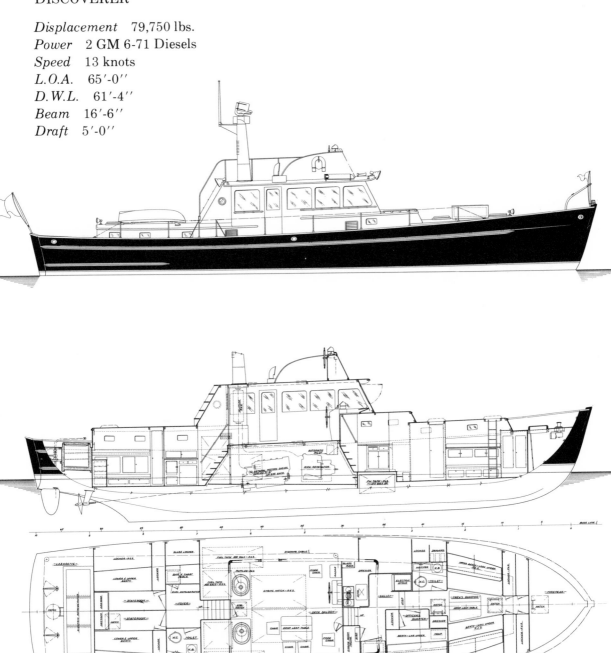

BEAYONDAN

Sail Area 2,580 sq. ft.
Displacement 113,640 lbs.
L.O.A. 82'-6''
D.W.L. 63'-8''
Beam 17'-10''
Draft 6'-3''

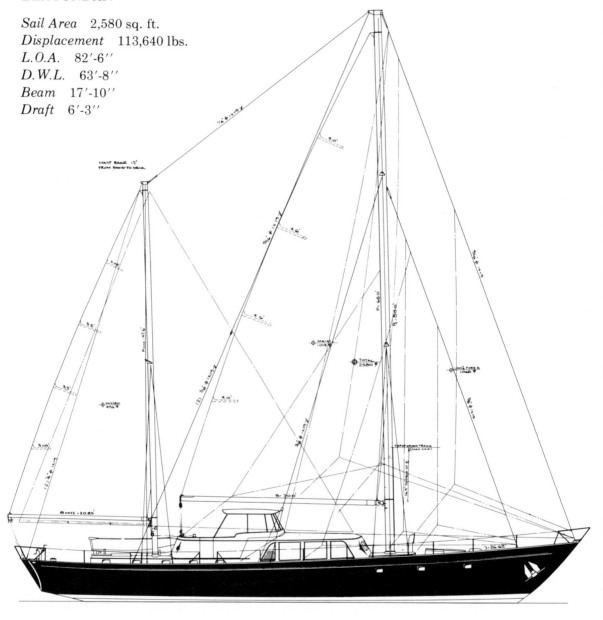

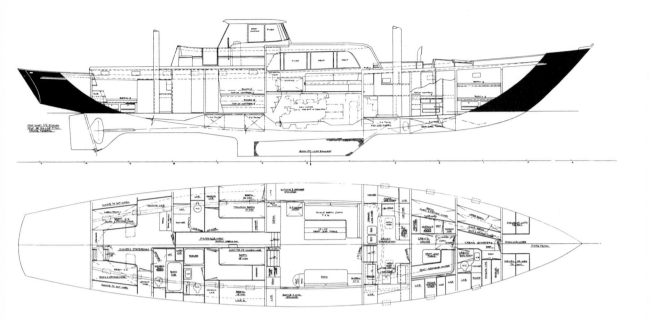

quite a study recently of gas turbines, finding that they are lightweight compared to a diesel but that the fuel consumption is considerably higher. So to cross an ocean the amount of fuel needed would offset the additional weight of diesels. Another factor is the high revolutions at which they operate, 10,000 to 13,000 RPM's. They must have reduction gears and reverse gears, which also offset the weight saving but not as much. Temperature has an effect on their power. As an example, at 59°F. they may have several hundred horsepower more than at 80°F. Another detrimental factor is that when they slow down the fuel consumption goes up, as high as .9 pound of fuel per horsepower per hour, even to 1 pound per horsepower per hour at low speed. This is very poor, because diesels only burn about .4 pound per horsepower per hour.

But the worst problem of all is the noise made by the exhaust and air intake, like a jet plane. "The exhaust sizes are immense," Gil said, "with 12 to 13 square feet needed for each air intake and exhaust section." That's 4' in diameter needed for *Double Eagle*.

In conclusion, for all the reasons just mentioned, the gas turbine may someday be the engine of the future for powerboats, but not yet for yachts.

Now to a different kind of craft.

Near the end of World War II, I watched a miniature submarine being built while I was working in the mold loft at Jakobson's Shipyard in Oyster Bay. It was a top-secret project for the O.S.S. She was built of plywood, a simple double-ended shape like the 110 and 210 Class sailboats. The idea was that it would be carried aboard a large submarine, transported to the enemy's shores, then launched. Her mission would be to put someone ashore in Japan.

WITCH OF THE WAVES

Displacement   26,800 lbs.
Speed   19.5 knots
L.O.A.   45'-0''
D.W.L.   42'-0''
Beam   12'-9''
Draft   2'-11''

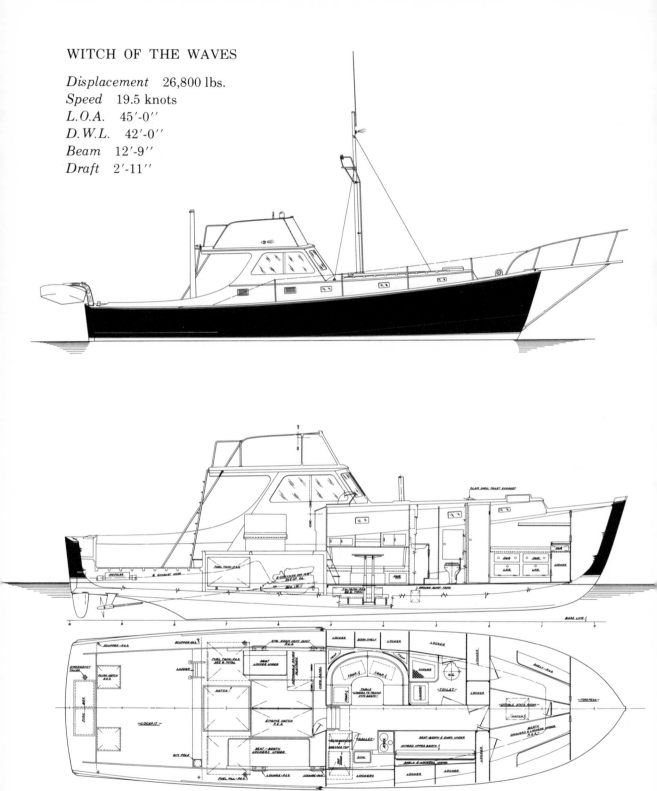

JARANE EX ELECTRON   (Barlow)

ELECTRON

Power   2 GM 6-71 diesels
Speed   13 knots
Displacement   174,000 lbs.
L.O.A.   82′-0″
D.W.L.   77′-0″
Beam   18′-6″
Draft   5′-0″

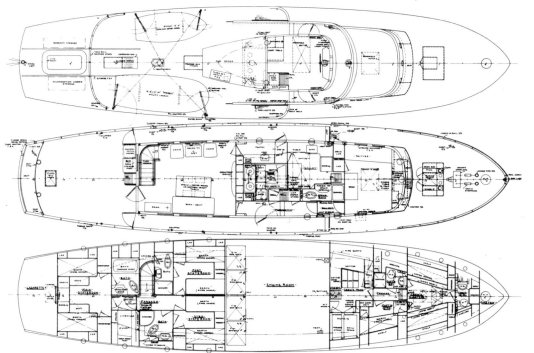

ADVENTURER

Displacement   43,970 lbs.
Power 2   *GM 4-71 Diesels*
Speed   10.5 Knots
L.O.A.   49'-2''
Beam   14'-6''
Draft   4'-1''

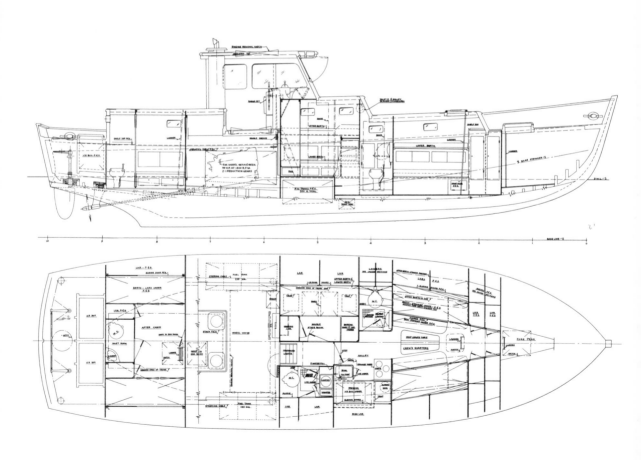

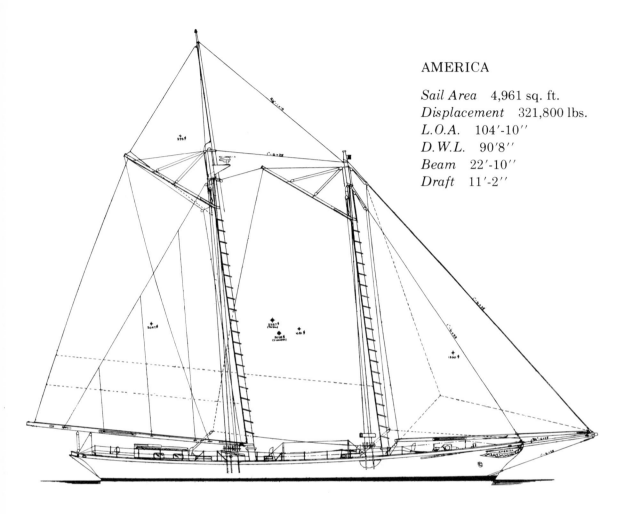

AMERICA

Sail Area   4,961 sq. ft.
Displacement   321,800 lbs.
L.O.A.   104'-10''
D.W.L.   90'8''
Beam   22'-10''
Draft   11'-2''

Gil Wyland went to the Atlantic Commander of Submarines in New London with some of the O.S.S. people to discuss the project with submarine officers back from active duty in the war. They knew what was going on. One of them told him, "We'll take you anyplace you want to go in Japan, except the Imperial Palace." He meant it, too.

Gil took her down on her first trial. "I got scared to death!" he said. "I was running with the hull submerged and the rim of the hatch was only a few inches above the surface of the water, when I realized I could see daylight between the hatch and its sill. I surfaced in a hurry!"

The engine used was a little Universal 4-cylinder gasoline motor, so popular in small auxiliaries today. It was in a tank and had an underwater exhaust system discharging in front of the propeller. She was a development based on a little sub the British had, called the *Sleeping Beauty.*

During the war Sparkman & Stephans served as design agents for the Navy and won the competition for the design of a wooden PT boat. A group of them

DJINN

Sail Area   1,507 sq. ft.
Displacement   77,000 lbs.
L.O.A.   61'-11''
D.W.L.   47'-0''
Beam   15'-11''
Draft   6'-0''

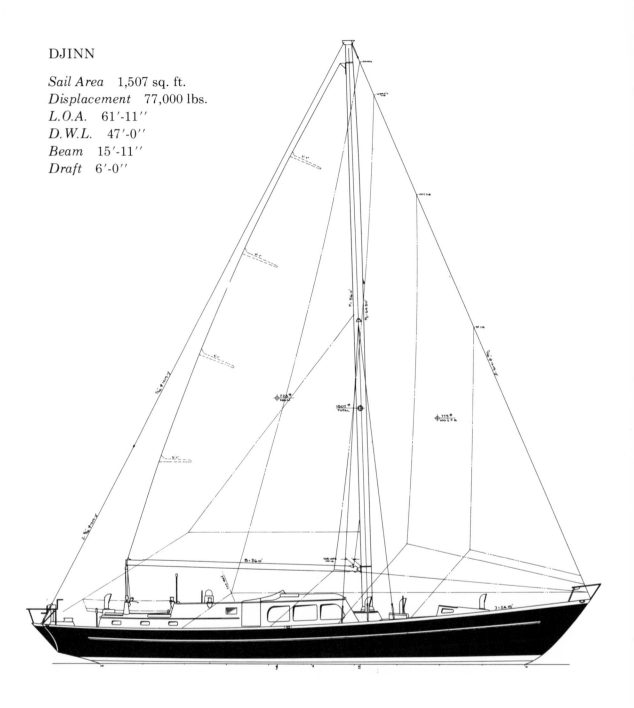

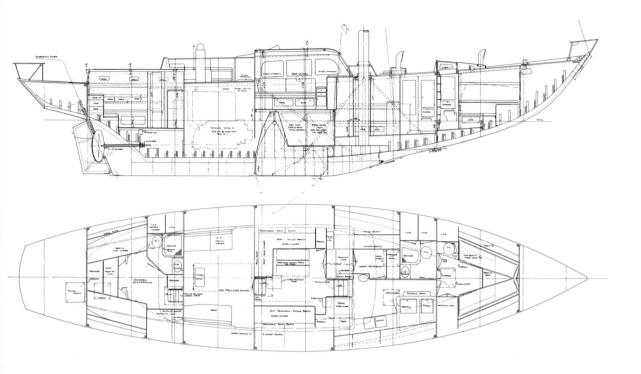

was built by Higgins in New Orleans. There were over 400 wooden submarine chasers built to S & S design. The firm was also design agent for 178-foot tankers, of which 100 were built; many are still in service.

Later for the Navy the firm had charge of overseeing the plan work and inspection on alterations of destroyer escorts for conversion to fast troop transports, APD's, used in the Pacific to carry the Marines. Very sensibly, the higher topsides were not welded on but were riveted the length of the joint, so that the destroyer escorts would not be pulled out of shape, moving their shafts out of line, which surely would have happened if welding had been used.

Olin supervised a lot of miscellaneous work, such as design for the lead landing craft used for the Normany and Sicily invasions.

Later, during the Korean War, the firm did the design work on the 145' wooden minesweepers that had to be nonmagnetic so they could sweep up magnetic mines. Ammunition transfer ships 580' long of 21 knots were built from S & S contract plans and specifications at the request of the Navy's Bureau of Ships.

To go back to World War II again, the Army had a design competition for a floating bridge, which Sparkman & Stephens won. Not only was it interesting, it also contributed to the Allies' victory. Because of loosing a lot of bridges and tanks crossing the flooding Arno River in the invasion of Italy, the Army set up a testing station in Yuma, Arizona, to try out the design we did. It was called a ponton bridge, and it was important that it should work.

YANKEE

Sail Area   1,323 sq. ft.
Displacement   62,500 lbs.
L.O.A.   50'-7''
D.W.L.   42'-6''
Beam   15'-4''
Draft   4'-0''

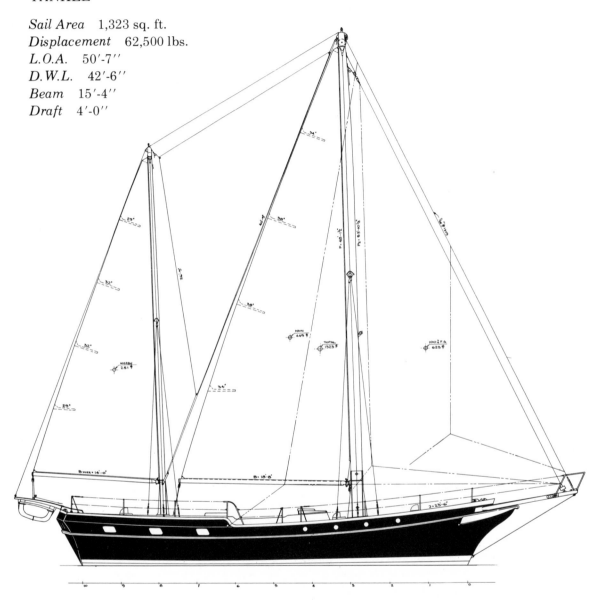

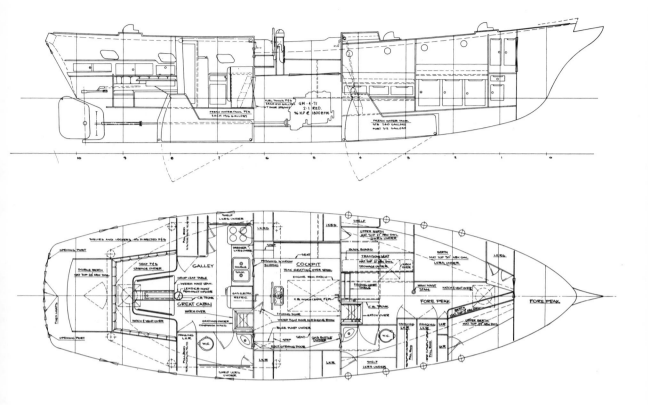

The boats in the floating bridge were aluminum and were connected stern to stern, their sterns being square across. The old ponton bridges before this design had always had boats, framework, and decking. Our design called for square box girders of hollow aluminum members, which could float, staggered over the gunnels to form both structure and deck at once. They lay longitudinally across the river at right angles to the boats that supported this deck, forming a bridge with elastic support. The Army used it for tanks as well as trucks, jeeps, and other vehicles. Because it was lighter and quicker to install, so much time was saved for this vital operation that it was a good contribution to our war effort.

Although the firm is noted for the boats it designs, there was a period after the war when Sparkman & Stephens took on a 563' ship, the *Atlantic,* an American Banner Lines ship formerly a Mariner cargo vessel, converted so that she carried 862 tourist passengers, 40 in first class, and a crew of 330. We had 7 inspectors on the job at Ingall's Shipyard and several design agents for this interesting job. Our job was to approve all their plans, then obtain the Maritime Administration's approval, and also approval from the Coast Guard on all the various calculations. The line is now defunct and the ship is at present a cruise ship in Mexican hands.

ESCORT   (Rosenfeld)

This is by no means a complete list of all the power, naval, and commercial vessels on which Sparkman & Stephens worked one way or another. There were a lot of small ferries (most recently the firm is serving as technical representatives and is responsible for plan approval and inspection of the 132' Fisher's Island auto-passenger ferry) as well as tugboats and barges that the firm designed—quite a contrast to the America's Cup twelve-meter sloops.

That brings to mind one very significant design project S & S received from Rudy Schaefer. He wanted to build and sail a full-size replica of the original 105' schooner *America*. The only change made was to put outside lead ballast on the keel of the replica. Otherwise she was kept to the same shape and had the identical rig, as well as a similar deck layout, to begin her new life. The first year in commission she was filmed for a half-hour movie commercial used on television to advertise Schaefer beer. The interior of the original *America* was quite stark, but belowdecks the replica was arranged to accommodate the owner and his guests as well as the crew in modern-day comfort. The original *America* had a round cockpit with a very long tiller, while the replica had hers only until after the movies, and then was given wheel steering. Her second year in commission, after the purpose of advertising was satisfied, saw a deckhouse added just forward of the cockpit, and a foretriangle change. To make her easier to handle, a double-head rig with forestaysail fitted with a boom was incorporated. She was built of wood with great pride by Goudy & Stevens Shipyard in East Boothbay, Maine.

A General Motors V-8 diesel powers her at a speed of 11 knots in calm weather, whereas the original schooner simply had to wait for a breeze. Some other amenities of the updated model that were not invented in the 1850's for the original are: electric lights, storage batteries, generators, a deep freeze and refrigerator, air-conditioning, a dishwasher, a laundry machine, an oil-fired central heating system, an automatic pilot, radar, radio telephone, loran, depth finder, etc. She is always a magnificent sight to see when under sail, with her two raked masts, old-fashioned gaff-rigged sails, and main topsail set. I am particularly interested as a yacht designer to observe the very flat stern wave she leaves behind when sailing.

There is another type of yacht, a motor sailer. S & S has done many. Their performance varies from that of mostly power, such as a seagoing powerboat with sails to assist and steady, as *Bird of Passage,* to a really well-termed "sailing" motor sailer such as *Cruzan* to an ocean cruiser such as *Palawan,* which is capable of going anywhere anytime, and does just that. They are comfortable boats to live aboard with their spacious quarters given prime importance, double the amount of power the same size auxiliary would have, and all necessary machinery to provide all the amenities of the good life.

It seems to have been my specialty for a time now at S & S to do this type. I like creating new ones, making them seaworthy, commodious, and able to sail well, but yet power better than an auxiliary. Carrying out the owner's ideas when working with him is good fun, especially as one is not restricted by rating rules, just good sense.

ROD   (Rosenfeld)

10 *Rod and the Seagoing Trucks*

Rejected, blacklisted, pigeonholed, scoffed at by nearly every general and admiral in Washington, "the truck that goes to sea" helped win World War II only because three determined civilians would not give up on it. For four years Rod was one of those three.

It was at dawn on a day in July, 1943, when Allied forces began to land on Sicily. That same night the weather turned ugly and a vicious surf built up, pounding the beaches, capsizing and wrecking landing craft, threatening to cut off Allied troops without food, ammunition, reinforcements, or supplies. Then through the darkness, like an answer to prayer, came a strange fleet of unique amphibious craft.

They were the secret DUKW's, the "trucks that go to sea." This fleet was composed of nearly 1,000 of them. For sixty crucial hours through that pounding, crashing surf they brought ashore nearly 90% of all cargo, directly from the transports, over the treacherous sand, and on the beach roads to the front lines.

General Eisenhower, in charge of the invasion, reported to Washington: "Amphibious truck 2½ ton, commonly called DUKW, has been invaluable. . . . Suggest commendation for officer responsible for its development."

Back in the Pentagon, General Marshall passed the message to his aide, noting: "I agree. Please determine what officer deserves this commendation."

His aide, after making a search, reported, "No one in the War Department had anything to do with the development of the DUKW except to oppose it."

It was true. The DUKW had been turned down at one time or another by every top-ranking general in Washington to whom it had been referred, including the chief of the Army Ground Forces, and the chief of the Corps of Engineers. Nor would the Navy touch it. The DUKW nevertheless was built, thanks to a trio of civilians who were willing to fight anybody, including our own generals and admirals, to win the war.

These three determined men were: Palmer Cosslett Putnam, a yachtsman, geologist, idea man, and the driving force behind the Weasel, a snow-and-mud vehicle. Next, Dennis Puleston, a Britisher who became an American citizen. He was an expert on small boats, having sailed across the Atlantic in a 30-foot boat and spent years cruising around the Solomons, the Gilberts, the New Guinea coast, and the East Indies; he knew the intricate passages, channels, and reefs of Guadalcanal, Luzon, and Tarawa. The third was Rod, selected because he was eminently qualified to serve with this pair by virtue of his first-hand experience designing, building, inspecting, and sailing small boats many thousands of nautical miles in every kind of weather and sea condition. Both he and Puleston separately became the finest and most successful teachers of troops assigned to the DUKW's. It was a staggering workload to take on.

At the start there was another yachtsman with them, Roger Warner, an industrial chemist and engineer very adept at solving mechanical problems. Later he was transferred to the atomic bomb laboratory in New Mexico and then to the Pacific, where he was one of the civilian scientists assigned to assemble that bomb and observe the attack on Hiroshima. All these men worked for the Office of Scientific Research and Development, headed by Dr. Vannevar Bush. The sum total of their combined knowledge of practical amphibious warfare was at the start roughly zero. But their knowledge of small boats, of marine engines, rigging, hull design, of tricky reefs, shoal waters, and pounding surf added up to a very great deal.

They came to know more about back doors in the Pentagon than the architects that designed the place. When they were turned down by one general they went over him, under him, or around him. If they had been under full military control, they would have been court-martialed. These men had vision. Remembering Clemenceau's warning that "war is too important to leave to the military," they forced on the services more than 21,000 DUKW's that these same services at first refused to order. Overseas they trained more than 15,000 American, British, Canadian, Australian, and Indian crews, and for months each of them risked his life in the battle zones. They did a job that the Army admitted years later was remarkable.

The idea of the DUKW was originated by Palmer Putnam and Rod Stephens, Jr. However, the necessity of discharging cargo directly across a beach had been clearly foreseen by their chief, Hartley Rowe, vice-president and chief engineer of the United Fruit Company and head of the government's transportation-research division, who took the idea to Dr. Bush before the war.

"As early as 1942 it seemed inevitable that we'd need something like the DUKW," Rod and Palmer Putnam agreed. "Foreign ports were being jammed—ships waiting two or three months for barges, barges waiting for trucks, trucks waiting for trains. If we could get an amphibian that could take cargo at high speeds from a ship lying off a coast and bring it right up to a road or railroad, it would speed up shipping so much that it would be just as good as adding millions of tons to the allied merchant fleet."

Rod and Palmer Putnam argued that it just did not seem logical that harbors or piers would be ready for the use of our invasion forces. Certainly not after bombings, sabotage, and enemy demolition. It seemed to them that landings, particularly in the Pacific theater, would have to be made on open beaches, perhaps through heavy surf over reefs and sandbars.

As far as they knew, in 1942 there was nothing in production or even under development that could handle the job. Dr. Bush ordered his men to design such an amphibian.

They received warm encouragement from General Jake Devers, then the chief of the Armored Forces, who was looking for a way to get his tanks ashore from ships lying near shore. Another general, Ted Dillon of the Transportation Corps, was also enthusiastic. It was suggested that they arrange to have General Motors Truck and Coach division at Pontiac, Michigan, build four pilot models. At this point the Army's purchasing department heard about the proposed new vehicle. "Don't do it!" they said. "It's just another special vehicle, and we've got too many already." One general said, "Even if it happens to be the most perfect vehicle ever built, we don't want it. It won't fit into our plans."

To which Dr. Bush suggested, "Maybe you ought to change your plans." The commanding general, Brenon Somervell, turned thumbs-down. "Nobody wants it," he told Dr. Bush. So Dr. Bush called Putnam and told him the bad news. "Better not start," were his words.

"We've already started," said Putnam.

"Then stop."

"That would be a pity. Those fellows out at General Motors have been working their hearts out. Besides, the first pilot model will be tested in the water next week," he replied. On the spur of the moment Dr. Bush put through a call to General Somervell and made a bargain. "If you give me your blessing on that first model, we'll cancel the other three." The general agreed.

GM, by working day and night, delivered Pilot Model No. 1 just thirty-eight days after receipt of the first go-ahead. In its initial tests at Pontiac it traveled at a speed of 45 mph on hard roads, and in the water the bargelike hull with six wheel appendages worked her way up to 6 mph. Not bad considering that shape.

"She's not very fast" admitted Rod, "but she's better in water than any truck, and she'll beat any boat on a highway!"

How did this strange creation get to be called DUKW? It was because of

GM's code system used in their engineering department. "D" stood for the year 1942, "U" for utility, "K" for front-wheel drive, and "W" for two rear-driving axles (thus the six wheels all powered).

Military observers watching the first trials were not enthusiastic. But it so happened that at that very moment the problem of landing supplies on the European beaches suddenly became vitally important. General Somervell ordered his aide to do something about it. Who was his aide? None other than the famous general who had been seemingly trapped on three sides by the Germans at the Battle of the Bulge and had replied, "Nuts!" when they demanded he surrender. This man, A. C. McAuliffe, then a colonel, outlined his new problem at lunch one day to his hosts in Washington, Hartley Rowe and Palmer Putnam.

"I think," said Putnam, "we have exactly what you want. You already know about it. It's the DUKW."

"The DUKW?" repeated McAuliffe. "But what about its wheels? Won't wheels get stuck in sand?"

"My business," said Rowe, "is landing cargo. I've been landing cargo and picking it up on the beaches of South America and Central America for more years than I'd like to count. I can assure you, Colonel, that a wheeled vehicle like ours will cross 90% of the beaches in the world. Don't worry about sand. If you keep the tire pressure high for hard roads, but keep it low for sand, you'll be all right."

Colonel McAuliffe was convinced. He ordered 2,000 units built at once.

But more and higher hurdles were still to come. When the first DUKW was completed and put through its paces before groups of officers in Michigan, Virginia, and Maryland, none of the spectators were impressed or enthusiastic.

Rod and Putnam knew that unless there was a warm and general acceptance, Colonel McAuliffe's 2,000 DUKW's might sit the war out in some Detroit warehouse. But there was still a chance. A big demonstration had been arranged near Provincetown on the ocean side of Cape Cod. Through friends in the War Department, a Liberty ship was provided even though there was a shipping shortage, and a detachment of recruits fresh from Midwest farms. They were then trained intensively for three weeks and began to operate like sailors.

Four days before the scheduled large demonstration, during a gale blowing on shore, a Coast Guard officer, drenched and seemingly in a state of shock, rushed through the door of the little inn that was headquarters. "I'm Commander Allison," he said. "One of my boats with seven men is aground on a bar out there. Do you think your DUKW's can get through this surf?"

Throwing on his foul-weather gear, Rod started the engine of one of the DUKW's and sped down the road to the beach. There a group of Coast Guardsmen were standing by helplessly, unable to use their surfboats or breeches buoy. When Rod looked where they pointed, he saw a 50-foot patrol boat a quarter of a mile offshore being pounded on the sandbar by the breaking waves. He headed his DUKW straight into the high surf. A breaker hit her, exploded into spray obscuring her. When it cleared, the powerless men on shore saw her behaving just like a seal slipping from shore and swimming out through the seas. On she went to the rescue. In six minutes Rod was back with all seven shipwrecked Coast Guardsmen. Their 50-footer vanished during that night.

Two days later, Secretary of War Stimson went to the White House for a Cabinet meeting. He rose and with a wink at Frank Knox, Secretary of the Navy, offered a bit of news. "Mr. President," he said, "two nights ago, from Cape Cod, an Army truck went to sea and rescued the men from a stranded naval vessel."

Four days later, when the DUKW's staged their big demonstration, there were 86 top-ranking enthusiastic officials on hand. Each thought, "I'm sold." So the Army ice was cracked.

The boss of the Navy's Atlantic Amphibious Forces, Vice Admiral Henry K. Hewitt, was working out his plans for the Sicilian invasion. He was invited to watch the DUKW's perform at Fort Story, Virginia, and was amazed to see the trucks competing with the conventional Navy combination of ordinary landing boats and sailors in a human chain passing the cargo, box by box, through the icy surf. The trucks were doing much better in every respect. Immediately he gave the order for 2,000 DUKW's for the Navy.

It was at this exhibition that Putnam demonstrated an air pump permanently connected to the tires, so that the driver could lower tire pressure for traveling over soft sand, and raise it to make the tires harder for roads or coral, without stopping. This device was adopted for all DUKW's, because it allowed them to keep going despite almost anything that happened to the tires.

Someone in the Navy turned thumbs-down on Admiral Hewitt's order. By Navy standards, it was thought, DUKW's were not seaworthy. So the DUKW's that saved the troops that first night of the invasion of Sicily were operated by Army men.

Before that invasion Putnam heard that the DUKW's were to be operated by green crews. When no one else in Washington paid any attention to his warning of what would happen if the DUKW's went into battle, and how a disastrous result might befall them without special training for their crews, he went to the British mission. The British were buying DUKW's, so they paid attention. They promptly asked for American experts to provide this training. Rod and Warner were selected and rushed to Scotland.

When the training was underway, Admiral Lord Louis Mountbatten called to ask if there was anything they needed.

"We don't have enough spare parts for repairs," said Rod, "and we have too many damn admirals asking for joyrides."

The training time was tight. Rod and Warner instructed almost around the clock, alternating with groups of crews. When the DUKW's went into their first action at Sicily and later at Anzio, they proved invaluable. For hour after hour they came through the surf, bringing guns and ammunition right up to the front lines, carrying high-test gasoline directly from ships to the planes on newly captured airstrips. The DUKW crews' training paid off. They were good, and they were cocky.

Off Anzio, one driver alongside a cargo ship saw an oversize load being lowered down to his DUKW. He started to move off. "I'm not taking that load!" he called back. "It's too big!"

"I order you to take this load!" came a shout from the ship's deck.

"Yeah? And who are you?"

"I'm the first mate of this ship! Now, damn it, get back alongside!"

"In your eye!" said the DUKW driver. "I'm the captain of this here DUKW, and you can keep a civil tongue in your head when talking to your superiors."

The DUKW was now accepted in the Mediterranean Theater, but Rod discovered that the creation he and his colleagues worked so hard on was blacklisted in the Pacific and regarded as a flop. In Noumea it had begun brilliantly, but afterwards it had been used by untrained men, put on jobs it could not handle, and finally discarded. So Rod went to the Pacific, taking DUKW's to Guadalcanal, Tulagi, and the Russell Islands to show overworked officers on jammed beaches how his vehicle could help.

Back in the United States, meanwhile, Putnam got wind of some disturbing news. It seemed that Admiral Mountbatten wanted to order 8,000 DUKW's for an invasion of Burma up the Irrawaddy River. Putnam sought out Mountbatten's representative in Washington and argued, "But the Irrawaddy is nothing but mud, and DUKW's won't work in mud. That's the one terrain they can't manage." Through his boss, Dr. Bush, Putnam got to meet Mountbatten at Quebec at a conference with Churchill and President Roosevelt.

"I understand you're uneasy about some of my plans," Admiral Mountbatten remarked a little dryly.

"I am, sir," said one determined civilian. "In the first place, I don't think the DUKW's can be produced as fast as you want them. Second, they can't operate in mud. And third, if you plan to use them without providing intensive training, your amphibious operations will fail."

After thinking a minute the Admiral said, "Come out to India. I think you can help us."

On his way out Putnam was invited to a series of staff conferences at Pearl Harbor about three months before the assault on Tarawa, then being planned by the Navy with the Marines. He was asked about the DUKW and tried his very best to convince them it would do the job well.

The Navy brass listened to the proposals he made and then turned them down. Once again he was told, "No amphibian can go where a landing boat can't."

Between this planning and the actual assault on Tarawa, two successful landings were made over worse coral using DUKW's. One was at Funafuti, the other at Nanumea, both with well-trained crews. After each, Rod and his colleague urgently requested the Navy to reconsider using DUKW's. But the commitment had been made to attempt the assault on Tarawa without them. When those landings were made, the Marine Corps lost a lot of good men. They came in aboard landing boats as far as the coral shelf, plunged into water up to their chests, and stumbled toward the beach. They were hit with mortar shells that exploded underwater with horrible concussion. Tarawa was the last major landing in which DUKW's were not used.

The battle-wise Marine and Army commanders saw clearly the fast, elastic kind of attack DUKW's used by well-trained crews could provide. In New Guinea, at Melue Bay, a demonstration was arranged for MacArthur and his generals. The DUKW's came in from landing three miles off the beach, carrying howitzers, ammunition, and gun crews. Landing on soft sand, they crashed through the jungle, found the rendezvous, unloaded, and went back to sea to pick up another load. It happened so fast the spectators were flabbergasted. "This," the generals said, "we'll buy."

A few weeks later at Arawe, the enemy was hit with DUKW's. Thereafter, this new and nimble assault became standard operating procedure. The Japanese never did solve a defense for it—not at New Britain, Peleliu, or Kwajalein, nor at Guam or Saipan. Nor at Tinian, where a storm struck just after the first landings, as in Sicily. The DUKW's kept the supply lines open.

Putnam and Puleston went on to India, where Mountbatten was waiting to confer on where and how DUKW's could be used in Burma. Puleston was put in charge of training the crews. After three weeks Putnam moved on to Algiers to work with the men planning the invasion of southern France, then to London to work on plans for the Normandy landings.

Puleston sweated it out with crews near Bombay, training them, rehearsing them, checking their equipment—and doing it over and over again until the men could do it in their sleep. He embarked and landed with them under fire on the Arakan coast in northeast Burma. Then one morning an enemy shell hit, a cargo boom snapped, and cargo came crashing down on him.

When he woke up in a British military hospital the doctors told him, "You're out of the war." Three weeks later he received orders to report to Eisenhower's headquarters in London. Although the doctors told him his spine was fractured in six places and his scalp was still wide open, he caught the next plane.

In General Eisenhower's headquarters he was told that Dr. Bush had asked Rod and him to help prepare the huge combined DUKW fleet, American, Canadian, and British, for the invasion of Normandy. The Americans were green and largely untrained. Thirty percent of them had never seen an amphibian before. Others had taken a thirty-minute ride in the cargo compartment while an officer did the driving. Still others had never used DUKW's in water rougher than a millpond. Their equipment was not in fighting trim. Spare parts were missing, and many vehicles lacked essential new modifications.

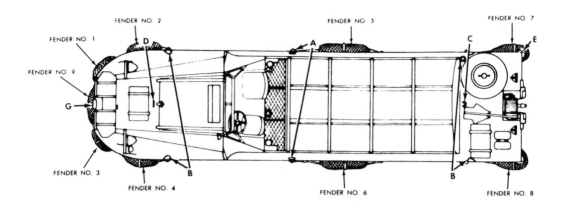

FENDER NO. 1 FENDER NO. 2 FENDER NO. 5 FENDER NO. 7

FENDER NO. 9

FENDER NO. 3 FENDER NO. 4 FENDER NO. 6 FENDER NO. 8

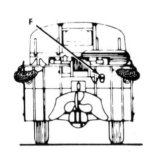

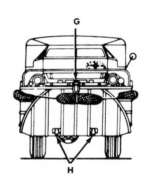

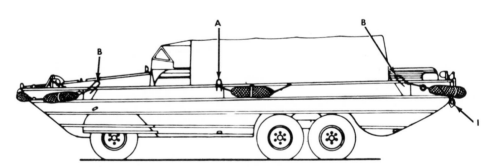

A MOORING EYES   F TOW CHAIN SHACKLE
B LIFTING EYES   G WINCH CHOCK
C LIFTING EYE (REAR)   H TOW HOOK SHACKLES
D LIFTING EYE (FRONT)   I PINTLE HOOK
E LASHING EYES

Puleston and Rod really pitched in. To give as much training as possible in the little time that was left, they split the men into two groups apiece. The first was handled from 4 A.M. (when it was just getting light) until 1 P.M The second from 1:30 P.M. until 11 at night. They took no days off.

The men they trained achieved a record at Normandy that perhaps will never be surpassed. For 13 weeks, despite enemy strafing, confusion, mistakes, and the unexpected storms that came to Hitler's aid by kicking up a treacherous surf all along the coast, they and their DUKW's landed more than 40% of all cargo brought across the beaches.

"The German High Command," said one American observer, "based its strategy on the delusion that we could not supply an army of several million men across stormy beaches. The DUKW had a major part in surprising the enemy and inflicting a catastrophic defeat upon him."

After Normandy, Puleston went back to the United States for a rest, he hoped. But Dr. Bush had urged the Army to establish a new DUKW school in Hawaii. "Do you think you possibly feel up to running it?" he was asked. The Marines needed him and, at long last, the Navy. So Puleston found himself training men of all three branches of the service.

In the meantime Rod was sent to the Philippines to consult on operations there and at Iwo Jima. Both he and Puleston were getting set to train men to roll up the beaches of Japan when the war ended.

Rod was justly honored by being awarded the Medal of Freedom, our country's highest award to a civilian in time of war, which can only be given by the President. The citation with it reads in part: "Mr. Roderick Stephens, Jr., American civilian, rendered meritorious service in England, Guadacanal and Pacific Ocean Areas. Having assisted in the design of the amphibious jeep and DUKW and related amphibious devices, he instructed higher commands in the technical use of this equipment. His characteristic enthusiasm and drive contributed materially to furthering the success of Amphibious warfare."

One day after the war was over, at the entrance to the harbor of Junsen, in Korea, a fleet of DUKW's was nearing port when they were overtaken by a flotilla of destroyers. As one captain to another, the skipper of the lead DUKW gravely signaled his respects to the lead destroyer. Watching for the reply he saw that narrow, fast vessel's lights blinking a two-word answer. It read: "QUACK-QUACK." He accepted it with a grin as a mark of well-deserved recognition of his craft's achievements.

11 Yacht Brokerage and Marine Insurance

What goes on in the S & S brokerage office is a different activity from the happenings at the firm's design office, where I work. Now both are together at 79 Madison Avenue, which is at 28th Street in New York City. I had a chat with Bob Garland about the brokerage aspect. He is the top yacht broker at S & S, and I wondered roughly what was the total yearly value of the boats he himself handled when buying, selling, and chartering for his clientele.

"Probably something over $3 million worth of yachts a year," he told me.

Then I asked, "Do you find that when there's an America's Cup Race you get more clients?"

"Well, I think there's a general heightening of interest in yachting," he replied, "and it's more apparent in the chartering of yachts during the summer, and a little more purchase and sale of boats going on. It's a big show, particularly the final trials, which seem to create more interest for knowledgeable yachtsmen than the Cup races themselves."

I asked Bob when he started with the firm and he told me it was in 1931, after the transatlantic race, 46 years ago. He thought for a minute, then said, "I didn't realize it had been as long as that. I got to know the Stephens brothers over there in England. Rod was at that time working for Nevins. He started out with Nevins, and was a very good yacht builder long before he ever came to S & S. At that time Drake Sparkman was running the business, and I joined up with him after I came back.

SHIELDS CLASS
(Rosenfeld)

"Roger Haddock started a yacht brokerage firm around 1920, and he decided in 1927 that he'd had enough and retired, and asked Drake if he wanted to take over the business, which Drake did, and did very well," Bob went on.

"I'm sure you must have some interesting stories," was my next question, "about some of these big deals you have handled and some of the extraordinary ways buyers have handled paying for them. Have you had any people pay you cash directly?"

"Yes, there have been a few of those, Frank. Not as many as you might expect, but we had one recently who bought a yacht in Europe for a sum of well over $300,000. We were surprised to hear from him one day that he was sending a courier to New York with the money. The courier showed up. She was an attractive young girl with a satchel, and it was filled with bills of fairly small denominations. We were somewhat nonplussed with that, but made arrangements with the Citibank to not only count the money, but I think the term is 'wash it': They looked over the money, and surprisingly enough it was not counterfeit. Hadn't been taken illegally from anyone. It was perfectly good money. The bank made their report to the IRS. It was a legitimate deal—the man just wanted to deal in cash. There was one thing that embarrassed the courier. When the satchel was opened up in the bank, the only article on top of the bills was some lingerie!

"There have been other peculiar instances," Bob related. "A long time ago we were outfitting the *Joseph Conrad,* a square-rig ship for Huntington Hartford, and he was looking around for a starboard launch. We found one at Fyfe's Shipyard, which seemed to be suitable, and discovered that it belonged to the yacht *Black Watch,* which in 1927 had been used to greet the Prince of Wales when he made his first visit to the United States. She went down the harbor and picked him off the Cunarder he came over on and brought him out to Glen Cove. When the owner of the starboard launch was approached with a bid of about $1,200, this was in the mid-1930's, he said, 'Well, I'll sell you the launch on one condition for this money, and that is if you'll take the *Black Watch* as well.' It's a hundred-foot yacht. Hartford didn't want the *Black Watch,* but his Russian Captain Trunan did, so the deal was made.

"For $1,200 Trunan got a handsome hundred-foot power yacht in sound condition and Hartford got the starboard launch.

"It just illustrates the fact that yachts weren't very negotiable items in the Depression and shortly after the Depression. There's another interesting thing. In 1931 we had a listing describing yachts that were offered for sale. We usually divided them into various types of sailboats and powerboats. But the distinguishing feature of this book, which was of fair size, was that it was comprised of auxiliary sloops, yawls, and ketches, each one of which was for sale at a price of $1,000 or under. I think the largest in that book was 52' overall.

"There wasn't much money floating around in those days. And the clientele changed from one which was principally stockbrokers to white-collar workers. They were the yacht buyers in the early 1930's."

"Bob, another question. I know that lots of clients you brought in for new designs seem to ask you later, when the boat is built, to help as part of the crew. For instance, I know that Lee Loomis was one of these with his new *Northern Light*. Who are some of the others?"

"Tom Watson, Porter Schutt, Bill Stocks, Jack Potter, Dick Reynolds. There've been a number," he recalled, "and I can't name them all, but they are a few that are prominently in mind. I've certainly gotten a lot of pleasure out of this. As an old ballad went, 'It's part of an officer's pay.'"

"What outstanding races have they won, when you were aboard helping out?" I asked.

"We won in our class several times with *Equation* and *Blitzen* in Bermuda races, and were first to finish twice aboard *Northern Light* and *Baruna*. There have been other races, too, such as the Queen's Cup, the Seawanhaka Cup, and in the Mount Desert Race, but not quite so prominent," he answered.

"It seems to me, Bob, it's good insurance for the firm to have excellent sailors, like Olin and Rod and yourself, taking part in active races and helping to win them. And speaking of that," I said, "don't you think the desire to win is what makes clients willing to pay almost any price for a fast boat?"

"The desire to win is very strong in many people, and it certainly has sparked a great development of the ocean racing fleet. Originally, when I started, I think that people were racing because it took them to sea. The cruising fleets were far from the present types that we have, but after racing a little while, the desire to win seems to have taken over, and many people build new boats every few years just for this purpose. I have a feeling that this era is coming to an end, and there may be more emphasis on cruising in the next generation than on the all-out racers, who may go in for 'Grand Prix' racing. That number will be very limited, I believe."

This was encouraging to me, because I seem to be doing the cruising boats and such types in the design office now.

"You have your own boat that you race at Seawanhaka. It's a Shields Class boat, isn't it, Bob?"

"Yes, I've been racing that since the class came out, Frank. We have a very good class, and there are a number of those boats in the western end of the Sound that gives us a very good fleet."

"These boats are a pretty sight when they're all together," I noted. "Each is beautiful with her long, graceful ends. She must be a very comfortable and well-mannered boat to sail."

"They're an excellent club boat, because they are stable. They're easily handled with not too many strings. You don't have to have a first-class crew

SHIELDS CLASS

Sail Area   360 sq. ft.
Displacement   4,600 lbs.
L.O.A.   30'-2''
D.W.L.   20'-0''
Beam   6'-5''
Draft   4'-9''

MAIN 222 ♦

TOTAL 360 ♦

100 % F △
138 ♦

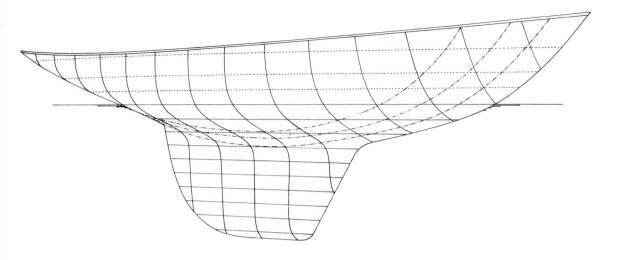

every time you go out. The boats can be sailed (but not raced) by one person without any difficulty, with pleasure and in a hard breeze. It's just a good, healthy type of boat," Bob added.

"To go back to the beginning of the firm, Bob, do you have some thoughts about six meters?"

"I remember the first six meter that Olin brought out was called *Thalia.* I first raced on her. Olin had gotten me a berth on the boat, and I raced her off Larchmont not very successfully. It was a very lucky thing for Olin that before *Thalia* was launched he was commissioned to design *Comet* and *Meteor,* two other six meters that came out the same year. They happened to be outstanding. If *Thalia* had been the only boat, it might have taken a little longer for Olin to get started. However, the great majority of Olin's other sixes worked out very successfully. I know from having participated in some of those Seawanhaka Cup and Scandinavian Gold Cup races, where *Goose* and *Lanoria* turned out to be winners."

Then I asked him what his job was as crew on them. He replied, "A very easy one in the after cockpit with the helmsman, setting up backstays mostly, and giving a little free tactical advice to the helmsman."

"I had the first half of that job on Phil Roosevelt's *Jill,*" I said. "We went to Scotland in 1936 and stayed in the Royal Clyde Yacht Club. My job was just the running backstays. Pat Merle Smith and I. One had the port one and the other had the starboard one. And that's all I had to do. Jimmy Roosmaniere was part of that crew, too, and his job was the genoa sheet. Also we had a paid hand, a Norwegian fellow, Olie, who set the spinnaker. But Phil was all alone at the tiller and the rest of us were down below sitting on the boards on the bottom of the boat, down under the deck, where crews on the twelve meters have been until recently. And all you could see when the boat heeled beating to windward

ANITRA

Sail Area   1,068 sq. ft.
Displacement   29,762 lbs.
L.O.A.   48'-5''
D.W.L.   33'-6''
Beam   12'-4''
Draft   6'-11''

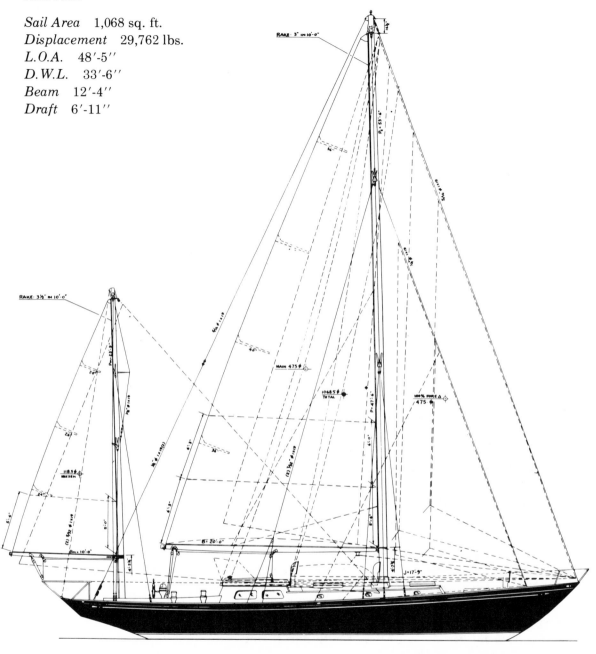

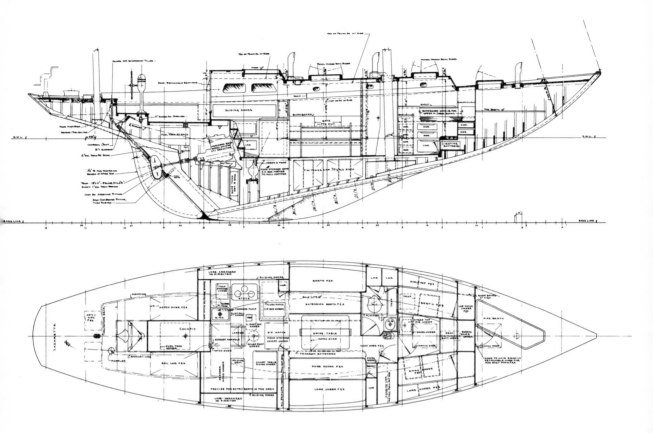

was out horizontally just above the coaming and just beneath the foot of the genoa jib through a little slot about 6″ high and 4′ long. You couldn't see much of any other boats, or anything else. You were just a machine pulling on one rope at the right moment."

"Well, you know, Frank, you speak of a professional on those six-meters. Some of them had as many as two pros on them, but I think that would be a subject for a very good book about the pros. Most of them were Norwegians who came from the island of Tisnis. You've mentioned Olie, with whom I have sailed many times, mostly on *Good News*. And he was on *Goose*. Olie Kalgraf. And there was Harry and Sandpaper Gus."

"Sandpaper Gus? Why that nickname?" I asked.

"Because they were all good at using 'Norwegian steam' very good on varnishing and sandpapering. But there were many of those men, quite an outstanding group. They were excellent sailors. Peter Hansen was another one. Despite the Scandinavian name, he came from Scotland. They did a whole lot to help the quality of racing back in the 1920's and early 1930's."

"I remembered I read somewhere that in 1937 the crew of *Ranger,* the big J boat, consisted of almost the entire population of a Norwegian fishing village."

"It could well be that little island of Tisnis," Bob said, "where the best of them seem to have been born and raised."

HEAVENS ABOVE

Sail Area 382 sq. ft.
Displacement 4,610 lbs.
L.O.A. 27'-11''
D.W.L. 21'-3''
Beam 7'-0''
Draft 3'-10''

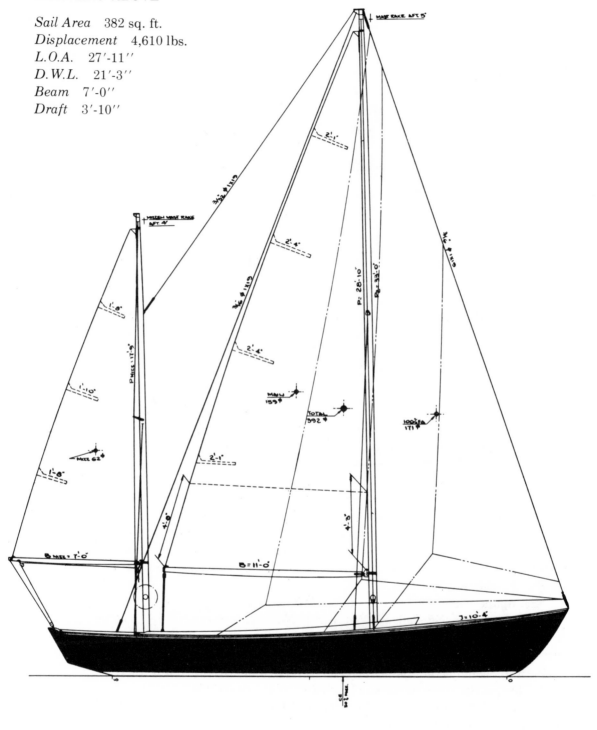

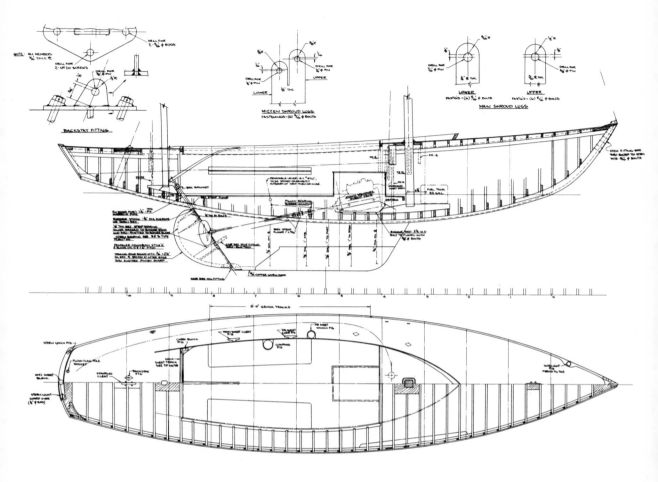

Because these boats did not have any winch to hoist the mainsail up, there was instead a cheek block at the base of the mast. They all lined up on the deck, tailed out on this halyard, and just gave it the heave-ho. It went up much quicker that way, of course, than it would if you had cranked it up by hand on a winch.

"It certainly is amazing," Bob went on, "to see those models in the New York Yacht Club of sailboats which had 90′ spinnaker poles, main booms that must have been 90′ or 100′ long. It seems incredible to have over 14,000 square feet in a Cup boat's sail area."

It is a lesson in economics to go around that room, especially for the America's Cup boats and the models in their showcases. All of a sudden it changes from 1937, with *Ranger* and *Endeavour*, the English challenger, to 1958, which was the next race, and they were so much smaller. The amount of money spent on the Cup races for individual boats has remained more or less constant, but the size of the boat has come down.

"It seems to me most people go out and buy a fiberglass stockboat nowadays, and they're getting bigger and bigger," I noted. "Have you had any

MERMAID

Sail Area 1,032 sq. ft.
Displacement 27,600 lbs.
L.O.A. 45'-8"
D.W.L. 32'-4"
Beam 11'-6"
Draft 6'-8"

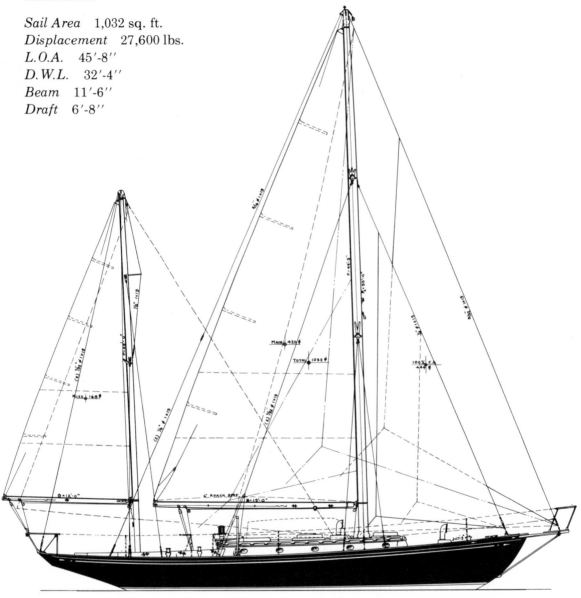

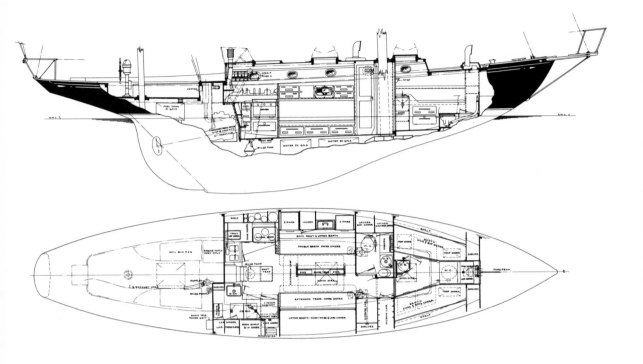

experience on any of these stockboats that are around? Of course your Shield's is a fiberglass boat. Do you prefer certain ones over others?" I asked.

"That's a leading question, Frank. There are a few excellent builders of fiberglass yachts, and then a large group that builds run-of-the-mill type, which may or may not be good for offshore water. There are many good ones. Swans from the Nautor Company in Finland I think are the best built. You can't just close the list, because there are always other good builders."

"There are some pretty hairy tales, Bob," I went on. "There was one fiber-glass boat that was sailed from this area around New York down to the Carib-bean and was approaching Granada, where there was a big yacht marina and shipyard. She was almost within sight of the island and was heeling over, sailing between the islands where the breeze is pretty strong and the seas run quite high. The skipper went below to look at the chart, and he saw water over the cabin sole. He got scared and started looking around to find out where it was coming from. He found the place, all right. It was coming from the joint between the hull and the deck! And as you know, most fiberglass boats are in two pieces—one piece is the hull and the other is the deck, and they have to be joined together. And here was practically one of the only joints that the boat builder had to make, and he made it so poorly that the deck was lifting off. If it hadn't been for the quick action of the skipper and his crew, she might have swamped and sunk right then and there."

"Well, it happens," Bob said. "I just sold a Swan to a Brazilian to sail around the world. He was very insistent that he get a strong, seaworthy boat,

FIGARO

Sail Area   1,092 sq. ft.
Displacement   27,550 lbs.
L.O.A.   47'-1''
D.W.L.   33'-0''
Beam   12'-2''
Draft   4'-5''

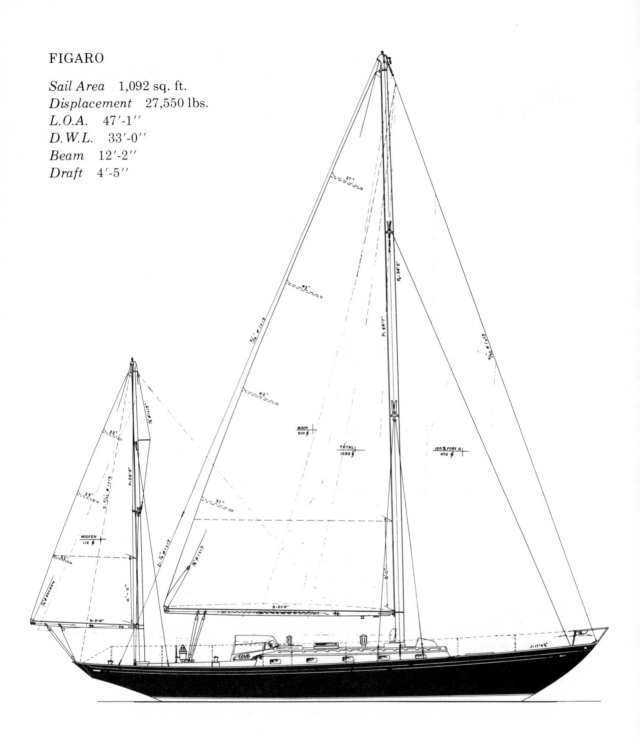

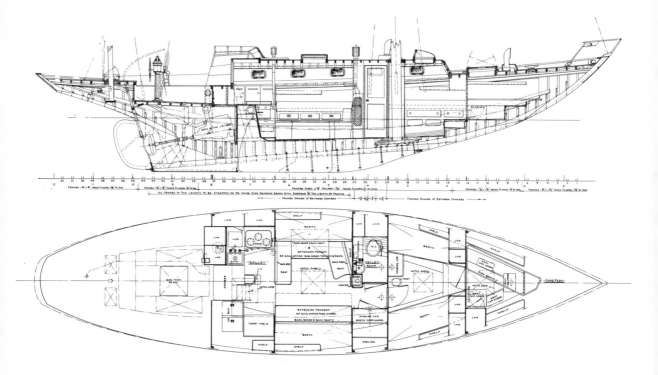

because he told me he had had a 45-footer (not one of ours) last year making a passage off the Brazilian coast when the rudder quadrant broke, and they had no way of controlling the rudder. It banged back and forth till it loosened the stuffing box on the rudder post, and it leaked copiously. Finally the rudder went through the hull and the vessel went down in a minute."

"How do you mean the rudder went through the hull?" I asked incredulously.

"The rudder actually banged itself through the hull as though it were breaking an eggshell. The top of the rudder was swinging completely from one side to the other in a rough sea, and there's no way they could control it, because the quadrant was gone. It wasn't just the cable breaking, the quadrant was gone. It finally ruptured the shell," Bob explained. "It's no wonder people look for sound construction."

The sea can be mighty treacherous. Nobody knows what happened to *Revonoc* when Harvey Conover was sailing around from the west coast of Florida to Miami on the east coast. The only thing they found was *Revonoc*'s dinghy washed up on the beach. It's still one of the mysteries of the sea. She certainly was very well built of wood by Bob Derecktor. She was one of the family of boats that was mothered by *Finisterre*, 29' on the water as against 27'6'', which *Finisterre* was.

"I have always felt that she was run down by a tanker or other vessel coming up the Gulf Stream. When a big ship hits a wooden yacht, I doubt whether

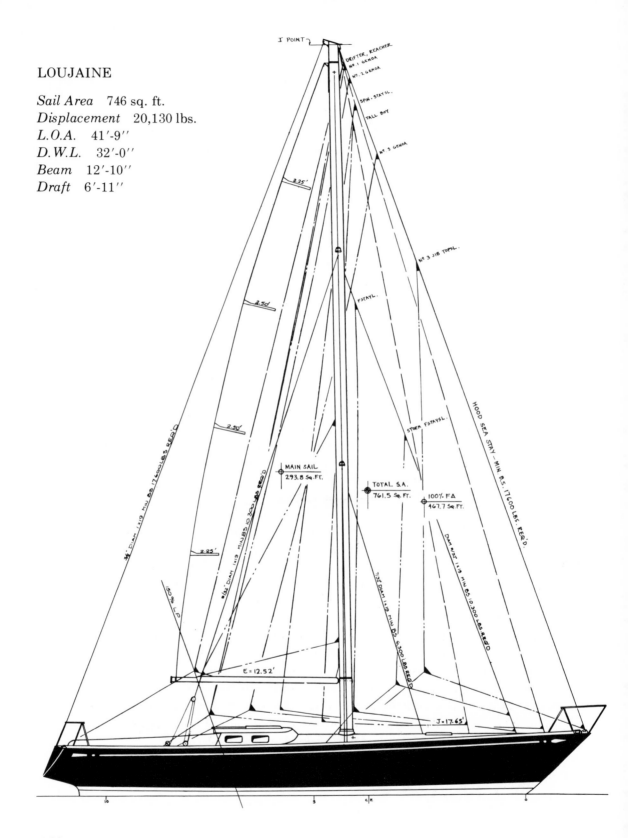

LOUJAINE

Sail Area 746 sq. ft.
Displacement 20,130 lbs.
L.O.A. 41'-9''
D.W.L. 32'-0''
Beam 12'-10''
Draft 6'-11''

I POINT

DRIFTER, REACHER
Nº 1 GENOA
Nº 2 GENOA

SPIN. STAY SL.

TALL BOY

Nº 3 GENOA

Nº 3 JIB TOPSL.

FSTAYL.

STORM FSTAYSL.

MAIN SAIL
293.8 Sq.FT.

TOTAL S.A.
761.5 Sq.FT.

100% FA
467.7 Sq.FT.

HOOD SEA STAY — MIN. B.S. 17,600 LBS. REQ'D.

E = 12.52'

J = 17.65'

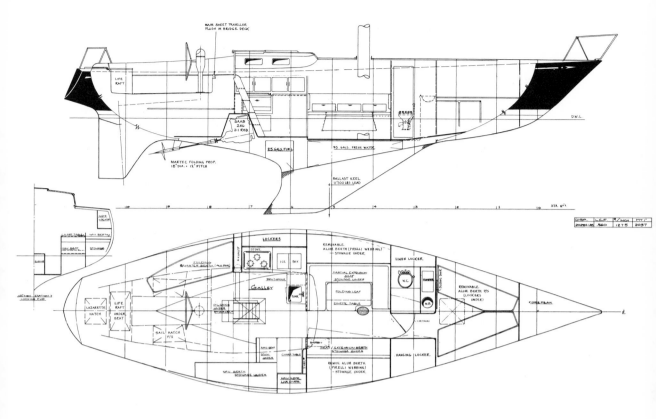

there's even a jar aboard the steamer," said Bob. "I've heard tales from Bill Moore of a Mooremac liner going across the fishing banks and hitting something, and that the only reason they knew they hit anything was a section of mast fell on the foredeck. They stopped the vessel and went back and picked up a few men.

"I heard an amusing story from a friend of mine in Rye, New York, who built a 37′ ketch in Nova Scotia and had it on Long Island Sound shortly after World War II," Bob went on. "We had a severe squall on July 4 reported to have blown 100 mph. He was sailing off Matinnecock Point when the squall hit. The vessel was flung on her beam ends. The airports in the trunk cabin were open, so she filled and went down. He was swimming around with his son, age about 9, and another man. They had a hatch cover that they were hanging onto. The squall was over, and the powerboats were streaming home down the Sound. One after the other would go right by them in the water and not stop. One powerboat came by with a man at the wheel and a woman in the cockpit, and they shouted to her. She threw over a life preserver on about 30′ of line, and it just missed them. The powerboat never turned back. She pulled in the life preserver at the end of the line, coiled it up, and they kept on going."

"That's terrible," I said. "He must have gotten to shore or he couldn't have told the story. Well, you know that very same weekend of the July 4th holiday, I remember it so well. It was in the early 1950's, wasn't it, Bob?"

"It had to be, because I was racing a Seawanhaka 21 at that time, and was also out in the squall. We were coming into Oyster Bay and I saw on the point of land, Rocky Point, that sand was being blown up into the air, and I realized we were in for something heavy. We took down our genoa at that point."

"We were in our little 28′ *Santa Maria* at that point," I recalled, "which was basically an open boat. It had a deep cockpit amidships. With two of my young children, we had started out from our mooring at Lloyd Harbor, taking two fellows on board who were going to charter the boat. In order to show them the ropes, I wanted them to come out for a sail before I turned her over to them. We decided we would sail around to the Beach Club, which we often do. It's a nice sail, about 10 miles, and you get all points of sailing on the same breeze. The wind was northwest. We started beating out behind Lloyd Neck and got out past Target Rock. I was just looking around to check things. It was absolutely a blue sky, not a cloud anywhere. And on the horizon looking out toward Stamford to the northwest I saw white water on the surface. Then I saw a fair-size yawl, 45′ or so, absolutely knocked down, with her mast and sails in the water. She was about 2 miles to windward. Without even stopping to do anything I said, 'Lower the mainsail and furl it.' Hap Johnson was on board—he was Henry Taylor's son-in-law, and was the navigator on *Baruna* in several Bermuda races. Well, he said, 'Did you say furl it?' And I said, 'Yes, and hurry!' He got it down.

"We just had a small working jib set then, because the boat had a ⅞ foretriangle. I bore away. So when the squall hit us, we were going before the wind with just this very small jib set. We had a little dory 12′ long. It was strictly for rowing, and 12′ of course was too long to stow on a 28′ boat. So we towed it everywhere we went. It was a very nice little boat. We were towing it when the waves started building up behind us.

"We saw all kinds of boats in trouble running before the wind. A powerboat passed, and she'd go down the front of a wave and her little bit of a rudder would come right up out of the water. It's a wonder she didn't broach. But she kept going downwind as best as she could. Anyway, the dory capsized. I had a ⅜″ nylon towing pennant on it with an eye splice and thimble on an eye bolt right through the stem of the dory. That was so strong it didn't part. So the dory was going along upside down almost like a submarine surfacing. Well, it acted as a beautiful sea anchor, and we slowed down. Otherwise we would have probably had to go down the Sound way past Eaton's Neck. But our overturned dory kept us from going too fast. Finally the blow subsided, and we came alongside the dory and righted her, bailed her out, hoisted the mainsail and sailed back in again. And there was poor Mary—she really must have been worried, standing on the bank in front of our house looking for us with binoculars. We showed up back at our same mooring about an hour after we set sail. It was quite an experience, I'll tell you, Bob."

"Yes, that's the hardest squall I ever sailed through," Bob agreed.

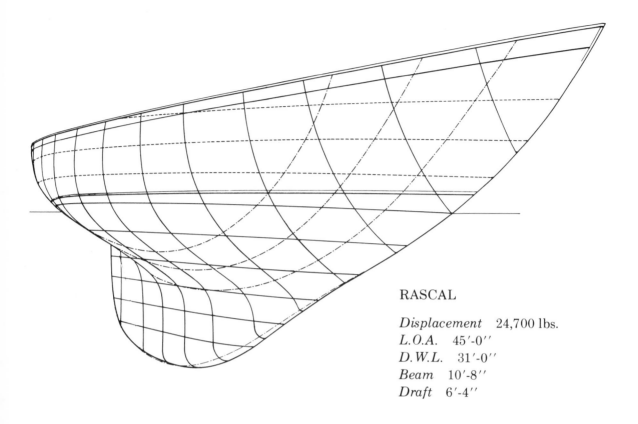

RASCAL

Displacement 24,700 lbs.
L.O.A. 45'-0''
D.W.L. 31'-0''
Beam 10'-8''
Draft 6'-4''

"You know, before we were talking about racing and six meters. It might amuse you to know," Bob went on, "that one of the people I sailed with was Herman Whiton, usually known as 'Swede,' who was an Olympic champion I think twice in the six-meter class and a very good sailor. But he was also a very volatile man and became very excited. If he became too excited, he didn't sail well. So one of my duties, as well as handling the backstays, was to keep him calm. We were sailing on the Sound in a big fleet and the Coast Guard was keeping the yachts away from the competing six meters. But one lone ship came down the middle of the Sound right through the spectator fleet. The Coast Guard couldn't handle this big ship, and Swede was getting more and more excited, and the vessel finally came alongside, and we read the name on it, *Herman Fresh.* The ship was owned by Swede's company, the Union Sulphur Company, and was named after his grandfather. I hate to think what happened to that skipper."

The other yacht brokers at S & S are: James D. Sparkman, Drake's brother, senior broker since 1929, in charge of powerboat sales. Then there is

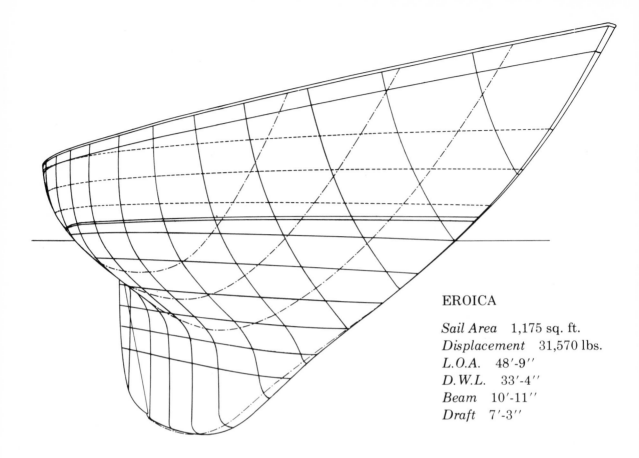

EROICA

Sail Area   1,175 sq. ft.
Displacement   31,570 lbs.
L.O.A.   48'-9"
D.W.L.   33'-4"
Beam   10'-11"
Draft   7'-3"

Roger Critchlow, who joined the firm in 1969. Carlos Echeverria has been a broker since 1974. Tom Curtis since 1975, and now Mitch Neff has recently come aboard. Among the old-timers were Porter Buck, now deceased, who was with the firm since the early 1930's, and Ed Payne, now retired. Ed suffered a heart attack and recovered at age 72 to sail his 25-foot overall S & S sloop *Pippin* to Bermuda with one other youngster of 65.

Marine insurance is a helpful service the firm provides for its clients, and this is handled by Drake's son, Bob Sparkman. He is the only one of the second generation of either a Sparkman or a Stephens who is now in the firm. The third generation is represented by his daughter, Annemarie Sparkman, now with us in the design department. Wanting to learn about this end of the firm's work, I queried Bob one day. My nickname for him is the "Benny Goodman" of Sparkman & Stephens.

"I can't tell you how much I enjoy that Basin Street music of yours when you play the clarinet with your group," I enthused, but then changed the sub-

IMPALA   (Fortier)

ject and asked if he would tell me about some serious happenings showing how necessary it is for an owner to protect himself against loss.

"One of the most spectacular losses was a near total one we had on Jim Wickersham's *Gannet,*" he said. "She was built in Holland, custom designed, balsa core, fiberglass construction, and was caught downwind of a fire aboard a powerboat in Yacht Haven West in Stamford, and was substantially damaged almost to the point of a total loss. But she was repaired and is back racing, and I think this is as good an example of functional marine insurance as anything I can think of today."

"It cost more than 90% of her current market value to repair her," Bob explained. "One of the big problems we have today is that with the older boats the spread between their insured or invested value and their replacement cost is so great it's hard to put numbers on insuring the boats.

"The insurance company can only respond up to the face amount of the policy. The big problem that marine underwriters are having today is what to do with the older boats, and a lot of them won't even insure them. They try to work out compromises by recognizing to some degree the aspect of replacement cost, but they don't wish to encourage losses either, by insuring a boat for more than an owner has in her.

"Before the war the Weekenders, for instance, that were built by Lawley in 1938, were sold for $5,700 each with sails. Wonderful boats. Simple. Some didn't have any electricity; they had kerosene lights, and magneto ignition on the engine. After World War II those boats were selling for $15,000. The same boats!"

If I lost my boat, I'd like another one exactly like her," I said. "I come to you and say, 'Now you've got my policy, please fix it up so I can duplicate this boat if she's a total loss.'"

"Well, there are two things to consider," Bob replied. "Number one, you don't have to worry about coinsurance, as you do with a homeowner's policy. Number two, the likelihood of total loss is very remote. Statistically it's not an impossibility. We'll have possibly one total loss every five years, and the recent ones we've had have been in one-design classes, where the values at which most boats are insured reflect the general market value.

"For instance, if you sink a Shields and have her insured for $8,000, you can pick up a secondhand Shields for $8,000 or maybe even less.

"One of the nice things about marine insurance is that it retains a consistency, which you don't find in other forms of insurance, because it's subject to Admiralty Law," Bob revealed. "And this has the effect of making the entire field conservative with regard to values and response to liability."

"During the October 1976 tornado, what about all those boats that were wrecked along the Connecticut shore? Did you insure many of them?" I questioned.

"Yes, we had our fair share of them. You remember Charlie Mower? He is in the salvage business now. One of Ed Greeff's former *Puffin* boats came adrift of her mooring line and went ashore, and Charlie did the salvage job on her. There's a little stone island sitting in the middle of the harbor at Greenwich, and she went right up on that, high and dry. There's a good example. She's a boat insured for considerably less than her replacement cost, and with the salvage bill added to the repair cost, the fact is that her repair bill will probably run fairly close to her total insured value by the time everything is in. But there's just nothing we can do."

"Will you pay the whole thing then?"

"Yes."

One of the Fort Schuyler Shields boats was racing when that same storm suddenly struck, and it started to blow very hard. One of the stake boats went out to call the fleet in. They got to all of them except the lead boat. She was knocked down and got hit by an 80 mph gust or better when the worst of the front came through. She swamped. There are hatch plates they have on the forward bulkhead to seal the forward flotation tank. Those compartments are used for storage a lot, and the covers don't get put back in place, so she filled up and sank in a few minutes."

"Did her people get off all right, Bob?"

"Yes, they got off, but they didn't have time to lower the sails or anything. The skipper had a tense moment when his foot tangled in the mainsheet, but he did get free. It was a vicious knockdown."

I asked, "Supposing a situation like this occurs: Two boats are beating to windward in good fair weather with fine visibility, and they have low-cut genoa jibs, so-called 'deck sweepers,' but the helmsman cannot see for half of his field of vision—that is, the entire leeward side. Suppose two such boats are coming on opposite tacks. They both have their blind side toward one another, and all of a sudden there's a collision. Who's at fault?"

"There's a principle of cross liabilities, which is more and more becoming applied in cases like this," he explained.

"Such a case happened in Cold Spring Harbor not too long ago, and I had to handle another in the middle of the Sound this summer. In these cases, when they're not racing, and there's no protest, the Coast Guard has held that where visibility is limited by low-cut genoa jibs, you're bound and liable to maintain a watch on the forward deck, to make sure that this doesn't happen. We had a case where there was a youngster up forward as a lookout. But there was a misunderstanding between the youngster and the skipper, his father, as to which of several white boats he was warning his father about. All of a sudden there was a collision. The father thought he saw another boat to windward approaching, and he thought that's the boat his son was referring to. But his son was referring to a boat to leeward, one the father couldn't see. And that case was settled on the basis of cross liabilities, with each responding to the other's damage in proportion to his degree of responsibility, determined by a Coast Guard hearing. Both parties were found negligent, because even though one party maintained a watch and the other didn't, the one without a lookout forward was a starboard tack boat, and the one with a lookout was a port tack boat."

"Were you involved at some time with explosions from gasoline fuel?" I asked.

"That has been the single biggest kind of loss over the past decade or so. So there's been a great attempt to upgrade ventilation in engine compartments," he said.

"Forced air requirements. As a matter of fact, the National Fire Protection Association makes no distinction between gas and diesel engines with respect to ventilation requirements. They do with respect to materials for tanks, I understand. But the problem has been that diesel fuel has been a sleeper as far as explosions and fires go. It was considered to be much safer than gas, but recent experience had indicated it may not be for reasons of which nobody is quite sure," continued Bob. "It's suspected that intense speeds and a lot of vibrations may cause a breakdown in the fuel system, and you might get a leak in a fuel line where diesel oil under pressure atomizes or vaporizes. It reaches a flash point that is comparable to gas leaks. A spark of some kind can set it off. There have been about a half a dozen explosions in the last 5 years on diesel boats, with no other kind of a fuel on board."

"That would astonish most people," I said. "We always specify that the fuel lines have a flexible fireproof section in them so that it absorbs the vibration. But a lot of these engine manufacturers put that down as an extra. I'm afraid that some of these stock boat companies that have to keep their price down in order to compete don't buy any extras like that. It seems to me they are of vital necessity to safety.

"Bob, can you tell me more about your dad? How did he get interested in being a yacht broker, and in the insurance of yachts?"

"Dad's interest was a natural one, which he acquired at a very early age, and I think it was perfectly natural for him to go into the yacht brokerage business. His interest in insurance I think started because he was a great friend of John Grimes, one of the principals of the Chubb organization and a good friend of Percy Chubb. Percy's father knew my grandfather. And I think when Dad opened the office, because of his friendship for those people, he liked the whole concept of service to his clients. And I think that's why he took a great personal interest in that end of the business.

"From a purely practical business standpoint, I don't think there's a better way to maintain a good relationship with a client after you sell him the boat than to handle his insurance. There's nothing worse than seeing a boat that's been grounded, or dismasted. On the other hand, there's nothing more satisfying than to see her sailing again," said Bob with a broad grin.

"There are so many people," I concluded, "that wonder how Olin and Rod Stephens could succeed so well. This teamwork of the brothers and their father and your father, Drake Sparkman, all pulled together and contributed something necessary. They worked so well together that it was a great success. You mentioned how much mutual respect they had for each other."

"I think that was the key to it, Frank, in addition to ability and a lot of hard work. The fact is, I have never seen the kind of unflagging mutual respect year in and year out that existed between the Stephenses and my father. Dad had the deepest kind of respect for Olin's personal integrity and his ability, and Rod's energy and his unequalled capability for hard work and thoroughness."

12 *Two New York Yacht Club One-Design Classes*

In my opinion sailboat racing is at its best when done in a one-design class. This is so, it seems to me, because from the time you start maneuvering for the best position crossing the line at the start to the time you finish the course, you always know where you stand in relation to the other boats in the race. The first boat to finish is number one and gets the prize. Each one-design class boat is designed and built to be exactly similar to the others in her class. The sport, then, is a fair competition.

Another thing that's fun about racing in a one-design class is that racing tactics are important. For instance, in beating to windward, getting the weather berth is important, or maintaining a "safe leeward position" just ahead of the four-boat length blanketed area, and avoiding "the hopeless position" in that area to leeward, as these terms were defined in Dr. Manfred Curry's old book on racing tactics. Going downwind there are many maneuvers like blanketing the boat ahead to take her wind, or on a reach never trying to pass close aboard to leeward, a tactic that will almost never succeed. Another trick is taking the long tack first on a windward leg in hopes the wind will change enough to give you a lift and thus eliminate taking the short tack. Rounding buoys has its good and bad tactics as well.

Even a knowledgeable race committee will lay out the starting line with the first leg of the race a beat to windward in such a way as to favor the port tack. Why? Because the

MUSTANG, Rod's New York 32
(Rosenfeld)

N.Y. 32 CLASS

Sail Area 990 sq. ft.
Displacement 26,750 lbs.
L.O.A. 45'-4''
D.W.L. 32'-0''
Beam 10'-7''
Draft 6'-6''

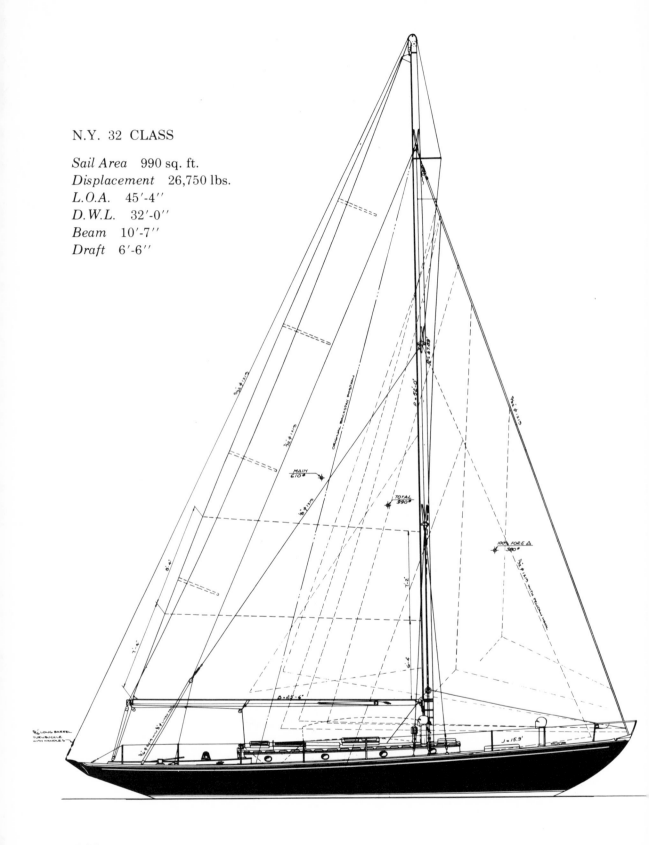

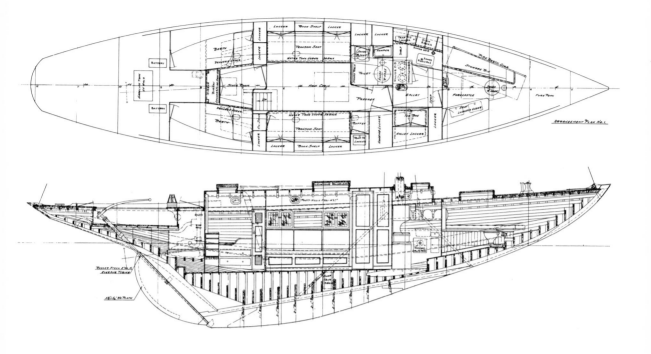

starboard tack boats have the right-of-way, and 99% of them will not take a chance on a port tack start. It is thus very exciting for the daring skippers, the other 1% of the fleet, to take this chance and with rare skill slip across the starting line on the risky port take ahead of the timid souls bunched together on the starboard tack.

And so with this idea of having more fun, yacht clubs have encouraged the development of one-design classes, the racing of sailboats being their primary reason for existence. One particular club has done this with quite large boats. It is the New York Yacht Club. There are two one-design classes that S & S has done for them just forty years apart in time. The first was the New York 32's in 1936, and the second the New York 48's in 1976. Comparing these two one-design classes is a lesson in the development of yacht design, construction, rigging, winches, materials for both hulls and sails, hull shapes, engines, and fuel used. A lot of improvements have occurred during that length of time, which you will see comparing S & S Design 125, the N.Y. 32, with Design 2281-C1, the latest N.Y. 48 Class. Line by line they are as follows:

The N.Y. 32 cost $11,000 complete with sails. Her dimensions were L.O.A. 45'-4½'', D.W.L. 32'-0'', beam 10'-7'', and draft 6'-6''. There were 20 boats built. (Rod bought No. 17 from the late Harvey Conover.) The latest N.Y. 48 Class dimensions are L.O.A. 47.9', D.W.L. 34.5', beam 13.76', draft 5.5' board up and 8.8' board down. Her draft is shallower because she is a centerboarder, but look at the big difference in beam—3′ more. There is a big difference in cost as well: about 20 times as much.

N.Y. 32 displacement is 24,550 pounds to D.W.L. Her underwater profile is like *Dorade*'s. The N.Y. 48 Class displacement is 27,952 pounds to D.W.L., and her underwater profile incorporates the divided keel and rudder with its skeg.

N.Y. 32 ballast is 10,200 pounds of lead. The new N.Y. 48 Class has 16,840 pounds of lead slotted for her centerboard, which is a 1″ thick stainless steel plate with an elliptical-shaped leading edge and a sharp trailing edge. It is hoisted by a two-part rope tackle through a pipe stanchion to a reversible centerboard winch on deck.

Sail area on the N.Y. 32 is 990 square feet total, with 610 square feet in the mainsail and 380 square feet in the foretriangle, which is a ⅞ foretraingle sloop rig. Because of this she has running back stays as well as jumper struts and stays, a complicated rig compared to the new class. Her mast, boom, and spinnaker pole are all hollow of "airplane spruce," as her specs read.

On the other hand, the new class is a simple masthead-rigged sloop with a total of 1,077 square feet of sail area, 483 square feet being in the mainsail and 594 square feet in the foretriangle—just the reverse emphasis from the N.Y. 32. The permanent back stay does the job of keeping her jibstay tight, so simple compared to the complication of her 40-year-old counterpart. Her aluminum spars, not available in 1936, are a great improvement over the wooden ones. Rod rigging and larger, more powerful winches are other improvements in standing rigging and the handling of genoa sheets. Then too, the material of the sails themselves is such good quality, being Dacron, which holds its shape and is stronger than the old cotton sails, which would mildew and rot, unheard of now. Ropes also used to rot. Manila, sisal, and even linen were nowhere nearly as good as present-day nylon and dacron. Just coming on the market now are certain dacron ropes so constructed that they hardly stretch at all. They are taking the place of wire halyards, eliminating the annoying fish hooks that develop in 7 × 19 wire, so unpleasant to handle.

Both the old and the new classes are auxiliaries. So it is interesting to note the improvements on engines.

The N.Y. 32 has a Gray Light Four gasoline engine of 16 horsepower at 1,800 RPM with a 2:1 reduction gear. It is rubber-mounted and turns an automatic two-bladed feathering propeller of 18″ diameter and 13″ pitch. The shaft angles aft to miss the rudder stock, and turns the propeller above and aft of the rudder. No aperture spoils her sailing qualities.

The new class is equipped with a Volvo Penta MD21A four-cylinder diesel engine of 51 horsepower at 3,000 RPM with a 2.9:1 reduction gear turning a two-bladed folding propeller of 21″ diameter. Her shaft, because of her cutaway profile, comes out ahead of the skeg and rudder and is held by a single strut. This combination of folding propeller and single strut has given other boats trouble, because if one blade refuses to unfold, so much vibration is set up that it breaks the strut. The old-fashioned Herreshoff folding propellers with teeth meshing together at the base of the blades prevented one blade from unfolding without the other doing exactly the same.

Small diesels were not yet invented in 1936 to suit boats of these two classes. Everyone knows of their greater safety and economy of fuel consumption as well as their being less troublesome, but since I can report on them from firsthand experience on my own boats, let me note it for the record. Our second *Santa Maria,* slightly larger than the third, cruised under power just above 6½ knots using 3 gallons of gasoline per hour. The third boat we had of the same name cruised at exactly 6½ knots under power using .85 gallons of diesel fuel per hour. There's the difference. In this case we powered more than three times as far on a gallon of diesel fuel as we had with gasoline. This gives a great extension of a boat's range under power. As for trouble, with a diesel you have only half as much as a gasoline engine has, because a diesel has no ignition system. So your only trouble comes from dirt or water in the fuel, or running the tank dry. It takes about 15 minutes, if the diesel supply line runs dry, to loosen about nine nuts and "bleed" them with the hand wobble pump on the engine, then tighten them and restart with a fresh supply of fuel. Good metal filters (never glass—it breaks) will keep out dirt and water.

Auxiliary machinery? The N.Y. 32 had little or none. But the new class has electric refrigeration for the chill space and freeze space in her built-in refrigerator. She also has a freshwater pressure unit with faucets at the wash-basins, galley sinks, and showers. Hot water is made by running the engine, and is stored in an insulated tank. These amenities were unknown on sailboats forty years ago. Imagine—a hot shower!

Electrical equipment? The N.Y. 32's had just a few electric lights below, that's all. On deck they had brass oil running lights on light boards, and oil anchor lights. There was little need to run the engine just to charge the batteries, a very desirable attribute.

The new class has two alternators on the engine. (There's another new invention, alternators. They are better than the old generators because they charge at lower RPMs.). One 38 amp is standard with the engine to charge the starting battery, and one 68 amp to charge the lighting batteries. Also there is a shore power system to use when plugged into 110-volt alternating current. The batteries are themselves quite hefty to do all the work they have to (95 A.H. 12-volt starting and 285 A.H. 12-volt lighting batteries), but are useful ballast.

Now for the comparison of the two galleys. The N.Y. 32 layout allows for a paid hand to live in the foc's'le, so her galley is forward in way of the mast, where the paid hand could easily do the cooking. It had a fixed two-burner pressure alcohol stove with an oven above and a tank in the base. There was an icebox, Monel-lined with block cork insulation, capable of holding ice almost all

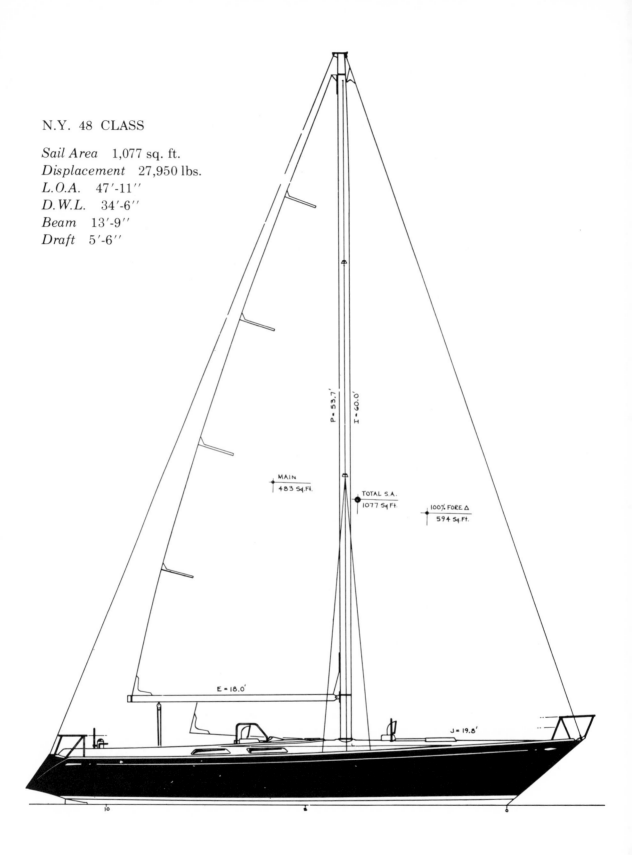

N.Y. 48 CLASS

Sail Area 1,077 sq. ft.
Displacement 27,950 lbs.
L.O.A. 47'-11''
D.W.L. 34'-6''
Beam 13'-9''
Draft 5'-6''

P = 53.7'

I = 60.0'

MAIN
483 Sq.Ft.

TOTAL S.A.
1077 Sq.Ft.

100% FORE △
594 Sq.Ft.

E = 18.0'

J = 19.8'

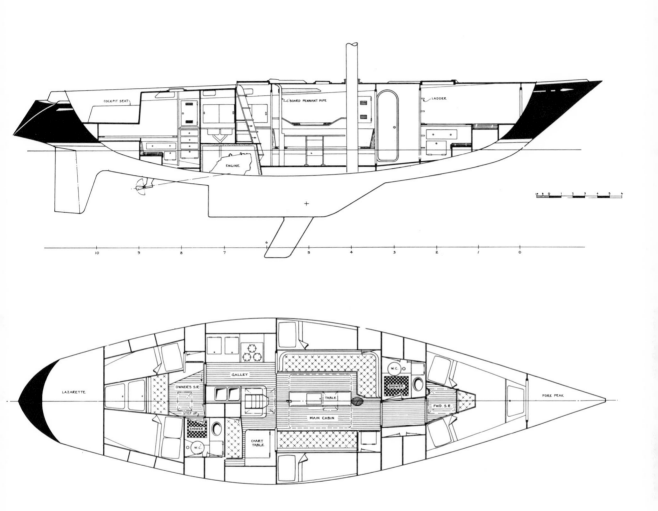

COCKPIT SEAT

C.BOARD PENNANT PIPE

LADDER

ENGINE

10   9   8   7   6   5   4   3   2   1   0

LAZARETTE

OWNER'S S.R.

GALLEY

W.C.

FORE PEAK

STEP UP

TABLE

FWD. S.R.

SHOWER

MAIN CABIN

W.C.

CHART TABLE

241

the way from Newport to Bermuda. It was a good galley with a large sink and lots of shelf and locker space going clear across the boat, but it had one bad drawback: too much motion that far forward.

The galley in the new class is just aft of amidships, the location in all boats where there is the least motion from pitching and heaving in a seaway. The stove's great improvement is that it can swing on gimbals. Also it uses gas as fuel, which is far more convenient than alcohol. For safety, the gas bottles are mounted in a drained and sealed metal locker under the lazarette hatch. The all-important shutoff valves are adjacent to the stove and at the bottles. A double sink is located in this galley very close to the centerline of the boat, so that it will drain directly overboard no matter at what angle of heel she sails. The refrigerator is top opening, built like the old N.Y. 32's but with plastic foam insulation instead of cork.

Steering on the N.Y. 32 is by an ash tiller with a bronze fitting keyed to the rudder stock to permit vertical motion, but no horizontal play. The compass is mounted in its binnacle on a shelf at the bridge deck. The compass specified had a 4½'' card underlighted with a rheostat-controlled electric light. A spare kerosene binnacle light was also specified.

The new class boats have steering gear consisting of a large-diameter destroyer-type wheel with rim covered by elkhide, mounted on a pedestal with compass and binnacle on top. Sprocket, nonmagnetic chain and cables connect it to the quadrant, which also can be fitted with an emergency tiller. To accommodate the large steering wheel, which allows the helmsman to steer from well to leeward watching the luff of whatever jib is set, the cockpit is laid out in a "T"-shape plan. This permits the helmsman to more easily sit facing forward, because it provides a well for his feet athwartships. To starboard, on the centerline, or to port he has that well for his feet. There is also a cockpit sole ramp sloped 20° on each side to have a flat, level surface for good footing when she is sailing hard close-hauled and heeling.

What about tanks? The N.Y. 32 had one tinned copper gasoline tank of 25 gallon capacity, and two tin-lined copper freshwater tanks carrying a total of 76 gallons. The new class has stainless steel tanks with a total of 53 gallons of diesel fuel in two tanks, and a total capacity of 92 gallons of fresh water in five tanks.

Now for construction. Here we find great differences. The N.Y. 32's were of wooden construction built by one of our best yards at that time, Nevins in City Island, N.Y. Their keels were 4⅜'' thick white oak. Frames were steam-bent white oak spaced 8''. Floor timbers were also white oak; those which took the lead keel bolts were wider than others. Limber holes throughout were fitted with brass chain, an old trick to free them by pulling it back and forth. Each boat was started upside down. After being planked with 1¹⁄₁₆'' Philippine mahogany in narrow widths (having white oak butt blocks well spaced throughout), they were turned right side up to receive their interior joinery, spruce deck beams, $\frac{7}{8}''$ cedar decking then covered with 8 oz. canvas laid in heavy paint, then the trunk cabin of $1\frac{1}{8}''$ Philippine mahogany was through-bolted to the deck. All fastenings were Everdur bronze (a trade name of a manufacturer of silicon bronze fastenings, still considered the best in the world today). Other members built into the hull were the clamp and shelf of Oregon pine, bilge stringers of three strakes of Philippine mahogany, and a ceiling of $\frac{5}{16}''$ Philippine mahogany.

The lavish use of Philippine mahogany needs some explanation. Like everything else, there are good grades and poor grades of it, depending on just where the trees grow in the Philippine Islands—that is, on which island, and whether on the plains or on the mountains. Some varieties have a course grain, which does not accept varnish or paint well without a priming filler. Nowadays Honduras mahogany is considered tops; it is close-grained and really lovely to see when well varnished.

A refinement in construction of these wooden N.Y. 32's was the hull strapping of $2'' \times \frac{1}{8}''$ Everdur flat bars—two on each side riveted to the $12'' \times \frac{1}{8}''$ chain plates of the same material and extending diagonally forward and aft down to the keel. They made the hull much stronger. One member, the mast step, was improved in later years by the use of metal weldments, but in 1936 the best practice was to use in this case $2''$ white oak logs bolted to 8 floor timers with a space just fore and aft of the heel leaving $1''$ each way for wedges. A tie rod of $\frac{7}{16}''$ Everdur extended from the mast partners down through them and through the mast step to hold the deck from heaving up under strain. All good sailboats are still equipped with this member regardless of the material used to build the boats, for the force is still there to be dealt with.

The toe rail was Mexican mahogany, but the rudder was Philippine mahogany and had an interesting fitment. Bronze plates $\frac{1}{16}'' \times 3\frac{1}{2}''$ were riveted through at the trailing edge to make it sharp and to eliminate chattering. For many years most S & S boats have had this.

The contrast is pronounced when we consider how the new N.Y. 48 Class boats are built. And in this case, too, the builder, Nautor of Pietarsaari, Finland, is considered by many one of the very best in the business.

The hull is built of glassfiber-reinforced polyester by the hand laying-up method with scantlings approved by Lloyd's Register of Shipping. Every yacht is delivered with a Lloyd's Register Building Certificate proving by inspection how strongly she is built. Structural bulkheads are of marine-grade waterproof plywood, laminated to hull and deck. For greater strength all door openings through structural bulkheads are semicircular at the top and have well-rounded corners at the bottom. There are not as many transverse members used in her wooden forerunners of forty years ago, but five longitudinal stiffeners on each side run fore and aft like bilge stringers. They are made of glass-reinforced polyester lay-ups over foam cores. Web floors of the same construction are laminated to the hull. Engine beds are similarly built and reinforced with steel inserts. Special care is taken to assure rigid foundation and proper adhesion to the hull. The deck is of sandwich construction using a foam core, thus eliminating deck beams. Teak decking is laid on top, making a good nonskid surface. Her spars are aluminum extrusions and her standing rigging is both Navtec stainless steel rod and 1 × 19 stainless steel wire with Norseman terminals (the kind that can be attached by hand, not machine).

The greatest difference with this new class over the N.Y. 32 is that of greater strength due to its two-piece construction of fiberglass, the hull, and the deck. There is thus just one joint, which is strongly fastened together by many closely spaced bolts. In contrast, the wooden N.Y. 32 has all those seams between planks, and joints like that between the trunk cabin and deck, with the possibility of leaking. Then too, an equally important advantage of this fiberglass material is greatly reduced maintenance. It is a lot less expensive just to wax and buff the topsides of a fiberglass boat than it is to completely sand and repaint a wooden boat every spring. Antifouling bottom paint must be applied at least once a year to all boat-building materials, but since fiberglass hulls do not have any planking seams to fill, painting the bottom also is less expensive.

Comparing the accommodations of the old and new classes is revealing, too, reflecting the change in living styles in forty years. In 1936 yacht owners of this size boat could afford and did have a paid hand to look after their craft. The fellow had mighty cramped quarters in which to live under the foredeck of those N.Y. 32's, because there was only a little headroom there. In the new class that foc's'le space has become a forward stateroom with two built-in berths, large lockers, drawers, and full headroom because of the higher freeboard.

Unlike the N.Y. 32 two-cabin accommodations, the new ones are divided into three cabins. Privacy is provided by separating the forward cabin from the main two- or four-berth cabin by a head with shower and a locker with bureau across the passageway. Privacy is also provided for the aft cabin by separating it from the main cabin by its own head and shower, by the large galley incorporating the accessible engine box, and by the chart table and navigator's seat. The aft cabin has a double berth and a single berth with drawer beneath and a seat between. There is a locker and a bureau here as well.

The main cabin amidships is quite commodious, being almost 9′ long with an "L"-shape seat to port and seat to starboard around a drop-leaf table on the centerline. There are stowage spaces under the two pilot berths accessible through the seat backrests.

This design utilizes the existing mold for the successful Swan 47, but incorporates the shoal keel and centerboard combination to permit cruising in depths slightly less than 6′. Her rig is 2′ shorter and her boom 2′ longer than the Swan 47, a desirable change. Her ballast is higher to satisfy the Yacht Club's requirement for 65′ bridge clearance.

She has good control with her large rudder and skeg. And with her generous accommodations, well-finished joiner work, complete equipment, as well as strong hull and rig, she is an excellent boat in every respect.

At this writing, 5 boats have been ordered to start the class. Long may they race together.

INTREPID   (Rosenfeld)

13 *Olin's Thinking on the Twelves*

Frank: Olin, I've often been asked by sailor friends just how you always produce a new twelve meter that is faster than the former one of your design. How is that possible?

Olin: Well, it isn't always possible, that's the first thing. It doesn't always work. Fortunately, it has worked several times. I think it's certainly not a sure thing, and I certainly wouldn't want to count on any one particular time, but I think you do learn something each time you study a boat carefully. It is nearly always possible to find something wrong with a given boat and possibly correct it the next time around. I think that is the main thing. We'll get to other points, the sort of relationship between intuition and computation between these things. But we are learning things about the computations all the time. The model testing has caused some difficulties as well as some very good results. In the present case, I certainly wouldn't count on anything; I don't know yet what we've learned. I think the ability to test a much larger scale model has been helpful, plus the ability to compute results and to make new allowances for the effect of the rudder and the trim tab. These things are much more clearly indicated on the large model tests than on the small ones. The better evaluation of especially the side force, which is related to rudder and trim tab effects—these things I'm sure can be more accurately done with the large model, and I think they have been helpful. So, I think there's a certain amount of luck in it. There's not any real magic, but I think

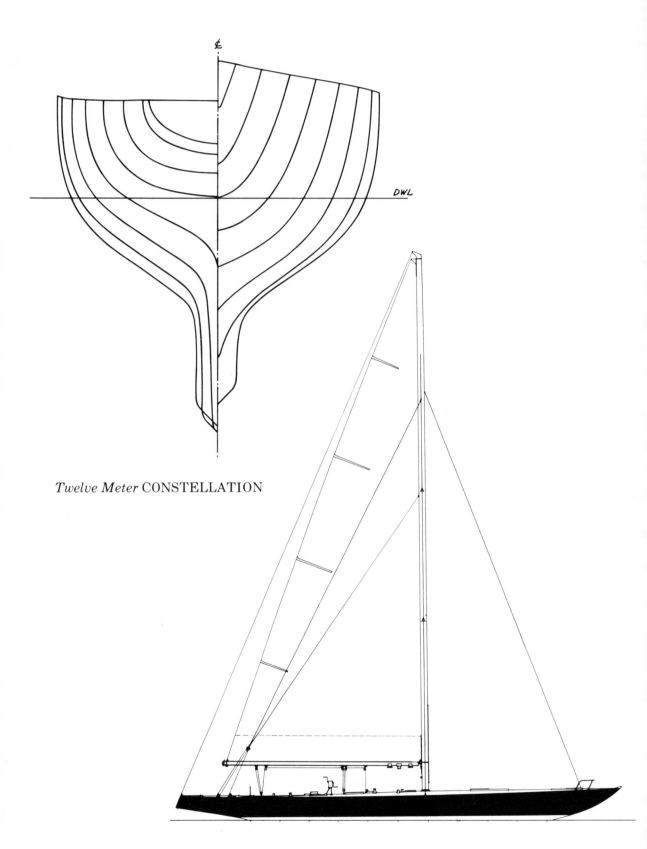

Twelve Meter CONSTELLATION

like any other vehicle you might say, or whatever, one does learn and there's a gradual improvement. Even strictly human sporting events like running and rowing and the like, human beings don't change they say. Yet the records do fall and the athletes do get better, and the technicians do get better, and it's unfortunate when the new boat isn't faster. I think that's about the best answer I can make right now.

Frank: Well, I'd like to ask a question right here, Olin. How did you come upon the idea of drawing the waterlines out underwater and moving the rudder further aft, sort of like a bulbous stern as opposed to a bulbous bow.

Olin: Well as I recall it, it was really through experiments having to do with the use of a bulb in a sailing boat, which were tried in connection with the twelve-meter designs. I think it was right after the time of *Constellation*, if I remember correctly, that we did have the means to do some experimental work on the twelves and tested bulbs or protuberances of some kind both forward and aft, and found essentially that these things were helpful only over a very limited speed range, and generally hurt the model's performance at other speeds. So it didn't seem a true bulb, or what was our interpretation of a true bulb, would be broadly helpful. Somehow, the possibility of increasing the length with something that's just a little bit like a bulb, that's been called a "bustle" or a "kicker," or whatever the name might be, this thing did seem to develop some real possibilities. It was strictly as a result of model tests started with experiments having to do with boats that the thing came about.

Frank: Well, that leads to my next question. Do you still think that moving the longitudinal center of buoyancy or center of volume or displacement a little farther aft improves the performance of the hull?

Olin: I don't think I can give a general answer to that question. Because you say farther aft, I immediately think of farther aft than what. If an extreme movement was advisable or even seemed promising, I'd certainly try it. I think that you have to use a compromise and that somebody's eye in a way has to judge. I think we have discovered, as is not really news to anybody, that the angle of entrance or, as it's often expressed, the half angle of entrance, has a certain importance in keeping down resistance. In other words, a relatively fine forebody does often tend to reduce resistance. On the other hand, if you get a boat that's too blunt at either end, I'm sure it's bad. So in extreme cases of fining up the forebody in order to get a certain displacement in the boat you have to fill out the afterbody, you have to fill it out somewhere, and I don't think it pays to go to extremes. I think you have to look at balance of the boat and judge either intuitively, or as a result of actual model tests, what is a reasonable balance. You have to be conscious of the effect of getting too much fullness at one end or the other or in the middle, and also think about the effect when a boat heels, because there are some boats which are quite good boats, which are very fine forward and very full aft shaped a little like a flatiron. We get this more on the IOR-type boats with dinghy-type hulls, but if those boats heel over too much they drop down forward, and the centerline of the hull no longer coincides in direction with the centerline of the keel, and to some extent the hull

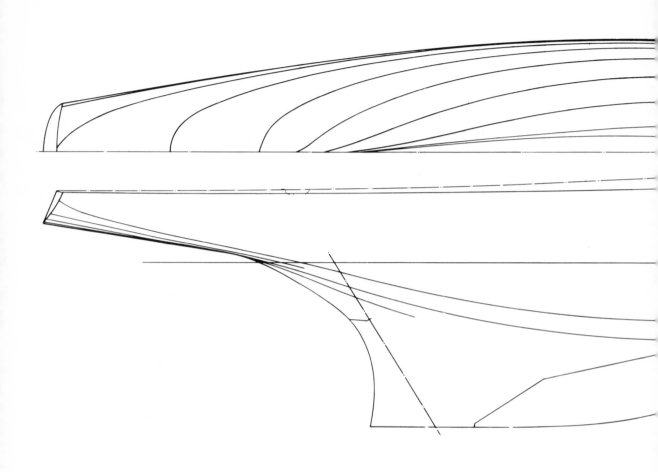

and the keel are working against each other. This is certainly not a good condition, so I really don't subscribe to the idea that the center of buoyancy should be continually moved aft, only that it seems best to have it somewhat aft of the center of the waterline. There's a very definite limit to the distance that you can go.

Frank: That bustle was a nice way of doing it, because you had quite fine waterlines, and creating that skeg effect did move the center further aft but in a very streamlined way.

Olin: I think you've made a good point there, because I was speaking about the difficulty of finding a place for displacement. It either has to be at one end or in the middle, but this bustle really gives you a fourth place where you can pack away some displacement that is necessary but results in a minimum increase of drag or, ideally, in a reduction of drag.

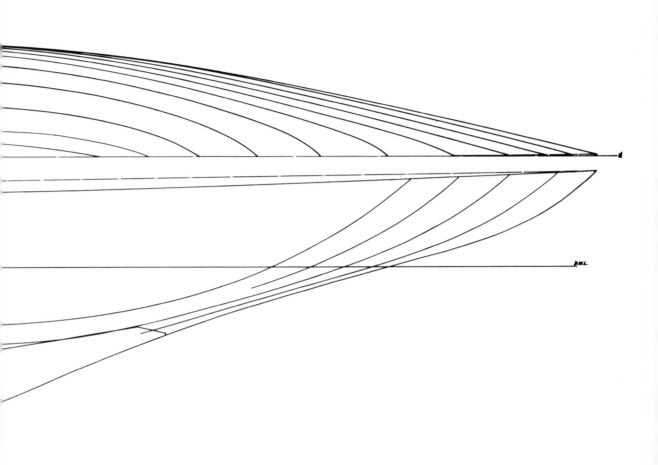

Frank: Well now, what about proportioning of sail area to hull length. Do you feel that the longer hull with less sail area does better than the shorter hull with more sail area?

Olin: Well, I think you have to answer this question with some consciousness of the history of the various classes, and if we're talking about twelve meters you can think of that class. The earlier boats were shorter, and the direction which has been progressive, and which resulted I think in fast boats for some time, was from the smaller to the larger hull, and consequently from the larger to the smaller rig. I think this reached an extreme in 1970 with the modified *Intrepid* and *Valiant* designs, which were both rather long heavy boats with moderate rigs. It's hard to draw these comparisons, but by and large I don't think either one was completely successful. And I think the 1974 boats were somewhat smaller. Of course this depends on one's judgment of the weather conditions. I think its pretty clear that the big boat with the small rig promises to give you good speed in a strong wind, whereas the reverse promises good speed in light airs. You have to know your boats and you have to know your weather conditions, and you can either solve it intuitively or by computation. As you know, in our IOR or offshore designs we look pretty carefully at stability indices, and calculations of that sort, and try to proportion them out in sail area so as to get a reasonable balance between the two, but in the direction of plenty of sail for a boat that will sail in a light weather area, and plenty of stability in a boat that will sail where we expect it to blow harder.

Frank: In the case of the America's Cup races which are off Newport, have you ever used all the weather information for the month of September and come up with an average wind speed which you use to design the boat for best performance?

Olin: Well, frankly not, because I look at the weather in September in Newport as being very uncertain and very changeable. You're apt to have very light airs and you're apt to have pretty strong winds. I'm afraid I've used more of an intuitive approach than anything else there, and have kind of felt that a certain size boat is apt to do pretty well, and also have had it very much in the front of my mind that the boat has to be selected before she's going to race for the America's Cup, and the weather conditions are apt to be pretty light in the midsummer off Newport. Fortunately in the twelve-meter class the differences don't seem to be nearly as critical as they are in some other classes. I think it's because a certain amount of displacement is required, and the boats seem to have sort of shaken down to the point where they're rather close together in size and sail area. We have avoided extremes, but I admit to being more conscious of the need of having a good light weather boat for the middle of the summer rather than anything extreme, and on the heavy weather side for the possible strong winds in September.

Frank: Now it seems to me that an America's Cup Race is the acid test for a yacht designer. But the sum total involves so many factors such as sails, crew, skipper, and hull that I wonder how you would evaluate them percentagewise for winning.

Olin: This is a hard question to answer. All of them are important, and I'd say almost equally important. Fortunately for the America's Cup races, the standard in all cases is a rather high one. So while it is of great concern to the designer to have the sails, the crew, and the skipper of the very top grade, all I can do as a designer is to have a certain confidence and a certain hope that these other elements will be good, and do the best possible part which is under the designer's control. I do feel, however, that I've always wanted to stay with an America's Cup boat in Newport because of the importance of everything else. Normally by the time the summer trials come along there's not a whole lot

252

that the designer can do about the hull, but maybe if he's had some experience he can be sort of helpful, and possibly sometimes a tempering influence, with the problems that do come up—and they always have, even though the standard is high. There have been problems with sail, crew, and skipper, which are all too well known, on which making the right decision at the right time or contributing toward it have certainly been decisive in connection with the selection of the boat. This was specifically true in the time of *Constellation*, and again in the time of *Courageous*. Actually there were changes in the skippers in both cases. It was the final selection of the skipper that influenced the selection of the boat. You might say in both those cases everything else was so close that the skipper was decisive. Whether this means you give him 100% or just a little larger percentage than the other items, I don't know. This is sort of a statistical matter, and I'm no expert in statistics.

Frank: Referring to the change of skippers, when Ted Hood stepped in, that changed the sails, too.

Olin: Well, that changed the sails also, and the sails were okay.

Frank: I'm going to pose a question that you don't have to answer, but which if answered may be the kernel of this book. The other day Mary had just returned from the Philharmonic and described how wonderful it was to listen to Beethoven's Fifth Symphony played there that afternoon. I said, "How could a man compose such lovely music? It must have been more than just hard work. He must have been born with the right genes." Then I added, "I wonder how such a young man as Olin was able to create such fast and able six meters in his first few designs? He was barely more than a teenager with little or no design experience. Then from his board came that masterpiece, *Dorade*, only his seventh design. How could he do it right off the bat?" How would you answer, Olin, if you could?

Olin: I don't know. It's again a lot of things put together. Of course at that time, although I was young, I had spent a lot of time studying boats in the six-meter class. I had sailed in the six-meter class some years, even at that time. I certainly knew the other boats very well indeed. As a youngster will do, I was very conscious, I had in my head all of their dimensions and all of the characteristics. I looked at all the good boats that came from abroad. I photographed them and studied their dimensions and everything I could learn about them. So I was very anxious to get into it, and even then the first boat I designed, the first six-meter, a boat called *Thalia*, really was unfortunately named, because she was pretty close to being a failure. Anyway, she wasn't all that good. She was fairly good in light weather. I was able to immediately pick up the faults in that design. She made enough of an impression that several people came to me during the following winter before the season of 1930 for new six-meter designs. I think Mr. Clinton Crane contributed a lot to helping me at that time. And I was fortunate in having had this one questionable design experience and in knowing the class very well. Then I came out somewhat intuitively with the plans of some successful boats. I remember, and I'm afraid I often think of it these days when I am conscious of things moving rather slowly, that I had an order to design two identical sixes for two friends from the Middle West, and I knew this had to be done of course, and was trying to keep to a certain schedule. I suddenly heard one day that they were going to be in New York the next day, and I drew the lines of that six meter in less than 24 hours. And she was a very excellent boat, so I obviously had some kind of feel for it, and just went ahead and put down on paper what I thought. I was lucky in the fact that it worked. With *Dorade* it was somewhat similar. I don't know how to explain it, because she certainly was a good boat, but she certainly was a boat which I was able to improve on later. I think in a way *Dorade* is more of an example about how a boat with a certain potential is still far from a perfect boat. But a good boat can be handled by a pretty active and skillful crew so as to get the best out of her. And I think the boats that came after *Dorade*, specifically *Stormy Weather* and *Edlu*, and boats which were beamier, were potentially much better boats. We were lucky with *Dorade* in that she was probably not up against quite the level of competition that the later boats were against. We did sail her hard, and we sailed her pretty well. I think the handling had a lot to do with *Dorade;* although she was a boat that was fun to sail. The first year she was certainly overrigged, but she certainly was fast in light air. During the winter before the transatlantic race we cut down her rig and she wasn't quite as fast in light air, but she then could carry this rig in quite a strong breeze. In distinction to existing boats, she could sail quite fast at a very wide angle of heel. And although she defied the present-day rule that it's wrong to have weight in the ends, she was so sharp and fine that she could slice right through a sea, and the widely distributed weight of her very long lead keel, and the interior accommodations too, didn't seem to slow her down at all. Otherwise she was an unusual boat and was great fun. I don't think she was really a masterpiece. She was a very lucky shot. That would be my thought, Frank.

Frank: Well, out of that very nice answer I picked one word, and I think it's the key to the whole thing. That is, intuition. Wouldn't you say so?

Olin: Well, I would say so, and I think this is a point which I mentioned before, maybe to you, and I've certainly mentioned it in one or two articles or talks that I've given here and there. My own direction in yacht design has been over quite a few years from intuition toward computation. I'd like to try to express pretty emphatically the opinion that neither one is altogether complete. You really need a combination of the two, which I hope we can use successfully and exhibit right here in the office these days. You need both, but you need a feel for both, and you need an eye for both. Then you need to know something about your weight and stability. To compare radically different boats you need a yardstick, which is very difficult to get intuitively. If you can run some numbers and some performance calculations and so on, I think it will guide anyone who has a good feel for what a boat should be. It will still guide him through the elimination of unsuccessful, unpromising patterns. So I hope this is the right way to go.

14 *Twelves Defending the Cup*

What cup? The cup the two-masted schooner *America* won racing a fleet of the top English yachts over there in 1851, since called the America's Cup after that craft, the swiftest yacht of her time. The New York Yacht Club has not lost that ugly prize, bolted to the floor in its specially designed octagonal room, to any challenger come-one, come-all. Yachtsmen from England, Canada, France, Australia, and Sweden so far have tried to no avail to win it away.

The amount of money spent by members and friends of the N.Y.Y.C. to keep it there every three or four years when a challenge is made is conservatively about 3,000 times its $500 value. It has thus become the single most important sailboat-racing extravaganza there is.

To continue these America's Cup races after the war, when the purchasing power of money bought half what it did before, it became necessary to reduce the size of the boats used. And so it was that the deed of the Cup was legally changed so as to allow twelve-meter sloops instead of J Class sloops of 135' length to be used. The first of these races using the 69' twelves off Newport, Rhode Island, occurred in 1958 when the Royal Yacht Squadron challenged with their twelve-meter sloop *Sceptre*. Twenty-one years had elapsed since the 1937 contest when *Ranger*, the superb J, defeated *Endeavour II* to keep the Cup in its small octagonal room.

Now in 1958 great energy was expended to produce the fastest possible twelve. That meant one that could beat Mike

COLUMBIA
(Rosenfeld)

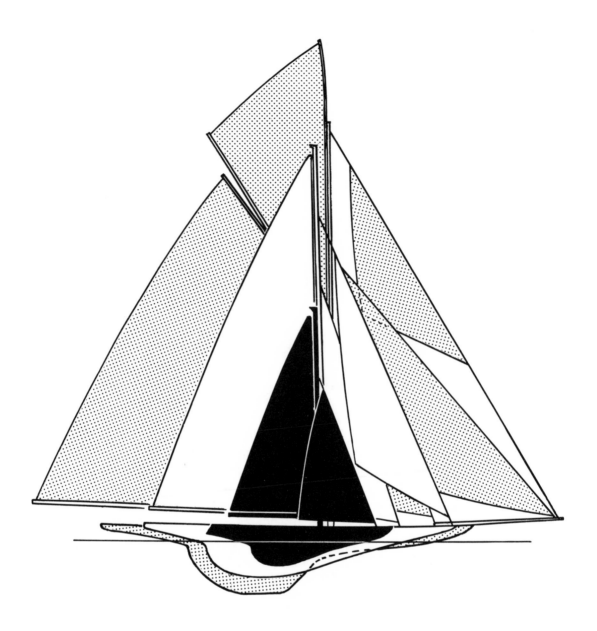

A RAFT OF
THREE TYPES OF AMERICA'S CUP BOATS

	J. Class Center	*Reliance to Port*	*Twelve to Stbd.*
L. O. A.	121 ft.	144 ft.	69 ft.
Sail Area	7,580 sq. ft.	16,160 sq. ft.	1,825 sq. ft.

Vanderbilt's *Vim*, and that was a very difficult thing to do because she was Olin's best for a very long time.

One of those times was when *Vim* was racing in 1939 on the Solent, the channel between the Isle of Wight and the English mainland. There is a strong current there, so if it is against your boat, when beating to windward, it is beneficial to stay out of it by hugging the shore and benefiting by back eddies in shoal coves. This was well before the days of depth finders as we know them now. Rod was a member of *Vim*'s crew then and volunteered to take soundings with lead and line from *Vim*'s bow. He kept the length of line exactly 9½' and swung the lead out ahead as *Vim* swiftly beat inshore. It worked pretty much like a pole thrust forward probing for the bottom. When the lead did touch the ground, there was an instant slackening of the line. Quickly Rod would turn his head at that moment with the command "come about." Mike Vanderbilt instantly would put the tiller down, and around she'd come. In this manner *Vim* was able to win against the British twelves, whose skippers had local knowledge of the currents and shoal shoreline. They could not get over how *Vim* could win in their tricky home waters.

Olin was commissioned to design a new twelve to outperform *Vim* by Henry Sears and his syndicate of contributors, and they agreed that Briggs S. Cunningham would skipper her. *Columbia*'s lines took shape on Bill Mavrogiannis' board after many refinements and long hours of overtime work—testing models, changing them, testing them again and again up to a dozen times, until Olin, analyzing each result carefully, finally thought he had a model that would perform just a little better than *Vim*'s model. He was proved correct when, after some of the closest racing ever seen occurred that summer between *Vim* and *Columbia*, *Columbia* was selected to defend. As so often happens, the trials were the best races to watch, because these boats were closely matched, flawlessly handled, and finished excitingly close together. It was a long trial series among four twelves, any one of which it turned out could have defended successfully, the best two being Olin's designs (*Vim* and *Columbia*). As with the J, the same system was used: The winner would be the boat that took four out of seven races.

Sceptre was an unknown quantity until the first few minutes of the first race. Within 20 minutes, as she pitched a great deal in what little sea there was, it was obvious that she could neither point nor foot with *Columbia*, which sailed as nicely as could be.

There was a huge spectator fleet for that first race, estimated at over 1,000 craft. They ranged from a few big excursion steamers, collectively carrying some thousands of people, and a Navy destroyer carrying President Eisenhower and his party, down to a horde of little outboard and sailing boats that had no business so far offshore. It was estimated that nearly 20,000 people saw that first race.

Almost unbelievingly, the spectators watched *Columbia* steadily draw away from her rival, finally to round the windward mark, a tugboat, after a slow beat

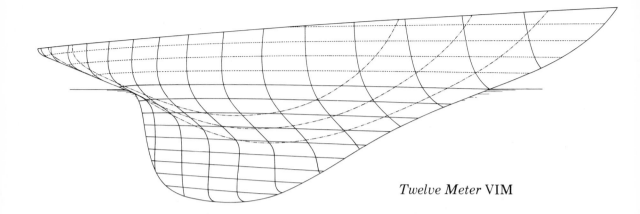

Twelve Meter VIM

of an hour and a half with a lead of over seven minutes. For the run *Sceptre* picked up a shift of wind and set a huge spinnaker. The new breeze soon collapsed, and both boats drifted along barely having steerageway. It was obvious that the race would not be over before the time limit expired, so the destroyer swung off for Newport and a presidential round of golf. You can imagine Ike saying, "So this is yacht racing!"

There was more wind for the second race, but the more it breezed up, the slower comparatively the challenger seemed to sail. There was nothing the British crew could do to catch up. To make a long story short, *Columbia* boiled over the finish line with a lead of over 11 minutes. During the trials she had been happy to beat *Vim* by half a second per mile, but now had beaten *Sceptre* by nearly half a minute per mile.

In the third race *Sceptre* had the strong breeze she wanted. It was a sou'wester blowing 22 and picking up at times. There was a lively chop from the wind but no real sea. The course was windward-leeward, twice around. *Sceptre*'s skipper, Graham Mann, made a perfect start crossing the line with full way on and a length to windward abeam of *Columbia*, which was not yet fully underway. But not for long. In just four minutes Briggs Cunningham worked her up under *Sceptre*'s bow and ahead of her, backwinding her. She had to come about. *Columbia* tacked to cover her. They made nearly 20 tacks in the 6 miles to windward, but Briggs covered every time and *Columbia* kept edging out to windward until at the mark (the Navy tug) she rounded 2 minutes, 23 seconds ahead.

By this time the breeze had increased and drove then downwind at 10 knots with *Sceptre* using her huge French spinnaker, again tacking downwind. She lost only 6 seconds on that run, her best point of sailing with her favorite wind strength. The second windward leg was a repeat of the first, and *Columbia*

VIM
(Rosenfeld)

gained a mile and a quarter lead. The final run to the finish gave an 8 minute, 20 second lead to *Columbia*.

The fourth and last race of this series was a sad one for *Sceptre* as mishaps plagued her. First, on the beat to windward her wire jib sheet fouled a cleat when tacking (for the first time in that season's sailing), holding her big genoa aback on the new tack until someone could cut this wire sheet. On the next, a downwind leg, in quick succession, her spinnaker guy parted, the end broke off her spinnaker pole, and she broke her main boom due to resetting the spinnaker on the other pole, which caused the guy to lift the boom up against the down-haul, which no one released. The boom broke in two parts, held together only by the metal sail track. British bulldog spirit came through. The crew decided to carry on. So they patched up the boom with the boom crutch and broken spin-naker pole and lots of line wound around them. What with all this it was remarkable that *Sceptre* lost only 2 minutes, 40 seconds. On the final reaching leg to the finish, British pluck was rewarded when she actually picked up over a minute.

But *Columbia* won that race, and the series, in the first four races. Why? To sailors with an eye for yacht design, it was clearly apparent that the hulls of these two boats had quite different shapes. This did not mean that one's eye could tell which would be the fastest, only that one shape had to be wrong. I may be wrong, but in my opinion it was *Sceptre*'s fullness forward that must have done her in. Because of his intuition, scientific analysis, and persistence in improving *Vim*'s design by the hard work of his designers, Olin came up with the shape that won, because it was right.

Four years later, in 1962, the Australians made it one of the closest matches in history with *Gretel* against *Weatherly*, the latter designed by Olin's former boss and competitor since 1931, the late Philip L. Rhodes. It was a series between evenly matched boats and crews, and a few breaks might have swung the balance of victory to Australia.

Men and boats race each other on the sea, and it was the sea itself that this time made the winner. To me the most exciting single moment in America's Cup history came at the beginning of the third leg of the second race of this series when *Gretel*, her new white spinnaker standing out like an inflated balloon in the fresh west wind, surged at 14 knots on top of first one, then two, then a third high swell cresting under her stern, and surfed into the lead. I can attest to that myself, because I saw it happen from close aboard on the top deck of the well-positioned steamer *Martha's Vineyard*. Just as *Gretel* picked up and began to surf, her crew let out with a wild fighting yell. The Aussies were used to doing this when a dinghy hits a plane, and couldn't resist the urge to give vent to a blood-curdling "Yeeee-hoooo!" that was immediately picked up by the startled, hard-pressed *Weatherly* crew, just downwind. They had been having trouble getting their own spinnaker to draw, and they were highly preoccupied on deck when the ear-splitting screech sped downwind to them.

Before they even knew what it was all about, *Gretel* had surfed on by into the lead.

At the steamer's rail next to me an Australian spectator turned to me just then and said, "This has really made my trip all the way here worthwhile!"

Now came her skipper Bus Mosbacher's moment to haul up across the challenger's wake and try to blanket her in turn. But as *Weatherly* attempted this maneuver, her after spinnaker guy parted, the aluminum spinnaker pole slammed against her headstay, and the pole buckled a few feet short of its outer end. By the time her crew had rigged the spare pole and had the spinnaker drawing properly again, *Gretel* was so far ahead, and the finish line so close, that there was no hope of *Weatherly* saving the race. *Gretel* won by 47 seconds, and the series stood at one to one. A roar of horns, whistles, and yells greeted *Gretel* at the finish line and again as she sailed into Newport Harbor.

The third race was in light air and *Weatherly* won by the large margin of 8 minutes, 40 seconds, putting the score at two to one. The fourth race was a thriller again. *Gretel* was outsailed to windward but regained nearly all of the distance on two reaches to finish so close to *Weatherly* that it was the closest margin in America's Cup history, a short 26 seconds. *Gretel*'s fine showing is the more remarkable when you consider that she was the first twelve-meter sloop Australia ever produced, and that few of her people has sailed in match races, or in yachts as big as the twelves.

A tactic that appeared in this series of races was the prestart merry-go-round in which Bus Mosbacher of *Weatherly* and Jock Sturrock, *Gretel*'s skipper, would chase each other around in a circle, each trying to force the other either away from the line or over it before the starting gun was fired. Bus was a past master at it and usually got the best start as a result.

Among the spectator fleet of over 2,000 craft this time was the Navy destroyer *Joseph P. Kennedy, Jr.* with the Kennedy family aboard. I remember so well watching her knife slowly in through the mass of boats at the finish line so that President Kennedy, who was standing way forward on her prow, could congratulate the skipper and crew of *Weatherly* immediately as she crossed, and then again *Gretel*'s company. He might have remembered then the fun he had racing his own gaff-rigged Wianno sloop as a boy at Hyannisport.

By the time the fifth race was run this spectator fleet had dwindled to a mere few. It was partly because lay days between races had been requested and granted, and because it seemed a foregone conclusion that *Weatherly* would win eventually. She won it four to one. And once again the Cup stayed in its room at the New York Yacht Club.

There was only a two-year pause before England challenged once more with a new twelve, *Sovereign*. At that time, in 1964, Olin received a commission from Eric Ridder, Walter Gubelmann, and a group of yachtsmen to design a new twelve to be named *Constellation*, which they hoped would be selected by the Yacht Club committee to defend the Cup.

Designwise she was unusual with respect to the sections through her keel. They were not the usual "U" shape at the bottom—which S & S boats had been since *Dorade* and as lately as *Columbia*—but were "V" shaped. This feature, decided upon after testing various models in the Stevens Tank at Hoboken, seem to improve windward performance by reducing leeway. This was one of many elements that combined to make *Constellation* the powerful, close-winded boat she became. As well as this idea of Olin's, incorporated in the lovely lines Mario Tarabocchia drew, there was an excellent job of construction by Minneford Yard; beautifully built Ted Hood sails; Rod's ability as a rigger, tuner, sail trimmer, and navigator; Bob Bavier's sure-handed helmsmanship; and excellent crew work under the administration of skipper Eric Ridder. No one of these was enough, but none of them could be missing in the complete picture, and they all fell together into an unbeatable winning combination.

The buildup to this year's series featured a recurrent theme in the press that the British would no longer be underdogs. Their earnest effort would certainly not bring a repeat of the humiliation of *Sceptre* in 1958.

Through the summer the trials to select the defender were exciting. The other twelves providing competition were *Columbia, Easterner,* and *American Eagle.* After close races all summer, one after the other were beaten by the new *Constellation,* and she was selected.

The Cup races in September were an anticlimax. Every race was firmly settled before the end of the first leg. I remember watching the first one from the steamer *Martha's Vineyard,* when the challenger and defender were close enough to visually compare their motions in the seaway that existed. *Constellation* seemed to forge ahead as steady as could be, while *Sovereign* pitched more violently and would almost be stopped dead as her bow slammed down on the bigger waves, and foam splashed forward. Her sails, not well fitting, would wrinkle and alter shape somewhat during a race.

This series of Cup races were mere parades, a severe disappointment to all who love sailing competition, with no suspense, no tactical maneuvering after the starts, and altogether as one reporter's phrase went, quite like "watching grass grow." *Constellation* won the first four races by margins of 5½, 20¼, 6½, and 15¾ minutes over the 24.3-mile course. The Cup itself never even quivered in its long-accustomed spot in the clubhouse on 44th Street.

Because models of both *Constellation* and *Sovereign* were tested in the same tank at Stevens Institute, before the rule was changed to deny challengers this privilege of using United States facilities, one would think that they would have been more closely matched. You might say the N.Y.Y.C. America's Cup Committee bent over backwards to encourage this. Why weren't they? Only those who worked with the tank tests of both boats know how their tests compared. Both Olin and David Boyd, *Sovereign*'s designer, felt they had improved on their respective 1958 antagonists, *Columbia* and *Sceptre.* That Olin had the bigger percentage of improvement is obvious. His special forte is the ability to translate tank test data into a design that behaves well in the far more complicated environment of a full-size twelve in the open sea encountering wind and wave action that was not duplicated in the tank.

The year 1967 once again brought a challenger from Australia. Her name was *Dame Pattie*, financed by a syndicate from the Royal Sydney Yacht Squadron. "Ah," it was thought throughout the yachting world, "here would be another colorful gung-ho affair, with some competitive fireworks between the twelves for the Cup." There was good reason for this after the stirring battle Australia made of it in 1962.

It was not long before the "hat was passed" at the New York Yacht Club again, and a syndicate formed with William Strawbridge as manager. They quickly signed up Olin to design, and Bus Mosbacher to skipper a new twelve to be named *Intrepid*.

Progress in design took a big jump ahead with *Intrepid*. Whereas Olin had a tough time improving on his *Vim* with the design of *Columbia*, and Phil Rhodes made just a slight improvement on *Columbia* with his *Weatherly*, and although Olin's *Constellation* with her "V" section keel was just enough better than *Columbia*, *American Eagle*, and *Easterner* to be selected to defend the Cup, Olin's *Intrepid*, again with her lines drawn by Mario Tarabocchia, was a breakthrough. Her great stability was the real key.

By studying her full form one is immediately struck by her quite different shape, especially in profile. The bow above the water has a knuckle similar to an Atlantic's, so as to lengthen her heeled waterline. She has two rudders. The forward one on the fin keel, misnamed a trim tab, could be set at a slight angle to give an extra lift to windward, or could be turned with the aft rudder to maneuver her in a tight circle, and the after one way back on a drawn-out skeg, (given the name of "bustle" or "kicker") all introduced some very desirable improvements. Olin's passion for excellence produced in *Intrepid* the fastest twelve of her time.

The trials for selection that summer proved it, as she easily outsailed *Columbia*, *Nefertiti*, and *Heritage*. The first ten minutes of the first Cup race told the same old story. The N.Y.Y.C.'s defender was superior in every department that counted, and the 116-year-old Cup was as safe as ever. The way she was handled was as precise as a drill team in every maneuver. Ted Hood sails that were perfection in action powered *Intrepid* to maintain an average advantage over *Dame Pattie* of 11 seconds per mile.

In the second race superior boat speed allowed *Intrepid* to work out ahead and cover the Australian challenger. This was the signal for Sturrock, *Dame Pattie*'s skipper, to start a tacking duel. He held his own for a while, but lost what chance he had by trying to pull off a false tack to fool Bus Mosbacher.

A vital part of match racing is to keep a constant eye on the opponent for any such maneuver, and *Intrepid*'s afterguard easily detected this one. While

Dame Pattie hung in the wind and lost all way before falling off again on the same tack, *Intrepid* made one flicker of response, then bore off again with full speed to cover, and the race was over.

The third race was notable for the most dramatic moment of the series, an odd encounter, worrisome to Rod, between a tiny catboat and a Coast Guard helicopter that capsized her and very nearly did *Intrepid* in, when trying to help clear her path. This Rod described as one of his anxious sailing experiences in Chapter 7.

Dame Pattie was designed to be at her best in 10–12-knot breezes (which the Aussies gambled on as being normal at Newport in September). However, the weather did not cooperate. Instead, there were two hurricanes behaving strangely offshore, causing continued heavy breezes off Newport. As a result, *Dame Pattie* was tender, taking in so much water that three men had to bail constantly.

Intrepid was so superior, being quite stiff, there was just no contest for the Cup in the third and fourth races. And that was the series, 4–0.

Three years later, in 1970, the Australians challenged again with *Gretel II*, and this time unquestionably they had the superior boat. The American twelve was the slower of the two. She was *Intrepid*, altered by Britton Chance, Jr., and she had beaten Olin's creation of that year, *Valiant*, in the selection trials. Even so, there was a great deal of discussion, when *Intrepid* was shown to be slower than *Gretel II*, as to whether she was actually improved over the way she had been before, when Olin originally designed her. She had undergone drastic alterations to her after underbody when the old *Intrepid* syndicate commissioned Chance to try to improve her, because Olin had decided to give his exclusive attention to designing a new twelve, *Valiant*.

The trouble was that there were no good twelves available against which the originally designed *Intrepid* had previously been tried. If it had not been for her skipper "Bill Flicker being quicker," we surely would have lost the Cup to the Australians then. As in the J Class year of 1934 when *Rainbow* battled *Endeavour*, a seemingly slower boat used superior tactics to fight off a potentially faster one. Protests and bickering in 1970 took the fun from actual sailing, and there was a controversy which reached far beyond sailing circles.

Never before in 100 years of challenges had a series been fought so directly on the water, rather than having been settled at the designer's boards, towing tanks, or sail lofts. The technology gap had been completely closed with designer Alan Payne's creation, *Gretel II*. This Royal Sydney Yacht Squadron challenger was not an underdog in design, sails, or rig. It was the way the boats were handled in competition that determined the outcome; it was match racing at its best.

Perhaps the most telling background statistic to account for *Intrepid*'s victory is this: In previous races under the tension of all-out competition, *Intrepid* had a 22–5 record, while *Gretel II*'s was 4–0. Her brushes at home against

Gretel I meant nothing in preparing her crew for the pressures of the real thing, and all she had behind her was the abnormal series against *France*'s eccentric threat. With 27 tough races under their belts, *Intrepid*'s crew knew almost automatically what the right move at the right time had to be. They knew every sail and exactly what it could do, and match racing could hold few surprises for them.

It was a 4–1 victory for *Intrepid*, with protests in the first and second races.

After the five-minute gun before the start of the first race there was general consternation when the red protest flags could be seen on each boat. *Gretel II* had protested *Intrepid* for a basic starboard tack situation, and *Intrepid*'s counterprotest was that *Gretel II* had attempted to obstruct her in the act of keeping clear by luffing up sharply at the last minute. Later the race committee disallowed both protests because there had been no contact.

Intrepid arrived at the windward mark of this first race a little over a minute ahead of *Gretel II*. This was close enough to make it interesting on the spinnaker leg downwind, but Aussie hopes for catching up were sadly wrenched when a horrendous spinnaker wrap developed. For more than six embarrassing minutes the unsightly mess stayed up there before it was finally cleared and a second spinnaker was set.

Despite this, the boats were going so fast in the nasty raw easterly that *Intrepid* added only five seconds in time but more in distance at the next mark, and there were still prospects of a battle developing, perhaps a slam-bang tacking duel on the next beat. There was even greater consternation, then, when *Gretel II*, soon after clearing the mark and changing from spinnaker to genoa, was suddenly seen to come about and head back along her track. There in the welter of wind chop and boat wakes was a bobbing head. Her foredeck man, Paul Salmon, who had just secured the spinnaker pole, had been caught by green water when facing aft, as he put her bow through the top of a wave, and his feet were swept out from under him. *Gretel II* missed him on her first pass, tacked again, and picked him up the second time, her sails shaking wildly, her lines tangled and flailing around. In all, she lost about three minutes, and that ended the contest for the first race, *Intrepid* winning.

After a lay day the second race was attempted. *Gretel II* got to the first windward mark a minute ahead of *Intrepid*. However, in the rapidly closing fog after the second mark was rounded, *Intrepid* swept by under spinnaker. The fog closed in thick shortly thereafter, and with the wind almost nil the race was abandoned.

In the next race *Gretel II* had just her weather, a 6–8-knot sou'wester, but she again sought a fouling situation. Prior to the starting signal, both yachts were approaching the starting line on the starboard tack. *Intrepid* was to windward and rapidly overtaking *Gretel II* from astern. *Intrepid* was on a close-hauled course to pass astern of the committee boat forming one end of the starting line. *Gretel II* was slowly luffing. After the starting gun was fired and before the yachts had cleared the line, *Gretel II* continued her slow luff until she was above a close-hauled course. During this maneuver the yachts became over-lapped and converged. *Gretel II*'s bow struck *Intrepid* just abaft her chain plates on the port side. Protest flags were seen on each boat again.

Had *Gretel II*'s skipper not been intent on forcing the foul, the irony is that she could have borne off and gathered way in a fine safe leeward position, so that she never would have been headed in the entire race. Despite her lack of forward way, she almost broke through on the first leg, and gradually the challenger ghosted by to a 50-second lead at the fifth mark, as Aussie rooters went wild. Few even knew that protests had been lodged at that time, and when *Gretel II* easily skipped upwind to cross the finish line 1 minute, 7 seconds ahead of *Intrepid*, bedlam broke loose in the fleet and rockets burst into the darkening sky.

The cheers turned to shouts of anger and tempers exploded when the race committee arrived at its final decision about the protests. *Gretel II* was dis-qualified because she did not fulfill her obligation under the rule to fall off to a close-hauled course, which could have allowed *Intrepid* to have room to pass between her and the committee boat. "*Intrepid* is therefore the winner," they decided.

The reaction reached to the Australian Parliament, so great was the public criticism. It even led to a statement by the United States Ambassador to Aus-tralia "regretting" the action. One Australian politician even went so far as to suggest that Australian troops be withdrawn from Vietnam. Packer, *Gretel II*'s owner, refused to let the matter die, fighting it in the press for days. It was not until the final press conference that any Australian had anything but criticism in public for a clear-cut application of the rules, and it was *Gretel II*'s skipper, Jim Hardy, who then stated, "The New York Yacht Club Committee acted with complete integrity."

The start of the third race in a 10–18-knot sou'wester was a masterful one on the part of Bill Ficker, skipper of *Intrepid*. He gained the leeward position out of some circling with *Gretel II*, and both boats headed for the line far too easily with about two minutes to go. Visser, *Gretel II*'s starting helmsman, had nowhere to go but to windward as Ficker kept forcing him there, and both were 200 feet over the starting line before the gun. The buoy end was favored, but Visser had to tack away to port and got back to the line far to leeward, while Ficker dipped back, just cleared the buoy on the starboard tack, and came about with a tremendous advantage. *Intrepid* remained about one minute ahead around the first three marks. On the run *Gretel II* again began to close in the freshening breeze. Both boats were almost at hull speed. *Intrepid*'s margin dropped to 53 seconds at the fourth mark, but finally worked ahead to 1 minute, 18 seconds as winner at the finish. It was a race in which one bad move on *Intrepid*'s part after the masterful start could have blown it. Once more the Aussies called a lay day.

The fourth race was won by *Gretel II*. Bill Ficker gave his fans fits by sail-ing his own race without covering on two windward legs. For the third leg he set a balloon jib despite *Gretel II*'s spinnaker. It worked, but the gamble caught up with him on the final leg. *Intrepid* began it with a one-minute lead and the Cup all but won. It looked as though she could almost fetch the finish after just one tack, but the direction of the wind changed slightly so she was headed with *Gretel II* well up on the windward quarter. Suddenly, and too late, *Intrepid*'s afterguard realized that *Gretel II* had a better slant and was being lifted. *Intrepid* had to tack over to cover at last in the new air, which headed her again. She could not clear *Gretel II*'s bow by the time the two boats approached each other. She was forced to come about on *Gretel II*'s lee bow, and lost out. Jim Hardy sailed the challenger full and by with great speed, and waited until he had one short tack to cross the finish. *Gretel II* made it by a margin of 1 minute, 2 seconds. It was one of the most amazing comebacks in sailing history, and the closest America's Cup finish in distance, only about 60 to 75 yards.

The score was now three for *Intrepid* and one for *Gretel II*, and this time *Intrepid* requested the lay day.

The fifth race was once more in exactly the weather for which *Gretel II* was designed to be at her best, a faint 8–10 knot northerly. It turned out to be one of the all-time great shows of match racing. From gun to gun it had just about every classic move of this type of sailing competition.

Gretel II got her best start of the series. A windward advantage made *Intrepid* tack to leeward of her in five minutes. Jim Hardy's hesitation in covering in the next few tacks finally let Bill Ficker break through. The clincher was an encounter when, with *Intrepid*, on the starboard tack, *Gretel II* tacked under her bow and watched *Intrepid* get a lift, then ease by into the commanding weather berth. *Gretel II* had to take two extra tacks to make the mark, which gave *Intrepid* a 44-second margin. Bill Ficker used every trick in the book to fight off the continuously surging, threatening *Gretel II* from then on.

On the reaches they seemed glued together. The second beat to windward then produced one of the tensest tacking duels in Cup history. Ficker almost let the same thing happen that lost him the fourth race, but he came back in time to cover closely when *Gretel II* started to get a lift. *Intrepid* blanketed her opponent from then on, while inching toward the lay line where the duel would have to end. During the next reach *Intrepid*, at her best point of sailing, drove for the mark with slightly started sheets and had a 51-second lead as they squared away for the direct run in a dying breeze. It was an agonizingly hour-long, suspense-filled leg. The yachts tacked downwind at radical angles, with *Intrepid* never letting *Gretel II* blanket her from aft. On the last rounding of the leeward buoy, *Intrepid* still had a 20-second lead. Just then there was a shift in the direction of the wind to the east, allowing the boats to fetch the finish line without beating. Precise crew work allowed *Intrepid* to tack, immediately rounding the mark, but *Gretel II*'s crew kept her spinnaker set too long, and did not douse it as smartly. So she had to stand off on the wrong tack for wasted distance, while *Intrepid* was headed for home! Jim Hardy tried desparately to lure *Intrepid* into some mistake on this last leg, but Ficker would have none of it this time, staying between the challenger and the finish line all the way to win by a margin of 1 minute, 44 seconds. It was a long-to-be-remembered series.

Perhaps the best way to sum it up is to use the prophetic name of the large power cruiser used by the race committee to mark the starting and finishing lines: *Incredible.*

Four years went by, allowing time for yachtsmen abroad and at home to prepare to finance a challenger and a defender. In the meantime the rules governing the Cup Races had been amended to allow the use of welded aluminum construction. So it happened that in 1974 the Australians challenged for the fourth time with their new twelve-meter *Southern Cross* of the Royal Perth Yacht Club, owned by Alan Bond, a 36-year-old real estate promoter who spent millions on the boat, advertising her predicted prowess with a bombastic buildup.

Once again a group at the New York Yacht Club headed by William Strawbridge and later Robert McCullough came to Olin for a new twelve to be named *Courageous*. It was also decided by another group from California, with Jerry Driscoll at its head, to rebuild *Intrepid*, giving back her old speed as Olin, with Mario's help, had originally done her, and possibly improving on that, so that the welded aluminum *Courageous* would have the fastest possible wooden twelve to try to beat out for selection to defend the Cup. This time Olin accepted the redesign job, not limiting his work exclusively to the new *Courageous* as he had with *Valiant.* Two irons in the fire were better than one.

Britton Chance, Jr., also received a commission to design a new aluminum twelve, to be named *Mariner*, by a syndicate headed by George Hinman. She was to be built by Bob Derecktor. This time it was hoped nothing would be spared to ensure that the United States had the superior boat, not the challenger.

I've often wondered why wealthy men here and abroad are willing to part with so much money to defend the Cup when challenged for it. I may be wrong, but in my opinion the challengers often use this opportunity to promote their products, as Sir Thomas Lipton did for his tea and Marcel Bich did for his ballpoint pens and Alan Bond did for his real estate. On the other hand, with us I think it is purely a matter of patriotic pride and the desire to be second to none.

For the first time the spring and summer trials of 1974 included a twelve financed and rebuilt by yachtsmen from the West Coast. This made it more of a national affair than just an East Coast club group, as before—all to the good of the sport of sailing.

Everyone except a few knowledgeable designers expected the new welded aluminum boats to be far superior to the old wooden ones. "Surely the would have greater stability, because the saving in weight of aluminum over wood would allow more weight to be put in the lead ballast keel, thus lowering the center of gravity," most yachtsmen thought. The once-more-redesigned wooden *Intrepid* proved the thoughtful few designers, who added up weights and moments constantly in their work, to be correct. *Intrepid*, rebuilt and skippered

COURAGEOUS
(Barlow)

270

by Jerry Driscoll, almost beat out the new aluminum *Courageous* in the selection trials, but at the last possible minute the latter was selected.

It so happened that one new aluminum boat, *Mariner*, unfortunately for her backers, was the slowest of them all. Well, nothing ventured nothing gained. It was not because of her material or construction, but because of her shape. The submerged step at her stern was supposed to let the flow of water separate as on a planing boat. It worked on the model in the tank, but not on the full-size boat. Model test data was misinterpreted.

After the excitement of the trials, *Courageous*, skippered by Ted Hood, and using the sails he built, won four easy victories over *Southern Cross* in defense of the Cup. "It was like watching a slow leak in a hot-air balloon," was the summation by one spectator.

This time the New York Yacht Club had a far superior boat than the challenger, *Southern Cross*, despite all the confident claims and advance bragging by Alan Bond. He ended up with a boat that was slower, had less effective sails, and was not so well handled. It was competition in "anger" that was the key to America's fully realized twelve-meter campaign in 1974, and *Courageous* as well as *Intrepid* had been tuned to a perfect pitch by the exciting summer-long battle for selection.

The Aussies had been at their preparations far longer, but without the stimulus of real competition. They had an easy victory over Monsieur Bich's *France* in the challenge eliminations. But the performance of *Courageous* was almost totally flawless, while in comparison *Southern Cross* fell far below that. This Cup series might by typified by calling it "the one with the luffing starts."

The start of the first race set that procedure. With little more than three minutes till the gun, both boats luffed dead into the wind alongside each other a couple of hundred feet to leeward of the line, *Courageous* with *Southern Cross* to starboard. Just before they both lost steerageway, they fell off on opposite tacks, headed for opposite ends of the starting line, with *Courageous* on the starboard tack at the buoy end. She then tacked over, and for 19 minutes with *Southern Cross* to leeward but slightly ahead, they remained thus together. It looked like a real boat race, because the maxim that the first ten minutes of the first race would show if one boat was clearly superior was not being proved out.

Southern Cross was the first to tack, and when *Courageous* came about without trying to pass in front, it looked like an Aussie lead and brought wild cheers from their sympathizers. Those died slowly to moans when it became apparent that Ted Hood was gradually squeezing *Courageous*. The moans changed to groans, when she suddenly bore off, easing her sheets and speeding down on the mark with *Southern Cross* in her wake. It was a classic tactic of leading your opponent further away from the mark than you are, thus getting there first yourself. From there on it was no contest. At the finish *Courageous* was nearly 5 minutes ahead.

The second race produced another luffing start, but not before there were protests from both boats because of a near collision. Jim Hardy, skipper of

Southern Cross, got the better of this start, but *Courageous* to leeward had her wind clear enough to squeeze up and make the challenger tack in 7 minutes. About 16 minutes later *Southern Cross* got a lift by coming about and crossing *Courageous*. But she then failed to cover the defender. Another mistake Jim Hardy was observed making was the way he rounded marks too widely, losing time.

On the second windward leg Alan Bond, who was aboard *Southern Cross*, manned a winch himself. He had quite a workout when she made 11 tacks in 11 minutes. But they were fruitless as *Courageous* accelerated out of tacks much better.

At the end of this second race the International Jury (thoughtfully selected in fairness to avoid possible prejudice by one consisting of N.Y.Y.C. members only) decided the protests saying that because both boats had complied with their obligations, both protests were disallowed.

The third race had the now standard holding luffs before the start. The rest of it was another parade, with *Courageous* gradually building a greater and greater lead at each mark. The margin of her victory at the finish was about 5¼ minutes.

In the fourth and last race the twelves staged another of their long, stalling luffs, even backing their booms to kill speed before the start. This time it was the most one-sided start of the series, because *Southern Cross* did not carry enough way to hold *Courageous*, which got clear to build up a lead at the finish of over 7 minutes. By the time *Southern Cross* made it to the line, the champagne bottles passed to the *Courageous* crew from her tender were just about empty.

The year 1977 brought together for the America's Cup races, so far, a total of nine. Four were foreign boats, *Australia, Sverige, France II,* plus the old *France*. And five were from the United States, the new ones—*Enterprise* and *Independence*—as well as the old standbys—*Courageous, Intrepid,* and *Columbia* (although the latter is now owned by the Swedes).

An impressive 4 out of 5 American twelves were Olin's brain children. *Independence*, the only one that was not Olin's, was designed by Ted Hood.

Independence and *Courageous* got a year's head start, beginning their private match races in the summer of 1976 at Marblehead. Lee Loomis principally financed them, with other tax-exempt contributions to the Kings Point Fund, Inc., United States Merchant Marine Academy at Kings Point, N.Y. *Enterprise* and *Intrepid* match raced early the next spring off the California coast. *Enterprise*, Olin's newest design, was built at the Minneford Yard in City Island (where *Independence* was built the year before). She was then shipped cross-country to California in two pieces, the hull (weighing roughly 20,000 pounds) on one truck and the lead ballast keel (weighing roughly 40,000 pounds) on the other. Upon arrival the two parts were bolted together with 75 bolts precast in the lead—it was a masterful job lining them up with their holes.

Intrepid was shipped to California by steamer from Hawaii. Both were financed by a West Coast syndicate headed by George G. Jewett, Jr., and Edward duMoulin, and with helpful tax-exempt contributions to the Maritime College at Fort Schuyler Foundation, Inc. Dave Pedrick was her project engineer. So much for the available defenders.

The possible challengers were *Australia* and *Gretel II*, Alan Bond of Perth, owner, and *France* and *France II*, Marcel Bich, owner. Then the mysterious *Sverige* from Sweden was financed in part by the Swedish Government and by the Volvo Company.*

The summer of 1977 for the defense turned out to be the summer of the sailmakers: Ted Hood of Hood Sails, designer and skipper of *Independence*, was one, and Lowell North of North Sails, skipper of *Enterprise*, the other.

Everybody was fooled when Olin slightly modified the hull of *Courageous*, his earlier creation, and when Ted Turner bought into Lee Loomis's syndicate and became her skipper. With her Hood sails daily improved by Robbie Doyle, and with the skillful sailing by Ted Turner, she outsailed the other three and was selected to defend.

In a way it was sad for Olin to see his new design, *Enterprise* not finish first in the trial series. She was not sailed quite as well, nor were her North sails as good as the Hood sails on *Courageous*; sailmaking mistakes were made by relying too much on instruments not sufficiently accurate and on computers fed faulty input. But as in 1970, when his new design *Valiant* lost to his older *Intrepid*, so it was the same this time when his older design *Courageous* won out and became the defender.

Olin faired up the underwater portion of *Courageous* in way of her rudder by using a straight edge and his eyes. This helped make her a little faster. He thought, and was told by many observers, that the scientifically developed and newer *Enterprise* had the swiftest hull. I may be wrong, but my own feeling is that perhaps yacht designing, sailmaking, and sailboat racing are still more of an art than a science.

Australia eliminated one after another of the foreign twelves and thus became the challenger. The foreign trials were run by the French too late in the summer off Newport; next time, if they are started earlier, it will be more of a contest.

---

* The last time the Swedes made a challenge was in 1852. It was with the original *Sverige*, a larger version of the schooner *America*. By enlarging her sail plan and lines, taken off by the English while she was in drydock, and by adding yardarms with square sails on the two similarly raked masts, the Swedes improved their schooner *Sverige*'s performance over *America* downwind.

In a 40-mile leeward-windward match race off England on October 11, 1852, the deeper fore-footed *Sverige* was beaten by *America*. The time difference? Twenty-six minutes. Why so much? Because *Sverige* lost one jaw on her foresail gaff, and because *America*'s windward sailing ability was so far superior she beat up through *Sverige*'s lead, made while running downwind, to finish first.

COURAGEOUS and AUSTRALIA   (Rosenfeld)

At the start of the first race it looked like Noel Robbins, *Australia*'s skipper, had the best position. Shortly before the final starting signal, Ted Turner came downwind to his rival and maneuvered to be between her and the line. But soon it was apparent that *Australia* had the safe leeward position and was starting to backwind *Courageous*. Both boats were on the starboard tack, heading for the long end of the starting line. When Ted realized he was falling off and dropping back, he instantly came about and headed for the other end of the line. *Australia* kept going, crossing just at the bouy end while *Courageous* crossed near the committee boat a few seconds afterwards. No tacking duel developed. Ted did not cover when the two came together on the first encounter, this time with *Courageous* just ahead. The knowledgeable spectators were aghast. Apparently the reason was that Ted, clearly ahead at that moment, felt he could let her go. But he did stay between his opponent and the next mark. The distance between each boat opened up. There in the first five minutes spectators could tell that *Courageous* was the faster of the two. I also observed that Ted Turner was frequently able to play the wind shifts better and point higher than *Australia*. Sharp eyes of experts saw that the challenger's genoa was easier in the leech and was sheeted too far aft, and that there was more twist in her main than need be.

In the two broad reaches on the next leg the boats set reaching spinnakers of the flat type. Both boats stayed the same distance apart.

On the second windward leg Ted, good sailer though he is, made another cardinal error. He overstood the weather mark, losing time to *Australia*. Both boats set different spinnakers on the next leg, dead downwind. They were fuller, the better for running before the wind.

Taking in spinnakers at the leeward mark was quicker than ever before because a small-boat technique was perfected racing the twelves the summer of 1977. By pulling in a light line attached to the spinnaker's center, it could be quickly collapsed like an umbrella folding the wrong way in a gust of wind. First the halyard is let go, then the deflated spinnaker is drawn below through a cloth chute by its center, quickly, precisely, and carefully to prevent tearing.

On the final beat to windward *Courageous* outdistanced *Australia* by 1 minute, 48 seconds.

President Carter promptly sent a hand-written note of congratulations on White House stationery to his victorious fellow Southerner, skipper Ted Turner.

After a lay day the next race took place in a dying breeze. *Courageous* was ahead by more than 10 minutes but could not quite make the finish line before expiration of the time limit of 5½ hours, because the wind was "up and down the mast." So the race was abandoned.

In the second resailed race the spectator fleet dwindled from about 500 for the first race to only 116 craft at the finish. The weather was cloudy with a prediction of rain, but there was a light to moderate breeze of 11–15 knots. This race was also decided in the opening beat to windward, as Ted Turner sailed *Courageous* beautifully.

Before the start the two boats joined battle early, a whole 10 minutes before the final gun. The 9 maneuvers they made rapidly must be studied in the accompanying sketch to best be understood. So precise was the timing, so skillful the execution, that *Courageous* crossed exactly 2 seconds after the gun with *Australia* only 1 second behind, but to windward.

Courageous could have taken *Australia* high of the line on the wrong side of the committee boat, but she did not. Ted opted for clear air and a safe leeward start. After a summer of tearing into opponents competitively and verbally, the exemplary demeanor of skipper Ted Turner on the race course seemed a measure of redemption.

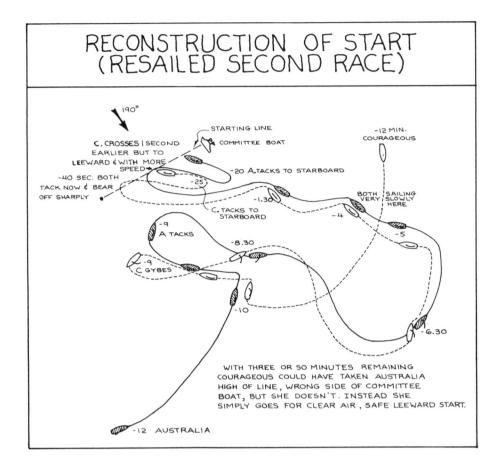

RECONSTRUCTION OF START
(RESAILED SECOND RACE)

190°

C. CROSSES 1 SECOND
EARLIER BUT TO
LEEWARD & WITH MORE
SPEED

-40 SEC. BOTH
TACK NOW & BEAR
OFF SHARPLY

STARTING LINE
COMMITTEE BOAT

-12 MIN.
COURAGEOUS

-20 A. TACKS TO STARBOARD

-25

-1.30

C. TACKS TO
STARBOARD

-9
A TACKS

-8.30

-9
C GYBES

-10

BOTH SAILING
VERY SLOWLY
HERE

-4

-5

-6.30

WITH THREE OR SO MINUTES REMAINING
COURAGEOUS COULD HAVE TAKEN AUSTRALIA
HIGH OF LINE, WRONG SIDE OF COMMITTEE
BOAT, BUT SHE DOESN'T. INSTEAD SHE
SIMPLY GOES FOR CLEAR AIR, SAFE LEEWARD START.

-12 AUSTRALIA

Ted's skill as a seat-of-the-pants sailor was evident as he began pinching *Courageous* up from leeward without losing speed. Then followed the classic racing tactic of working cagily upwind by playing the lifts in advance of your rival, and gradually backwinding him as you point higher and foot faster.

At the end of the 4½-mile first leg to windward, *Courageous* held a substantial lead of two minutes. After *Australia* rounded and squared away downwind, she caught a freshening breeze, which had not yet reached *Courageous*. She gained. In the last 9 miles the lead was cut in half. This time *Australia* had her best combination of jib and mainsail for the existing breeze. There were 19 tacks on the final windward leg to the finish line.

Ted Turner did not fail to cover, for he was getting anxious and knew he could not get away with it, as he had in the first race. After the twelfth tack and cover tack, the gap between the two twelves stopped closing. They stayed evenly apart from there to the finish. Just before the finish Noel Robbins made a last gamble, hoping for a favorable wind shift. When it failed to appear, he ended up taking two extra tacks and losing about 20 seconds.

It was a heartening performance for the Aussies. After trailing by 2 minutes, 38 seconds at the end of three legs, they caught up so fast as to be only 1 minute, 3 seconds astern at the finish. It was an indication that *Australia* had the potential to win.

The third race was sailed on a foggy day with visibility less than a mile, and in a light southerly of 4–10 knots. *Australia* suffered going to windward in light conditions, so Ted Turner was able to sail *Courageous* easily out in front. He leisurely covered every time Noel Robbins tacked *Australia*, and arrived at the first windward mark 1 minute, 50 seconds ahead of the challenger. The Aussies never recovered. The distance between the two twelves kept opening up, until at the finish in the smooth sea the final margin was 2 minutes, 32 seconds, with *Courageous* 600 yards ahead.

What happened to the promise *Australia* showed in the second race? She was well designed. Her deck is much lower, something no one else thought of, not even Olin. She has much less freeboard than any other twelve meter to date. Her bow is sharper, allowing her to cut through the waves more easily. The deck layout is simple and effective. Her center of gravity is thus lower, especially because of the weights of her rig (which have to move down with the deck), her lower deck and hull sides, and her lower weights of the crew on board. As Olin said, "She is a very fast boat." She comes from the drawing board of Johan Valentijn, a young Dutch-born yacht designer who learned the tricks of the trade for 5 years at Sparkman & Stephens doing IOR ocean racers. All the S & S twelves, except *Vim* and *Columbia*, came from Mario Tarabocchia's board there, under Olin's personal direction.

There were two other points of comparison: the sails and the skipper and crew. The sails on *Courageous*, from Hoods' Marblehead loft, were superior, and Ted Turner and his men were in that category as well. He always plays the lifts for all they are worth, and he tacks, if a header looks particularly damaging, to avoid falling off to leeward. I observed this closely just after the start of the first race. *Australia* stood out as being very slow to do this, or more often not doing it at all.

Practice makes perfect. But there again our boat and her people had more through intensive trials all summer long against top-rate competition. The challengers got going quite late, and because of less time had less practice. Match race practice brings out tactics exclusive to those two boat contests. Ted Turner and his 10 shipmates have been exceptional at it. In this type of racing you rarely can make a mistake and get away with it. Let your opponent make it. You avoid it, and you will win.

The fourth race of the series was much like the previous three. After a start with *Courageous* about 2 boat lengths to windward, she sailed slowly but surely ahead of her opponent in the first 15 minutes, and was free and clear to cover every move *Australia* made. Just staying between her and the next mark on each leg was sufficient.

But the reeason for her lead was not all because she was just a little faster. Her skipper and crew spotted a wind shift, and the Aussies did not. *Australia* actually was sailed in the wrong direction for a minute and a half, about half an hour after the start. Ted Turner tricked the challenger by purposely neglecting to cover a tack Noel Robbins made.

Courageous's lead increased to 44 seconds at the first mark. Then the same parade of the series began. The next mark was rounded 56 seconds ahead, the next 2 minutes and 11 seconds, the next 2 minutes and 35 seconds. At the finish *Courageous* won the race and the Cup by a margin of 2 minutes and 25 seconds.

For Ted Turner this was a magic moment. This victory had special meaning, because in 1974 when sailing the impossibly slow *Mariner*, he and his crew had been eliminated early in the trials for the selection of a defender. On the way back to port after winning the Cup he held up the procession until the defeated challenger could pull alongside for the wild welcome. On the volcanic rocks of Aquidneck Island, 1,000 spectators waved and shouted in a display of favoritism for a defender rarely seen in Cup racing. The underdog challenger usually takes the public's fancy, but with the colorful Turner, owner of the Atlanta Braves, grabbing attention wherever he went, and whenever he opened his mouth, the public did have a colorful winner.

He had some nice words to say about his shipmates after the finish: "Best crew ever. We worked our behinds off, and we won." About his boss, Lee Loomis, he said, "I do what I'm told and shut up. And I find both very difficult."

During the celebration with many rounds of fine French champagne distributed by his generous boss on the crowded pier, the victors pushed each other, or jumped overboard into the waters of Newport Harbor. Along came the Aussies in a powerboat, and they too went swimming, led by Alan Bond, the 38-year-old real estate promoter from Perth. His twelves—*Southern Cross* in 1974 and *Australia* in 1977—were both beaten in 4-0 clean sweeps by our own *Courageous*. But "Bondy" was undaunted. "We improved enough to come back in 1980," he predicted at a wild news conference.

Hurrah! rang out the cheers, as all hands heartily approved, defenders and challengers alike.

I wonder if that 126-year-old cup will ever leave its secure refuge at 37 West 44th Street in New York City? It is a tantalizing challenge in the yachting world because, like climbing Mount Everest, it is there.

15 S & S Boats in Bermuda Races

The first race to Bermuda started from Gravesend Bay (at the entrance of New York Harbor) in the year 1906. There were just three starters. A race followed every year through 1909, when it petered out. Then, after fourteen years, *Yachting* Magazine got a group of prominent yachtsmen in conjunction with the Royal Bermuda Yacht Club to revive the race, starting from New London with 22 starters. The distance is 660 miles from there to the island. Another race followed in 1924, then was omitted in 1925. The next year the newly organized Cruising Club of America became interested in oceangoing boats, and the backers of the first two races asked the club to take over and sponsor the event. This it did, and as before, with the assistance of the Royal Bermuda Yacht Club. It has been run since then every other year, except for the war years of 1940–1944.

It is a test for men and boats. Sometimes it can be as easy as crossing a pond on one tack all the way, or there may be a calm, as in 1976 when the last boats powered in. At other times the Gulf Stream, which must be crossed against the current, brings squally weather. In one Bermuda Race the sloop *Djinn* was suddenly caught in a Gulf Stream squall, taken aback, and knocked down on her beam ends. She could not free her genoa sheet in time when the squall instantly struck from the leeward side. Also, as in 1936, a northeast gale gave the fleet a good "dusting." Thus the boats must be strong and seaworthy, with good sails and gear, and

RUNNING TIDE
(Rosenfeld)

ARGYLL

Sail Area 1,456 sq. ft.
Displacement 47,750 lbs.
L.O.A. 57'-4''
D.W.L. 40'-0''
Beam 12'-9''
Draft 8'-0''

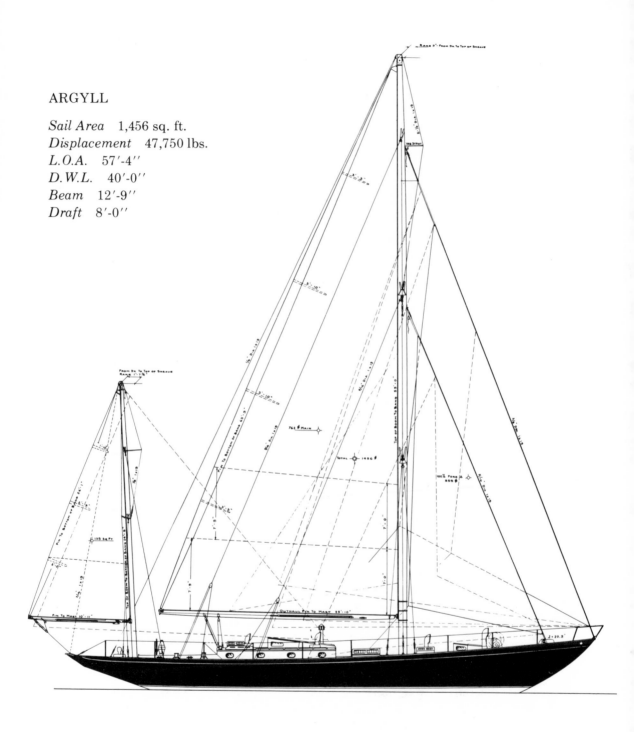

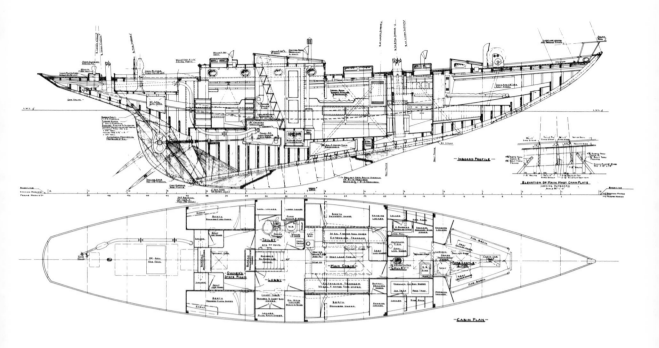

the men must be able sailors ready to take what comes at sea. The skippers and navigators must be experts to lay the proper course to win.

Because of modern electronic navigational instruments, it is easier to find the island than it used to be. Several boats have missed the island in the past—it is so low they went right by and had to turn back in search of it after going too far.

One boat, *Elda,* ran aground making her landfall on a black night. She struck the shoal coral reef just offshore and foundered. Her people got off in the rubber dinghy and tied it to the top of her mast still above water. They were picked up next day. She was a good boat with a competent crew. I can attest to that, because her navigator is an old friend of mine.

The first year a boat designed by S & S sailed in a Bermuda Race was in 1930, when the Stephens brothers' own yawl, *Dorade,* won second place in Class B. There were 42 starters then. The record to follow covers a period of 46 years and highlights the successful S & S ocean racers, showing how consistently well they have done.

S & S BOAT	OWNER	POSITION
1932	27 starters	
Dorade	Rod Stephens, Jr.	1st in Class B
1934	29 starters	
Edlu	R. J. Schaefer	1st overall and Class A
1936	44 starters	
Stormy Weather	P. Le Boutillier	1st in Class A
Brilliant	W. Barnum	2nd in Class A
Edlu	R. J. Schaefer	3rd in Class A
1938	38 starters	
Baruna	H. C. Taylor	1st overall and Class A
Avanti	W. Rothschild	2nd in Class A
Edlu II	R. J. Schaefer	3rd in Class A
Blitzen	R. J. Reynolds	1st in Class B, 2nd overall
Revonoc	Harvey Conover	3rd in Class B
1946	31 starters	
Gesture	A. H. Fuller	1st overall and Class A
Good News	Mrs. Barbara Henry	2nd overall and Class A
Baruna	H. C. Taylor	3rd overall and Class A
Mustang	Rod Stephens, Jr.	2nd in Class B
1948	36 starters	
Baruna	H. C. Taylor	1st overall and Class A
Royono	J. B. Ford, Jr.	2nd overall and Class A
Lord Jim	J. J. O'Neill	2nd in Class B
1950	59 starters	
Argyll	W. T. Moore	1st overall and Class A
Bolero	J. N. Brown	2nd overall and Class A
Mustang	Rod Stephens, Jr.	2nd in Class B
Egret	C. P. Schutt	3rd in Class B
Loki	G. B. Pinchot	1st in Class C
1952	58 starters	
Mustang	Rod Stephens, Jr.	1st in Class B
Cyane	H. B. du Pont	3rd in Class B
White Mist	G. W. Blunt White	2nd in Class C
1954	77 starters	
Bolero	J. N. Brown	1st in Class A
Good News	A. L. Loomis, Jr.	3rd in Class A
Circle	C. Hovgaard	1st in Class B
Stormy Weather	J. J. O'Neill	2nd in Class B
Gesture	A. H. Fuller	3rd in Class B
1956	89 starters	
Finisterre	C. Mitchell	1st overall and Class D
Figaro III	W. T. Snaith	1st in Class C
Gesture	A. H. Fuller	2nd in Class B
Argyll	W. T. Moore	3rd in Class B
*Bolero**	Sven Salen	2nd in Class A
Good News	A. L. Loomis, Jr.	3rd in Class A
Revonoc	H. Conover	3rd in Class C

* Fastest elapsed time (new course record)

S & S BOAT	OWNER	POSITION
1958	111 starters	
Finisterre	C. Mitchell	1st overall and Class D
Golliwogg	C. E. Ratsey	2nd overall and Class D
Legend	W. Morss	1st in Class A
Gesture	A. H. Fuller	2nd in Class A
Argyll	W. T. Moore	3rd in Class A
Cyane	H. B. du Pont	3rd in Class B
1960	131 starters	
Finisterre	C. Mitchell	1st overall and Class E
Dyna	C. Ewing	1st in Class A
Jubilee	F. D. Wetherill	2nd in Class A
Palawan	T. J. Watson, Jr.	1st in Class B
Baccarat	G. J. Coumantaros	2nd in Class B
Cyane	H. B. du Pont	1st in Class C
Solution	T. Ramsing	3rd in Class C
Katama	F. Adams	1st in Class D
1962	131 starters	
Northern Light	A. L. Loomis, Jr.	2nd in Class A
Dyna	C. Ewing	3rd in Class A
Mustang	Rod Stephens, Jr.	2nd in Class B
Loon	G. Pinchot	2nd in Class C
Reindeer	E. N. Smith	2nd in Class D
1964	143 starters	
Carillon	W. Morss	1st in Class B, 3rd overall
Salmagal III	A. B. Homer	2nd in Class B
Reindeer	E. N. Smith	2nd in Class D
Gesture	J. L. Madden	3rd in Class A
Dyna	C. Ewing	4th in Class A
1966	167 starters	
Kialoa II	J. B. Kilroy	2nd in Class A
Good News	J. Isbrandtsen	3rd in Class A
Palawan	T. J. Watson, Jr.	2nd in Class B
Inverness	R. W. McCullough	1st in Class C
Solution	T. Ramsing	3rd in Class C
Noryema IV	R. W. Amey	2nd in Class D
Puffin	E. R. Greeff	3rd in Class F
1968	152 starters	
Good News	J. Isbrandtsen	1st in Class A
Kialoa II	J. B. Kilroy	3rd in Class A
Yankee Girl	S. Steere	2nd in Class B
Dyna	C. Ewing	3rd in Class B
Baccarat	G. Coumantaros	3rd in Class C
Cyane	H. B. du Pont	3rd in Class D
Prospect of Whitby	A. Slater	2nd in Class E
Privateer	E. Trimingham	2nd in Class F
1970	152 starters	
Running Tide	J. Isbrandtsen	1st in Class A
Equation	J. T. Potter	1st in Class B, 3rd overall
Bay Bea	P. E. Haggerty	2nd in Class B, 3rd overall
Palawan	T. J. Watson, Jr.	3rd in Class B
Harpoon	M. C. Ewing	1st in Class D
Firebrand II	D. P. Miller	2nd in Class D
Pageant	J. H. Page	1st in Class F

TEMPEST   (Ross)

S & S BOAT	OWNER	POSITION
1972	178 starters	
Noryema	R. W. Amey	1st overall and Class C
Charisma	J. Philips	1st in Class B, 2nd overall
Dora IV	L. A. Williams	2nd in Class A
Saga	E. S. Lorentzen	3rd in Class B
Aura	W. J. Stenhouse, Jr.	3rd in Class C
1974	166 starters	
Dora IV	L. A. Williams	1st in Class A
Charisma	J. Philips	2nd overall and Class B
Siren Song	J. S. Wright	3rd in Class B
Kate	R. W. Hubner	2nd in Class C
Weald II	F. J. Cummisky	3rd in Class C
Diane	J. R. Mattingly	1st in Class D
Pride	R. N. Jayson	2nd in Class D
Shadow	F. Batten	3rd in Class D
Reindeer	E. N. Smith	2nd in Class E
1976	157 starters	
Running Tide	A. Van Metre	1st overall and Class A
Pride	R. Jayson	1st in Class D
Circe	E. Green	1st in Class E
Tempest	E. Ridder	2nd in Class A, 3rd overall
Good News	J. Pedersen	2nd in Veterans Class
Dora IV	L. Williams	5th in Class A
Charisma	J. Philips	5th in Class B
Pageant	J. Page	5th in Class E

FLYER, Winner Whitbread Round the World Race 1977–78   (Bremer)

16 Rod's Ideas on Construction

Rod uses an inspection checklist on trial trips of new boats and on his many visits to the building yards when the boats are under construction. This check list is published in *Skene's Elements of Yacht Design,* but it covers about 100 different items very briefly; a book could be written about the purposes and reasons behind each. It is a matter of the designer's attention to detail and the builder's know-how that can make the difference between losing a boat at sea or enjoying one that is a pleasure to own and sail. I asked him to elaborate on that checklist with his always straightforward answers and good reasons, so that yachtsmen who own a sailboat or are about to buy one may benefit from his knowledge and experience.

"Looking at new boats today is sometimes a lesson in misplaced priorities," said Rod. "The builder who proudly advertises carpeting throughout as standard—isn't that what people want?—may grudgingly put a stern pulpit, an emergency tiller, and even a bilge pump on the list of options. The swank 35-footer that's drawing oohs and ahs with its lavish teak appointments may have a deck as springy as a trampoline. No wonder the new buyer is confused. What should he expect?

"It's a complex question," he continued. "But there are certain measurable, observable points he can look for.

"Above all, keep simplicity in mind when looking over the new boats. The push-button temptations of our age are fine, but don't forget the fundamentals—strength and craftsmanship—are a better investment for most sailors than go-fast gadgetry," suggested Rod.

"Hull strength is one area where no compromise is acceptable and where the best is never too good. Unfortunately it is not possible to walk through a boat and come to a clear conclusion about its basic strength. As a result, the builder's reputation and the opinion of sailors who own his boats are the key."

Frank: Rod, I know you like to have the steering gear on a boat just as free as possible. Could you tell us why you like it that way?

Rod: Well, Frank, it seems that excessive friction is present in a majority of boats. A really free steering system makes any boat easier to sail properly, because you can feel whether she has a weather helm or a lee helm, and you can make her sail faster as you steer according to feel. Also, it is much more enjoyable to steer that kind of a boat.

Frank: How would you define just how free a steering system should be to work this way?

Rod: I would place the lower limit at one foot-pound. It should be enough to move the wheel. In other words, a one-pound weight one foot from the hub should move the wheel. When you step into a boat the wheel should move, because as she heels a little bit the rudder would turn. And if the system was free enough, so would the wheel.

Frank: I know you always insist on having big limber holes for good bilge drainage. What size do you recommend?

Rod: The capacity of the limber holes must be such that they can get water to the pump intakes just a little more rapidly than the properly operating bilge pumps can take out. A teacup full of water put in at the forepeak and another one just inside the transom should find its way immediately to the lowest part of the bilge, where the pump intakes are located.

Frank: We always specify flotation reference marks, but I wonder what importance you attach to them.

Rod: To permit intelligent study of trim or optimum performance rating, it is desirable to have reference marks on forward and after centerlines, one pair at each end on the datum waterline, and a second pair 12″ above those. By measuring from the surface of the water to these reference marks, it is possible to ascertain with considerable accuracy just where the boat is floating in relation to the datum waterline. In a fiberglass boat these points should be marked in the hull mold. In a metal boat they can be marked with a small welding bead, and in a wooden boat with round-head wood screws.

Frank: Another question about the steering gear. Shouldn't there be guards over the cables and sheaves?

Rod: Yes, Frank, because unfortunately the cable is not always properly adjusted, and under great stress considerable slack can occur. Without effective guards there is the possibility of the cable jumping, which will immediately render such a steering system inoperative. Proper sheave guards and deeply scored sheaves prevent a slack cable from jumping.

Frank: How about access to the steering gear?

Rod: Yes, it's important to have it easily accessible for adjustment, lubrication, and cable replacement. With a chain-and-cable steering gear it is a good idea to remove and replace chain and cable when there is ample time to provide necessary access, which all too often has not been provided originally. Then, when the situation is difficult and quick replacement mandatory, it will be an operation that has been properly rehearsed. Better than that, I would advise replacing the cable once every three years.

Frank: When you're backing a boat and put the rudder part over, it seems to me there is such a great strain on the system there should be some sort of stop.

Rod: Yes indeed, there should be one 40° from the centerline on each side, properly cushioned. Another poor thing about so many quadrants is that they have shallow grooves and sharp corners where the cables come round the ends.

Frank: You know, Rod, lots of my friends who are sailors have asked me how a boat should be protected from lightning, and I must admit everytime I've been out sailing in a sailboat in a lightning storm I've been kind of scared myself about getting struck.

Rod: On a metal boat—that is, an all-aluminum or an all-steel boat with an aluminum mast—there's nothing to worry about, because the boat is grounded to the water by its own material, metal. But on a wooden boat or a fiberglass boat, the mast and the rigging must be grounded to the water. The best way is to use either a high-capacity copper wire—that is, No. 8AWG, 5 pounds per 100'— or ⅜'' copper tubing flattened at the ends and connected to the chainplates to ground the shrouds. Also from the head stay and back stay fittings. Then these copper wires or tubes should lead to the ballast keel bolts, presuming the boat has outside ballast. On a fiberglass boat, where the ballast is inside, there should be a ground plate about one foot square of copper on the outside of the hull, to which these lead wires or tubes are connected. One theory behind this is that if the water is giving off a certain polarity, it is thought that it will go on up in a protective cone around the boat. The rig and hull will thus be of no greater attraction than the water itself. Hence the lightning will not pick this particular mast or boat to strike, because it is not any different in attraction than the water. Another theory is that if the lightning is led to the water with the least resistance, it will do the least harm.

Frank: How does one keep a solid propeller of two blades vertical in an aperture for least drag when sailing?

Rod: By having clear marks on the propeller shaft, when the propeller is in this optimum position for minimum resistance. As well, a simple, effective, safe shaft lock is necessary when the motor may be required for generating purposes. A relatively lightweight brass pin that can be sheared in an emergency provides the possibility of quick use of the engine without damaging anything. A friction brake that had not been fully released might cause damage by creating heat.

Frank: I like well-rounded corners and no sharp edges on a boat, don't you?

FLYER

Sail Area   1,827 sq. ft.
Displacement   55,300 lbs.
L.O.A.   65'-2''
D.W.L.   49'-9''
Beam   16'-4''
Draft   10'-0''

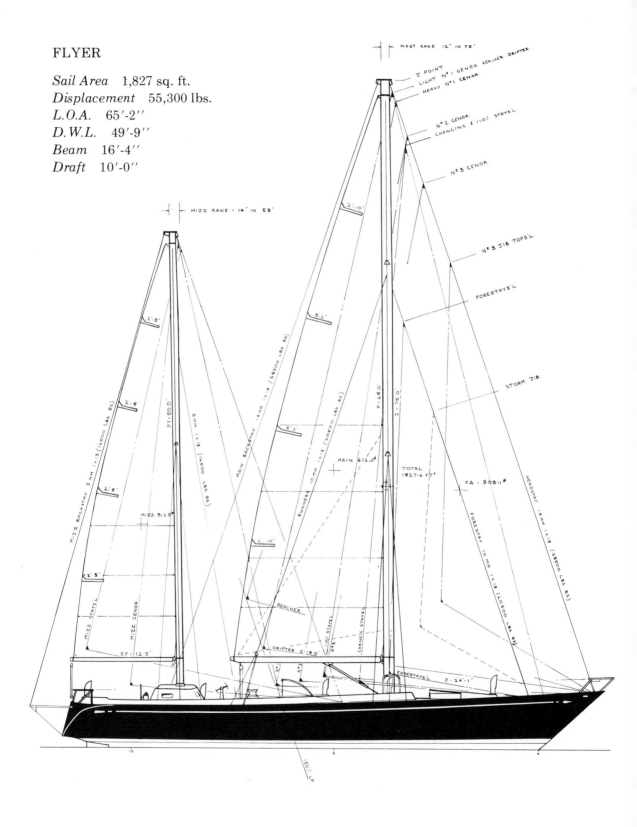

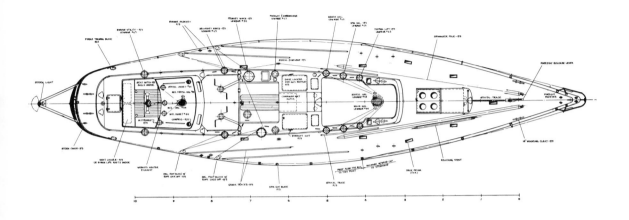

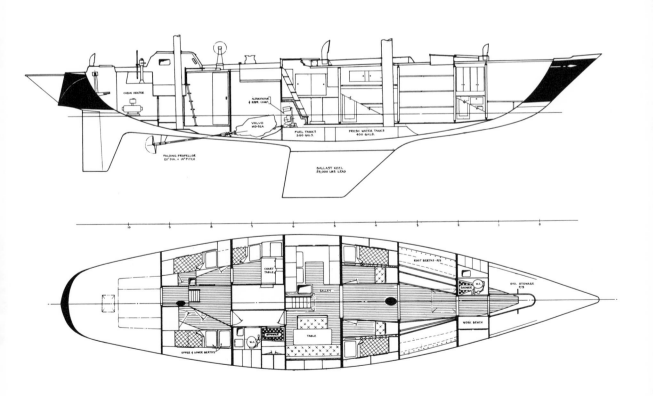

CHARISMA   (Rosenfeld)

Rod: Yes, that's a detail that pretty well reflects the experience of a builder, both in wood and metal, throughout the boat. Anything sharp is not only potentially dangerous, particularly if it is metal, but it is also hard to maintain, particularly if it is wood.

Frank: I've seen bilge water slosh right up on the side of a boat to the underside of a deck, haven't you?

Rod: Yes. That's why it is most important to keep the bilges clean and dry. In order to do this, they should not have a rough finish, because then it is virtually impossible to properly clean them.

Frank: Rod, why do you dislike interior liners on many fiberglass boats?

Rod: Because there are too many that are complex. These liners look nice and are quick and cheap to build, but they prevent adequate inspection of the interior of the hull and deck. They make deck leaks nearly impossible to locate and fix, and also they complicate changes and additions to the deck layout.

Frank: Rod, what are the key points to a good exhaust system, and how can an owner avoid expensive repairs.

Rod: In the first place, an exhaust through hull outlet should be well above the waterline, when the boat is traveling at full speed, allowing for a good-size stern wave to build up. The system should be quiet, and it should not give off a lot of heat into the cabin. The latest system we are using is the so-called water lift system. It basically is a tank or pressure-resisting muffler, into which the exhaust fumes and the cooling water are passed. Then they are discharged upward to a loop as high as possible, and out through the stern. Although they may go out the side, through the stern is better in case you are underway with a beam breeze, for less fumes would come aboard. This system is quieter, absorbs vibration better because of the use of rubber exhaust hoses, is less expensive, and will last longer.

Frank: Rod, I know you have frequently chatted about owners with compass problems. Could you briefly say what is the best way to avoid problems with a compass.

Rod: In a nutshell, take out any built-in correctors that are furnished in the binnacle beneath the compass and never return them to that spot. Throw them overboard.

Frank: Why so?

Rod: There is a great myth in the boating industry that the compass adjuster is omnipotent. There is absolutely no question that the best results are obtained when the compass, as installed, is not subject to any items creating deviation—hence, correct without magnets. This goes a long way toward reducing the possibility of any heeling error and is a great blessing to the navigator. Built-in correctors are prone to create heeling error. When the boat heels they change position, because they are beneath the compass. They're too close and quite powerful.

In a well-built yacht of fiberglass or wood there should not be any magnetic material near the compass, and there should not be any error. The greatest

SAYULA II, Winner Whitbread Round the World Race 1973–74   (Rosenfeld)

SWAN 65 CLASS

Sail Area   1,797 sq. ft.
Displacement   56,370 lbs.
L.O.A.   64'-10''
D.W.L.   47'-0''
Beam   16'-4''
Draft   9'-2''

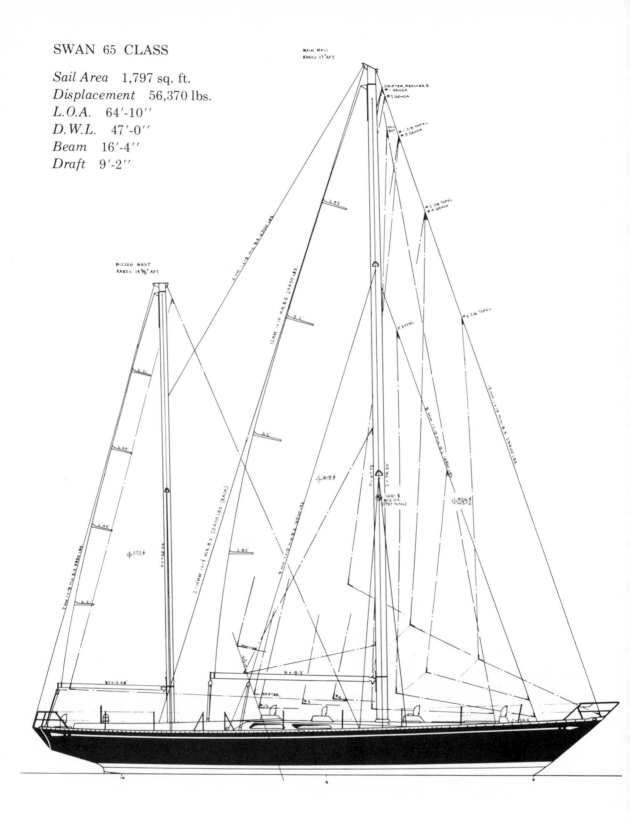

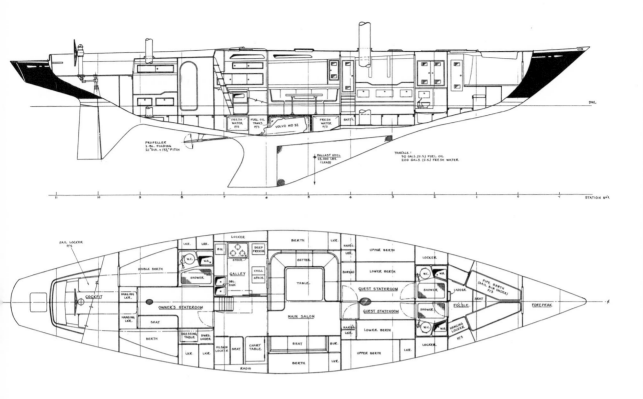

chance for error comes when the boat is heeled and where built-in correctors have been used for adjustment.

In steel yachts, or in yachts where there is need for some compass compensation, the correcting magnets should be far from the compass card outside of the binnacle, minimizing the probability of heeling error.

Frank: Rod, there's so much moisture on a boat that people have trouble with electric switches corroding and not working. In your opinion, what is the best location for an electric switch and the best type to use?

Rod: With relation to exposure to salt water and salt spray, it is much better to have to reach a little farther and to have the switches work. The right switch cleverly located can go on ad infinitum without any special maintenance. Spray-proof circuit-breaker-type switches are desirable.

Just a thought here, going back to steering gear. A strong nonmagnetic emergency tiller is a must complete with convenient stowage, including necessary tools for quick installation. Here again it is good to have rehearsals from time to time with the boat peacefully at anchor. The emergency tiller should be installed and a reasonably strong person should treat it very roughly. If there is any tendency to show distortion, the tiller should be suitably reinforced, or replaced with one that is adequate.

Frank: So many boats have wheel steering nowadays, Rod. Perhaps you could give us a few more pointers.

Rod: The current popular destroyer-type steering wheel is pretty useless in cold or wet weather, except where the rim has been covered tightly with elkhide, rough side out. This is the only covering that doesn't seem to change whether it is wet or dry, hot or cold. And it provides just the right grip without being hard.

Steering gears should be so adjusted that with the rudder straight on the centerline a spoke is on the centerline vertically. And this spoke should be marked first on the rim with something that can be felt easily at night. Secondly, the king spoke, as this is called, should be marked with something that shows up well in the daytime all the way along the spoke, so that from anyplace on deck it is possible to observe the position of the wheel and know the position of the rudder. This immediately helps indicate the necessary adjustments in sail trim to provide the best possible balance. To permit checking the adjustment of the king spoke, there should be a very precise centerline reference mark on the rim of the quadrant visible from where the cables are adjusted, so the wheel can be locked or secured with the king spoke on center. Then the cables can be adjusted so the quadrant is also registering on its appropriate centerline marking indicating that the rudder is exactly straight fore and aft.

Frank: After we had left the 57′ motorsailer *Baraka* in the Caribbean, we heard that one of her chain plates had broken off at the deck. This was for the bridle of the backstay. How could this happen, Rod?

Rod: Because it was not aligned properly, I'll bet you, which leads to fatigue. Chain plates for all standing rigging should line up precisely with the rigging that is attached to them. Above the deck the chain plates should be short, just high enough to accept the toggle.

Frank: We've been talking about items on the hull. Let's turn to the cabin.

Rod: Okay. First I'd like to say something about oversize cabin windows. This is fundamentally a matter of design, although it is an area where some builders will take liberty in an effort to accede to opinions expressed frequently by people observing a boat in the security of the main hall of a boat show, as opposed to a situation where the boat is fighting for survival at sea, where the cabin house may be subject to a terrific battering—fortunately not probably, but of extreme importance.

Frank: What about holding doors shut?

Rod: Magnetic catches or any type of friction catch can never be satisfactory except possibly in an apartment house in a nonearthquake area. A boat is uncomfortable enough in extremely rough weather without having to make temporary provisions to hold doors shut and at the same time pick up gear that has been dumped out on a wet cabin sole. This is a detail that would seem perfectly obvious, but one which is wrong on many installations. The best catch looks something like a woodpecker made in bronze. You put it on the inside of the door and have a hole through the door so that you can reach through with one finger and flip the catch open.

Frank: Isn't access to the bilge denied on most boats because the floorboards are too tight?

Rod: Yes, they are universally too tight. Great relief can be provided by the simple expedient of a 10° under bevel. The floorboards will still fit reasonably, but with the slightest lifting will free up immediately. They will also be easy to replace. Any floorboard that is adjacent to a vertical surface must have a margin piece, otherwise the adjacent surface will always be scratched when the floorboard is raised. The access to the bilge on the majority of fiberglass boats is unsatisfactory, because inadequate lifts are frequently provided. A simple keyhole-shaped plate strongly bolted through the floor and two T-shaped keys with oval handles will permit adequate force to be applied in the almost inevitable situation where the floorboards have become tight, generally after the first time the boat has gotten some water on the cabin sole. It should be easy to inspect all parts of the bilge.

Frank: Besides the Dorade vents, what are other good ways of getting ventilation in a boat?

Rod: For the quarter berth the best ventilation is to open the lazarette hatch, even when the boat is underway. Ventilation can be supplemented by opening ports in the side of the cockpit well. As is the case with any natural ventilation scheme, something that tends to draw the air out as, for example, a good dodger over the main companionway, will add greatly to the effectiveness of any type of air intake.

Speaking about berths, there are an unnecessary number of people who find sleeping difficult, and some are injured falling out of bunks in rough weather due to inadequate bunk boards. Generally bunk boards are too weak and too low. In my opinion, the best scheme is to use canvas that stretches under the mattress and up on the exposed side, where it may be secured to strong eyes overhead.

Frank: Rod, haven't there been fires on boats started by their stoves, and what in your opinion is the best way of preventing them?

Rod: The most important item is the master valve for the stove. It should be located where it is easy to see, to reach, and to operate. Also, it should be clearly marked so that anyone passing by can observe that it is in fact turned off when the stove is not in use. Of course it must be in a location where it is not necessary to reach across the top of a burner or through high flames in a bad situation to be shut off. Individual burner valves should be clearly marked for the same reason.

In connection with the frequently installed swinging stove, where the tank is not on the stove, a flexible feed line must be installed so it never comes against the hot body of the stove yet does not restrict the stove's motion. Incidentally, the stove ideally should go 50° each way from horizontal to take care

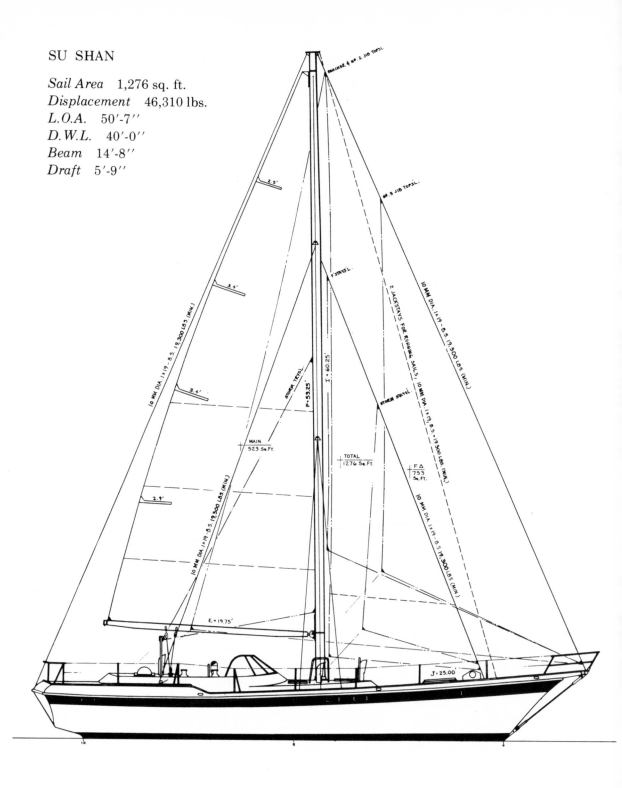

SU SHAN

Sail Area 1,276 sq. ft.
Displacement 46,310 lbs.
L.O.A. 50'-7''
D.W.L. 40'-0''
Beam 14'-8''
Draft 5'-9''

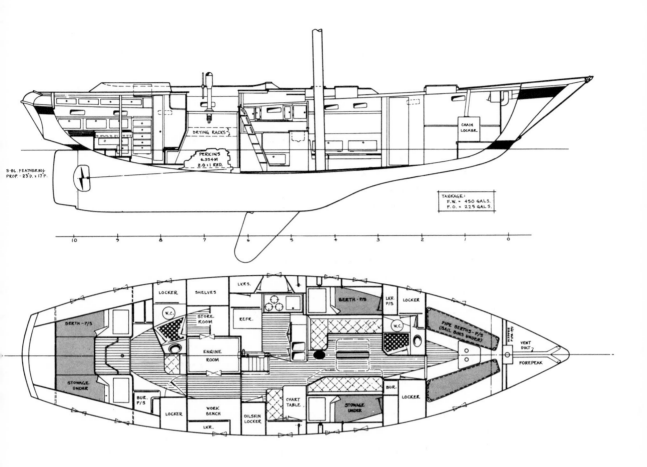

of any surge in rough weather. There should be an adjustable friction brake in the pivots to sufficiently dampen the stove reaction to overswinging.

In connection with alcohol stoves, pressure pumps are generally inadequate. The system generally fails to hold pressure, which then requires excessive pumping. A pressure gauge should be easily visible, with clear indications of the operating range, and there should be a valve to close off the pump to eliminate pressure loss back through the pump. With correct installation, the pressure should drop slowly only as a result of fuel used by the stove, and there should be absolutely no pressure drop when the stove is not in use. Before lighting the stove it should be checked carefully to be sure there has been no fuel leak.

Frank: How do you keep stuff from sliding all over the place and dropping onto the floor when the boat is heeled under sail?

Rod: There should be lots of fiddles. Few boats have really adequate fiddles on tables, dressers, and counters. They have to be high and strong and planned with the realization that the boat may sail considerable periods with a heel angle of 30° or more with a lot of incidental motion.

Speaking about dresser tops and fiddles, there must be adequate dresser area in the toilet room so toilet articles can be laid out for use. In addition, there should be individual stowage for personal articles. A series of small drawers, one for every member of the crew, is a good idea. Then too, a scrap basket should be there to minimize the temptation to put foreign objects in the toilet bowl, which may cause flushing problems.

There should be adequate dresser area in the galley combined with adequately high fiddles.

Frank: How do you keep a drawer from opening athwartships when a sailboat is heeled well over?

Rod: The drop sash is a very practical method of retaining drawers, but all too frequently there isn't adequate clearance. So if the drawer swells, there is no way to open it. The only cure for this is an axe. The clearance above should be twice the height of the keeper. Also, frequently the catch is too close, so that unless the drawer raises or lowers with the drawer face perpendicular, it will not actually catch. This particularly applies to drawers that are short, which with the necessary clearance creates some angle to the drawer face. Unless the lower part of the drawer face is pushed in, which has the effect of raising the back of the drawer, it will not get on the catch. If this drawer is heavily loaded, it will appear impossible to get it off the latch, and it can be done only by pushing in very hard at the bottom of the drawer. At the same time the drawer front is raised. The cure is adequate angular clearance in the latch.

We put in all our specs that "drawers must be made of the type which must be lifted $\frac{3}{16}$ of an inch in order to pull out."

Door clearance is important, too, because of the fact that the boat will work somewhat, particularly doors in transverse bulkheads, and these must be provided with ample clearance.

There is one more thing I would like to mention before leaving items in the cabin, and that is that the galley is certainly useless unless it has a really large trash container to accommodate the necessary refuse for an adequate period of time. It should be a container that accepts a plastic liner.

Frank: Yes, Rod, I know how important this is because we have worked it out quite well on *Santa Maria.* We have the usual kitchen-type container on the inside of the engine room door beneath the galley sink. This accepts a plastic bag. Then we have a great big one, like we have in our garage at home, under the cockpit seat hatch where the fenders and lines are kept. Into this from day to day we put the plastic bags from the galley until a garbage boat comes along in some harbor to take it away, or till we go ashore and dump it in a trash container there. It has worked out quite well.

Let's discuss the importance of proper scuppers and drains. Although a boat does float in her element, water, it is important to keep it out of her. Either salt water from the sea or fresh water from rain must be kept out of a boat, not only to make her habitable, but also to prevent her from swamping. What type of copper cockpit scupper guards do you recommend, Rod?

Rod: All too often the scuppers are either dangerously restricted by the use of a plate with a few round holes, or perhaps totally unprotected. The logical arrangement is the use of a lightweight cross that prevents large objects from stopping up the scuppers. Yet the cross made of two rods, say ⅛'' in diameter of bronze or copper, creates no measurable restriction to the outflow of water.

The cockpit should drain in three minutes when flooded by a wave. Chances are that you won't get another big wave that soon, and after 1½ minutes your cockpit is half empty. A full cockpit depresses the stern, and the water is bound to get belowdecks. Keeping the stern down for a long period presents many dangers. It is amazing how much faster straight tubing will take water out, opposed to tubing with even a slight turn in it. Make a time check on this sometime.

Frank: How about the water that lies on the cockpit seats? Shouldn't there be scuppers there, too?

Rod: Oh, yes. Inadequate drainage of cockpit seats, which results in carrying undesirable quantities of water inside the lee coaming, is particularly dangerous if there are related cockpit seat hatches. Even when the cockpit is at deck level, it is no cure to cut through the coaming, as this merely lets in water from the windward deck. Large-capacity scuppers that lead athwartships outboard with a very minimum pitch do a good job, as they only come into effect when the boat is heeled in the direction of the scupper. If the seat area can drain well into the outboard edges of a T-shaped cockpit, this is the best solution as it provides almost instantaneous drainage.

A great many boats have a useful and convenient locker in the wide type of coaming, which is associated with fiberglass construction. Again, there is no shortcut to draining such lockers. You need a locker with a bottom shape so that at any angle of heel the water will drain. Again, simply cutting holes to the outside or into the cockpit areas will let in as much water as it lets out.

Frank: How about pump intake screens?

Rod: There are many excellent diaphragm pumps, exemplified by Edson, Henderson, or Whale. These pumps have a pretty good capability of handling unavoidable foreign matter. But this in no way helps the fact that anything that gets into the pump intake may block the pump hose before it ever gets to the pump itself. So no matter how invulnerable is the pump as demonstrated at the local boat show, it is most important that there be a cross bar or similar device to prevent large objects from getting into the intake piping without reducing the important maximum capacity of the pump.

Frank: What's the proper routing for a pump discharge?

Rod: Laying out of bilge pump discharge piping is a critical detail. There are a great many boats that appear to leak in heavy weather, and in many cases some of this water is coming in through the pump system, as the pump valves themselves are not completely foolproof, particularly in view of the fact that a certain amount of miscellaneous solids can and will go out through the pump system. These may temporarily hold pump valves open. The only sure cure is to have the pipe looped up high close under the deck and as near the centerline as is feasible. And, where possible, pump discharges should be above the waterline, which in turn will prevent any tendency for the water to siphon back in. Also, the discharge above the waterline will permit you to observe how well the pump is operating. If discharge is below the waterline, the loop should be vented to prevent siphoning into the bilge.

Frank: Rod, I like your policy of specifying two bilge pumps on each ocean-going boat.

Rod: Yes, it's worked out well. Pumps must be located so that they can be used without admitting any water into the boat. One pump should be near the helmsman, arranged so that it can be pumped through a tight gland in the cockpit well. Thus, when shorthanded, the helmsman can be sure that the bilges are dry without having to go belowdeck to check and he can do the pumping at his station. The second pump should be located belowdeck so that in extremely heavy weather it is possible to pump without going on deck, and in an emergency both pumps can be used at the same time. Ideally they should be the same type to minimize the requirement for spare parts; in extreme emergencies one pump can be cannibalized at a time when both are out of operation, which may permit you to come up with one that is still usable.

You know how I feel about electric pumps. They cause more problems than they cure. Their capacity is minimal, and battery drain is immeasurably high. When the boat is heeled over, water often siphons in or just pours in through these electric pumps. They are far better left ashore.

Frank: What about tanks and their plumbing?

Rod: All tanks, both water and fuel, should have provision for sounding. Appropriately marked sounding sticks should be provided. Tank vents seldom get the thought they deserve. Freshwater tanks should never be vented on deck. This just provides the possibility of saltwater contamination. The vents should be located reasonably near the centerline and, if possible, arranged so they discharge into a sink or washbasin that drains overboard. And there should be a separate vent for each tank. It is then possible to make very sure that each tank is completely full by continuing to make water until each vent clearly overflows. On the other hand, fuel tanks should invariably be vented to the deck and in a position where the normal flow of air would not carry fumes from the vent back into the cabin. And they should be positioned where the possibility of seawater flooding is minimal.

Frank: I remember on a little 28' long boat we had the fuel tank vent was only on the after side of the cockpit coaming in an inverted U shape. We frequently found we got water into the fuel tank—fresh water and sea water. So on our present *Santa Maria* the builder located the fuel tank vent in the same spot, but instead of having it "U," he had it in a coil that went around two or three times. Well, we never had any water in our fuel with this arrangement.

Now back on the subject of plumbing. How about the location of through hull fittings?

Rod: The well-thought-out arrangement of all through hull openings can add to safety and facilitate proper operation. For example, the toilet's intake seacock should be in a point where it will be well below the waterline under all conditions, especially when the boat is heeled under sail. The same is true for the engine cooling water intake. Cockpit scuppers, where possible, should be above the waterline. This not only decreases the possibility of leaking but also means that any fuel vapor in the cockpit will drain away. It has already been mentioned that the exhaust should be above the waterline when going full speed. Again, pump discharges should be above the waterline. Finally, seacocks should be located on all underwater through hull fittings. They should be located as well so that they are reasonably easy to service and to operate. In all cases they should be clearly marked in the full open–full shut positions.

Now about freshwater systems. One of the most universal shortcomings in the freshwater systems is failure to install a high-grade check valve in the lowest part of the supply line leading from the tank to the galley or sink pumps. Such a check valve keeps water in the line, ensures satisfactory operation of the pumps, and eliminates many unnecessary strokes otherwise required to get air out of the line and raise the water to the outlet.

Frank: I'd like your opinion on the optimum way to build things on deck.

Rod: Let's start with the cockpit seat hatches. A most common fault is leaky cockpit seat hatches that allow a great deal of water to get below. Once below, the water is made more troublesome by the current tendency toward very flat midship sections and shallow bilges. While it is difficult to build a really tight hatch, reasonable gasketing can help a lot, as can large-capacity drains to minimize the time during which the hatch seams are under pressure.

Slack life lines are another common fault, perhaps characteristic of fiberglass boats. They are largely a byproduct of inadequate diagonal bracing on bow pulpits and stern pulpits as well as gangways. They are further weakened by inadequate dimensions of the stanchion socket base and by an inadequate size firm reinforcing piece belowdecks. Occasionally the stanchions are too light and bend in themselves, creating a further fault. Another dangerous fault is the almost universal use of close-barrel turnbuckles and/or turnbuckles without toggles on the life lines.

Frank: What about tillers nowadays?

Rod: There are so many poor ones now. Since the days of Herreshoff and then Nevins there have been relatively few nicely made tillers. The average tiller is too heavy in the grip area and too weak in the hinge fitting area, which takes the greatest load. The end that one holds in one's hand should be down to about a 1″ diameter, with a reasonable ball or knob on the extreme end. And the section should increase with more or less straight taper to the appropriate size in the hinge fitting. There should be absolutely no lost motion athwartships so that the response to one's hand when sailing is instantaneous.

With the present-day racing boats really having their decks designed around winches, it is strange that so few of them have adequate winch handle holders. It should be an absolute necessity that they be well located.

Frank: Rod, I know that cleat positioning on deck is one of your specialities. Could you give me a few tips on how to do this correctly?

Rod: Let me say first that the correct angling and spacing of cleats with relation to the winch that they are normally serving can contribute a great deal to the ease and efficiency of sheet handling. To create a simple rule, cleats should be turned 10° counterclockwise from the oncoming line so that the first turn around the cleat is made clockwise. It is desirable to have a minimum of 2′ between winch and cleat, although frequently this has to be compromised due to insufficient space.

Frank: What do you consider the best type of bow chocks?

Rod: Again, we have to look back on Herreshoff and later Nevins to find boats built with really useful bow chocks. In general the chocks are too small, too weak, the edge is too sharp. And many of them are designed apparently with the thought that the line will always pull straight out ahead, whereas in reality it is just about always going downward and may swing in an arc of more or less 180°. European boats suffer from rollers with inadequate and sharp cheeks, which work moderately well for a chain if it is leading straight ahead but from which the chain can jump if the boat is swung around by the tide, as so often occurs. In view of the excellent results that can be gotten from the inherent spring of nylon anchor rodes, it is most important that there be no sharp corners associated with either the chocks or the chain rollers.

It is most important to have a piece of heavy hose, either rubber or plastic, around your nylon mooring pennant in way of the bow chocks in order to prevent the rope from chafing through as it springs in and out when the bow rises and falls or the wind gusts to gale force. This vital pennant should be well protected. If it severs, you will suffer when the boat is lost.

Frank: Rod, it's most annoying to have hatches leak below on a boat. What do you suggest to solve this problem?

Rod: Hatch covers. Despite many ingenious arrangements, there are relatively few hatches that are in themselves really tight in extremely bad weather. There is also a desire to get ventilation, and the only way that a hatch can be kept watertight and also offer some ventilation in moderately bad conditions is to fit it with a tent-type cover that is absolutely tight on each side and across the forward edge. A rabbet to retain the edges of this cover with a continuous inner lip around three sides of the hatch, and with the outer lip simply broken at each corner to facilitate installation of the cover, is a very necessary basic provision in connection with all hatches, with the exception of the lazarette hatch, where any small leaking can be much better tolerated.

Frank: Another source of annoying leaks is at the place where the mast passes through the deck or cabin top. What do you think is the best way to stop these leaks?

Rod: With proper mast coats. Few boats have really effective and tight mast coats. It is basically pretty simple to install a good one, demanding the use of neoprene as a water barrier, and then a coat of Dacron to protect the neoprene from the deterioration created by sunlight. The most vulnerable joint is where the upper end of the coat fits around the mast itself. The extra long stainless steel hose clamp in turn protected by the Dacron cover and backed up with some silicon sealer can make an absolutely tight joint. The mast surface must be smooth. If the mast must be removed, the joint should be opened around the deck collar without disturbing the seal around the mast which, as stated, is the more difficult one to keep absolutely tight.

Frank: Are there any other areas on deck that present problems which good design can solve?

Rod: Yes, Frank, three more come to mind. First, genoa sheet tracks. These should have numbers presumably on every fifth location hole, and the sliding members should travel easily without having to resort to kicking, the use of a hammer, and/or profanity. Best results can be obtained when the locating unit or stop is divorced from the actual sheet-lead member. With this arrangement the locating unit can more easily be released and relocated, while the heavily loaded sliding member is temporarily kept just clear by winching it forward just a fraction of an inch. Once the virtue of this arrangement has been experienced, one will never be satisfied to go back to the conventional scheme, where the location pins are one with the member that carries the sheet itself.

Second, spinnaker pole chocks. These are frequently less than optimum. The right type has a sort of streamlined sheath that fits over the inboard end of the pole, and then the outboard end is held in place using its own latch. The pole should be placed where it interferes least with the usable deck space. The old-fashioned saddles, each located about a quarter of the way in from the ends of the pole, leave pole ends vulnerable to jib sheets, which not only can cause a back tack but may actually tear the spinnaker pole from its chocks, and the pole can easily be lost overboard.

Third, proper stowage of boat hook and reaching strut. In general, provision must be made for a boat hook just as it is for the spinnaker pole. Certainly on deck forward, and a reaching strut in an out-of-the-way place. Where possible, it's good practice to stow the reaching strut belowdeck, but handy to the forward hatch.

Frank: I've heard of several people who drowned because they were unable to climb aboard their boats. In your opinion, what's the best ladder design?

Rod: A very desirable and relatively new development is the provision for swimming and emergency boarding over the stern. A good system is a hinged stainless steel ladder that folds up against the pushpit and swings down for boarding.

Frank: Now we come to the rig and its fittings. Could you give us some hints on how to improve these fittings?

Rod: To start off with, let's talk about cotter pins. A cotter pin can provide a very safe way to secure many connections in the rig, but because of failure to live up to several simple expedients, most people dislike cotter pins. For good results the pin should be cut so that from below the head the length will be 1½ times the diameter of the pin, or turnbuckle, into which it will be inserted. The ends must then be carefully rounded with a smooth, flat file so that there are no sharp corners. When cotter pins have been put in place, they should be open very slightly, each side bent only about 10°. Never bend them sharply back because they cannot be reused or easily removed. By properly controlling the length, the sharpness, and the amount they are opened, there is little likelihood of damage. All cotter pins should be taped. There will be much less tendency to come out through the tape when there are no sharp corners, and they will require less tape. A good gob of silicon is a wonderful guard for any rough fitting that is difficult to tape.

Frank: Where should toggles be located?

Rod: The lower end of all standing rigging should have toggles, and the toggle should be included in the upper end of any stay on which a sail may be set, as it may be pulled considerably out of line by the headsails that are attached to it. Toggles should also be included on life line turnbuckles, as turnbuckles are strong in tension but very vulnerable to bending loads.

Frank: What are the problems with mast tangs and turnbuckles?

Rod: Many mast tangs are improperly beveled so that considerable basic strength is lost. On the commonly used double plate mast tangs the inner plate is brought out close to the line of the shroud, which will be fitted to it. The outer plate has additional bevel to bring it out enough to allow for the thickness of the upper eye terminal on the shroud, and then it is bent down again parallel to the lower plate. So all the offset, or most of it, is in the outer plate. When such a tang is heavily loaded, the outer plate gives more as it tends to straighten out, and the underneath plate is already straight. So the pins then are no longer square with the load.

On the subject of closed-barrel turnbuckles, it is my firm belief that they should be outlawed. This opinion also applies to compression locknuts, which inherently slack up when the turnbuckle is heavily stressed. If the locknuts don't slacken up, then they must be so tight that they apply additional load to the turnbuckle threaded section. Furthermore, there is no way of looking at locknuts to tell whether they are doing their job or not, as compared to the cotter pin, which is either in place or not. Another important defect of the closed-barrel turnbuckle is that it is impossible to see how much thread is buried. Often when it is necessary to slack a shroud or stay to get the correct mast trim, one may unknowingly get dangerously near the end of the threads. This has caused many unnecessary accidents.

A similar situation prevails in the rod rigging fittings, the majority of which are what could be termed "closed-barrel" as opposed to having slots that enable you to observe whether there is sufficient thread in the terminal to be safe. The same comment applies to them.

It seems logical to install terminals and turnbuckles on rod rigging so the right-hand thread is downward. This is so that when tightening one performs the normal motion that one does when putting a screw in. When all turnbuckles and terminals have been installed this way, it is very simple to tighten or loosen any piece of rigging. But all too often it is hit-and-miss, with some one way and some the other, and occasionally all installed upside down. After carefully studying the mast, you may want to tighten one turn here and slacken half a turn there. You think you're doing this, and then you look at the mast and find it is considerably worse. This means that the turnbuckles have been carelessly installed, which makes the adjustment problem unnecessarily difficult.

Frank: There are many fittings on a boom. What in your opinion is the best way to solve the problems there?

Rod: Let me take these fittings one by one. First, outhauls. A great majority of present-day boats were rigged with internal wire main clew outhauls with various schemes for applying tension. But almost none of them has a good scheme for replacing the wire short of a real shipyard job. If you have the good luck to have wire that lasts a reasonable length of time, it will be all the more difficult to get the end fittings off the boom, as is generally necessary for wire replacement. Where roller reefing is involved, the safe screw-type outhaul should last the life of the boat. Where roller reefing is not involved, the old-fashioned wire with rope tackle on the outside of the boom is best, because it is very easy to observe its condition and, when necessary, to make a replacement. If inside, it must be so arranged as to be easily replaced at sea.

Goosenecks—it's astonishing how many boats, particularly those equipped with single lower shrouds aft, risk a broken gooseneck when the boom is all the way out. Obviously the boom applies such extreme leverage over the shroud that the gooseneck is going to break. Again an unnecessary and disabling accident occurs, because fittings have not been well thought out prior to manufacture.

Tracks and slides—there are inumerable places where one piece slides on another, as for example the main gooseneck, spinnaker gooseneck, genoa leads, and luff and foot slides. In all cases both the track and the sliding member must be well polished and all exposed edges adequately beveled so that minor temporary misalignment will not cause a hangup.

Gooseneck track—this somewhat complicates the very necessary and desirable arrangement where the sail track and slides should come right down to the top of the boom, when the boom is in its lowest position. Provision has to be made inherently in the design of the gooseneck track, and the sliding member that goes on the track. But, presuming it is provided at the outset, there is no particular difficulty, and it is the only way the sail can be neatly furled, and the only way it can be safely furled in heavy weather, particularly when offshore.

Frank: What about slides on tracks or in tunnels versus grooves.

Rod: The racers like grooves with tapes on the luffs of their sails to fit. Trouble is, when lowered these sails come adrift and require a number of men to manage. The cruisers like slides, especially nylon ones, that move freely in an aluminum tunnel. The sails stay stacked when lowered, and can be managed more easily.

Frank: Hasn't roller reefing been superseded by jiffy reefing?

Rod: Yes, for two reasons: Main booms are shorter now, and sailcloth is dacron now, far more stable than cotton. So reefing this way (a streamlined method based on the old way using reef points) can be done in a jiffy. With the use of a fixed gooseneck with two inverted hooks welded to the top, a mainsail can be lowered so as to engage the tack reef grommet, then hoisted just a little to tighten the luff. Next the clew grommet is hauled down and aft lightly by winching in a two-part pennant. Usually there is no need to do any more, because dacron won't stretch. At most there need be only half the number of reef grommets for points, or a lace line, than with the old system reefing cotton sails.

Frank: What about boom lifts either fixed or hoistable?

Rod: Both types should be fixed aloft with a toggle. If a block were used at the masthead, the line would cross the main halyard and chafe on its wire hooks. The tackle for a boom lift is best located on the boom end for inspection. A good way to prevent it from wrapping around the backstay is to use a thin shock cord with figure-eight-type hook. It then can be sprung forward to the lower shroud. A snap hook in this system might catch on the leach of the sail, but the figure-eight type can't.

Frank: What about track gates and track switches?

Rod: There should always be a gate on the track just above the stacked mainsail. This is to permit setting a storm trysail and also, with roller reefing, to permit sail slides to be taken off in case very deep reefing is required. Also, of course, for bending on and unbending the mainsail. Unfortunately these track gates are seldom properly aligned. Rarely are the edges sufficiently beveled. Frequently they are located so high that they are unnecessarily difficult to operate, or else so low that the trysail cannot be bent on without letting a good part of the mainsail come completely adrift. Retaining pins, or whatever scheme is used for locking the gate, should be secured so there is no chance of losing them. The gate occasionally must be operated under adverse conditions.

The same general comments apply to track switches, which can be helpful on large boats in order to permit a trysail to be set on deck on a track that is off to one side. As the trysail goes up it can feed back into the mainsail track instead of having a separate track up for the luff of the storm trysail.

Frank: Rod, what in your opinion is the best way to wedge a mast where it comes through the deck?

Rod: Great importance must be attached to a proper securing of the mast as it passes through the mast partners. Fore and aft positioning should be very secure, because there is generally a long panel from the deck up to the headstay, and as the boat works through a head sea, there is a tendency for the mast to "pump" fore and aft. This can be minimized by proper wedging. At the same time, fore and aft stability can be coupled with a provision to let the mast move slightly sideways. This is in order to reduce the inevitable localized bending and fatigue as the mast moves over athwartships to take up the stretch in the windward shrouds. By all odds the best material for mast wedging is live rubber (density 35 durometers). This is rubber that a reasonably strong person can squeeze from, say, a 1″ piece down to ¾″ between thumb and forefinger. There should be two wedges, each with a width 25% of the mast circumference and each with a depth 5″ more than the depth from the top of the mast collar to the underside of the partners. Also each wedge should have a thickness 1¼ times the space available for it. One wedge should be installed on the forward centerline and the other on the aft centerline. Extreme pressure has to be applied to the first wedge to permit the second to be slid into place. This can be done with a strong block and tackle led to a winch. When properly installed, this system will be quiet in rough weather and provide optimum support for the mast, and for the deck as well.

Frank: What about electric wiring for masts?

Rod: The majority of the larger boats have considerable wiring for lights and instruments in their spars. It is generally pretty vulnerable. Wires tend to be damaged when the mast either is stepped or is removed under other than ideal conditions. A good arrangement for mast wire exits is to have a longitudinal hole that permits the wire and all terminals and connectors to be stuffed inside the mast where they are adequately protected from any damage while the mast is being stepped or removed. The wires can be fished out, after the mast has been stepped. The necessary connections can be made preferably on the underside of the deck and sufficiently away from the mast partners to be unaffected by leaking.

One more thing I would like to mention is about mast position. The average boat, particularly the one that is not used for racing, generally has the mast heel too far forward in relation to the position of the masthead. Assuming the mast is kept in the center of the partners, the fore-and-aft adjustment of the heel has a profound effect on the position of the midpoint of the mast. When the middle of the mast tends to come aft under pressure, this can be rectified by moving the mast heel further aft. This immediately tends to push it forward at its midpoint without any adjustment to fore-and-aft rigging, other than the lower shrouds, if these are double.

Frank: Rope to wire splices require great skill, don't they?

Rod: These splices are, more often than not, very badly done. When done properly it requires no external serving, and the splice should last just as long as either the rope or the wire. Done correctly, the splice's maximum overall diameter will be just less than the sum of the diameter of the rope plus the diameter of the wire. All too often the splice is very bulky, stiff, and rough. It will start to come apart the first time the boat is sailed. Often it is dependent on yards of external serving, which also starts to come off early. Such a splice is invariably bulkier than necessary, and usually too wide to go through the sheaves or blocks provided. A poor splice is apt to jam up completely when one strand of the wire pokes out and gets on the wrong side of a halyard block or sheave. The right splice does take more knowledge but doesn't take any more time or material, and is basically not any more expensive. An experienced sail-maker is a good source for this work.

The length of the wire for a halyard is very critical. It should be neither too short nor too long. The headsail halyards should have 3½ turns of wire on the winch when they are 5% of the foretriangle height down from the maximum possible hoist position. The main halyard should have enough wire to have 4 turns on its winch when close-reefed. Usually headsail halyards have too little wire and main halyards too much.

One of the most unnecessary difficulties is for the halyard to come unrove. This is only possible when there are inadequate bitter end attachments. With internal halyards, a properly tied figure-eight knot will do the job. With external halyards there should be an eye that the end of the halyard can be passed through, and the same figure-eight knot should be made in the end. With such treatment it is easy to take kinks out of the halyard when it is being coiled down, but under no circumstances can the bitter end get away. This invariably happens at a time when it is much needed and quite difficult to reeve again.

Frank: Rod, I know you like to mark wire halyards. Will you tell us why it is important to do, and how a dangerous situation can occur if this is neglected?

Rod: It's a necessity nowadays, because we now have masthead foretriangles and stretchy luff headsails. Main halyards should always be marked to indicate when the headboard of the mainsail is just at the underside of the black band aloft. The use of this mark is to exactly meet the measured area under racing rules. The jib halyard or halyards should also be marked, for a different reason. Here the marking should indicate when the maximum hoist has been reached. To go beyond the mark does not create a problem of exceeding the racing rule, but it does cause mechanical damage to the halyard or masthead. In extreme cases there is a possibility of making it either difficult or impossible to get the headsail down again. This can happen when the halyards are not clearly marked.

This mark can be done with nail polish or with red or black paint. For genoa halyards it's particularly effective to add reference marks on the mast or on the deck adjacent to the wire marking indicating the maximum point. Numbers, perhaps 1 to 10, on increments of 2″ to 3″, depending on the size of the boat, could also be used, keeping a record of the optimum position of the mark for each particular headsail under different wind conditions.

The internal halyard is pretty much accepted now, but all too often the exits are arranged with no relation to where the halyards enter the mast aloft. This can create difficulty in replacing internal halyards. It will invariably be necessary from time to time to do this, and frequently it results in the halyards wrapping around one another during replacement, creating undesirable friction and wear. The ones that enter the forward side of the mast should come out the forward side of the mast. The ones that enter the aft side of the mast should come out aft of the middle of the mast. The best exits are also the simplest— that is, an oval slot with simple half-oval bars to prevent chafing as the wire exits. These slots should be covered with rain shields to keep out any undesired water running down inside the mast.

Proper internal halyard arrangement, as just mentioned, means that friction of the halyards is low and replacing or clearance is greatly simplified. Using a messenger with a thin heavy weight to lower it down inside the mast is a simple matter. Take a bent coat hanger and fish out the messenger, then pull through the new halyard.

Frank: Shouldn't the aft side of the mast be straight?

Rod: Yes. Whether the mast be wood or, as is more common today, aluminum alloy, it is imperative that the mast be straight before any steps are taken to rig it. If the mast is delivered with a straight track, it is very easy indeed to adjust the rigging so the mast will stay essentially straight under a wide range of conditions. On the other hand, if there is some misalignment because of warped extrusions or butts, or tapers that are not fair, it is not feasible to overcome this inherent defect by any adjustment of the standing rigging.

Frank: Getting aloft requires a good bosun's chair. What are your thoughts on this?

Rod: First of all, boats must have a bosun's chair. The rig of any modern boat with internal halyards tends to defy effective climbing aloft because there is less to grip, and puts a lot of importance on the bosun's chair. Unfortunately, these chairs have several common faults. The worst one is when the rope straps are too long, so when the halyard is two blocks aloft you are still far short of the area that you want to inspect or work on. These straps should be synthetic to eliminate deterioration from being stowed in a moist atmosphere, and they should be short, so the chair is pretty tight for the biggest person who may use it. Properly done, it should get a man good and high up on the mast. The straps should have a metal ring sufficiently small that it will be easy to use in connection with almost any type of end fitting on a reasonable halyard. The seat part of the chair should not be varnished because it would make it slippery. Nor should it be made overly rough, which would destroy the pants of the unfortunate individual who has to use it. For offshore work you should have a canvas bosun's chair, with a safety line on a belt.

It is all but impossible to properly sail a boat without access to a reasonable number of small lines and sail stops. All too often there is nothing but a coil of large, expensive line, which is entirely unsuitable for securing the boat hook or the ice tongs, or for tying up a genoa jib after it has been folded. A small bag marked "small lines" and filled with a reasonable assortment of diameters from $\frac{3}{16}''$ to $\frac{3}{8}''$ and lengths from 1 fathom to 2 or 3 fathoms will be worth its weight in gold.

Frank: Rod, what's the best way to prevent turnbuckles from freezing up, so that when you try to turn them with a long lever they don't break?

Rod: Lubrication is a very important requisite of the modern rig. The best material for threaded parts and pins is anhydrous lanolin, which is available in drugstores. If turnbuckle threads are thoroughly coated prior to initial installation, and if afterwards the entire turnbuckle, including upper pins and terminal and lower pins, toggle and chain plate, is covered with a dacron boot, it will always be easy to make any necessary adjustment by temporarily removing the cover. One good job of lubrication should do for four or five years using anhydrous lanolin. The same applies to pins that connect the toggles to the chain plates and the upper terminals of the standing rigging to the mast tangs. All parts of the rig, where there may be motion and where, without lubrication, there will be unnecessary and considerable wear, should be lubricated. Thorough pin lubrication plus correct installation of cotter pins as mentioned before could literally save your life if you must clear up after a dismasting offshore.

Frank: Why is it poor to use a snatchblock for a headsail sheet lead block?

Rod: Use of a snatchblock will only invite the block to flog open, generally in just the worst circumstances, when the sheet is badly needed both to keep the boat in control and to save the headsail from flogging itself to pieces. A sliding lead sheave is effective and reliable for genoa sheets. For small headsails there is too often simply a conventional diamond-base padeye and a snatchblock. Better a block made right into the screw eye, which should go into an otherwise almost flush padeye. This protrudes above the deck only the thickness of the surface flange.

This leads to a thought on splicing running rigging. A considerable economy can be accomplished by eliminating splices in running rigging. Splices are really only necessary in connection with wire halyards. All rope eliminates the need of splicing. Tie in rope halyards, sheets, and guys using the bowline knot permit "end-for-ending." In the event of chafe damage this will equalize wear. In the case of the mainsheet it is very simple to unreeve the sheet by simply taking out the knot and pulling it out a short way. If there is an eye splice, the end first has to be unshackled, then the entire sheet pulled out through the blocks. This must be done if the sheet is to be stowed below, as it should be.

Frank: What are your thoughts on sheet leads, winches, and cleats?

Rod: Lines should approach them from at least 5° below the plane of the bottom of the winch. This minimizes the tendency to throw on foul turns when someone is pulling in slack rapidly, and probably with too many turns already on the drum.

A cleat ideally should be at least 2′ from the winch, but this is often impossible because of tight quarters. In any case, it should be angled about 10° counterclockwise from the direct line between it and the winch. There must always be a cleat, incidentally, even with that desirable accessory, the self-tailing winch.

Frank: Now on the final topic, namely sails, how can a sailor accomplish worthwhile gear improvements?

Rod: Let's start with battens. They are almost invariably too light for the three lower pockets in a mainsail, and too stiff for the top pocket. The best arrangement is a more or less indestructible, considerably tapered fiberglass batten for the top one. It must be very flexible at its inner end. The center batten can be well-tapered wood or fiberglass and should be considerably stiffer. The lower batten should be generally similar but should be fiberglass to minimize damage when deeply reefed.

Leach lines generally create an unnecessary requirement for more corrective work. They need adequate provision for adjusting and securing. They should be the proper size in keeping with the job they are intended to do. And the length should be reasonably controlled to save the need of cutting at the time of trials and the attendant need for heating to prevent the line unlaying. No sail, with the exception of spinnakers, should be without leach lines. These lines should be used to prevent noisy, undesirable fluttering. This will seriously wear the stitching, as well as make it more difficult to trim and steer the boat effectively. Also there are problems when people try to sleep below: too much noise. A new plastic clam cleat has been developed that is probably the best solution.

Frank: What about stowing sails?

Rod: There is a standard complaint about the lack of good space for sail stowage. It is much easier to sell a boat with staterooms that have many berths. Big headsails are still necessary to make the boat go, but if the whole boat is filled with berths, where can you stow them? All of this points up the desirability of learning to fold the sails, generally by the foot, flaking them down, and then tightly rolling them. You can roll them either from the tack or from the clew, then clinch them tightly to hold or even to reduce the size of the roll prior to bagging them. When this is done the sail occupies less then 25% of the volume an unfolded sail requires stuffed into a sail bag. With a little practice flaking is pretty easy to do, and it is certainly worth it to let you enjoy what space you do have belowdecks, and help you find the sail you may be looking for when you are in a hurry to make a change.

All headsails more than 5% or 6% short of the full hoist on the luff should be fitted with appropriate head pennants. In the case of a storm jib there is frequently a tack pennant. The pennants should invariably be shackled on with the shackles moused, so an overenthusiastic crew member will not remove them, which causes unnecessary confusion. A shackle facilitates any necessary adjustment of the pennant. If the pennant is spliced into the sail, the whole sail must be taken ashore to have the pennant changed.

Last but not least are mainsail stops. The final step after any type of sailing is to furl the mainsail, for which adequate sail stops are needed. The best thing in the world is to have them really long and have them all the same. They should be synthetic, so they will dry more quickly. There should be a full set of spare stops to replace those that blow away or may be used for other purposes.

Frank: Rod, I've found that a handy rig is the use of shock cord through eyes on one side of the boom, which can be pulled over the mainsail and hooked into hooks, alternately placed on the other side of the boom.

On another subject, Rod, that experiment you performed near my board the other day was most impressive. It was to find out if a piece of wood that looks like white oak really is. "This is the way you can be sure," you said, taking a cup of water. Wood in mouth, you dunked it, then blew through the end grain. Bubbles came out in the water. "If you can blow through it, then it's not white oak," you said. "There's no other easy way to tell."

As a final question I asked Rod, "What does someone who wants a sailboat look for in the electrical system in particular and the outstanding overall characteristic in general?"

"To sum up," Rod said, "remember that salt water and electricity aren't good bedfellows, so electricity should be used only for things you can't do by hand, such as lighting and communication. The most desirable characteristic of an electrical system, and the one most seldom achieved, is simplicity.

"And that brings us back full circle to the idea we started with. It is most appropriate to end with a final plug for simplicity. What you don't have saves weight, space, and cost, and will never need service—some very sensible thoughts to keep in mind."

"AMEN."

Index